WITHDRAWN

WHAT TO DO WITH ITALY

Other books by GAETANO SALVEMINI

THE HISTORY OF THE FRENCH REVOLUTION

THE ITALIAN COMMUNES

THE FASCIST DICTATORSHIP IN ITALY

BANKRUPT MACHIAVELLI *(in preparation)*

UNDER THE AXE OF FASCISM

ITALIAN FASCISM

CARLO AND NELLO ROSSELLI

HISTORIAN AND SCIENTIST

By GEORGE LA PIANA

CHURCH AND STATE IN FRANCE IN THE 18TH CENTURY

THE CHURCH OF ROME AT THE END OF THE SECOND CENTURY

THE IMMIGRANT GROUPS IN ROME DURING THE FIRST THREE
CENTURIES OF THE EMPIRE

WHAT TO
DO WITH ITALY

By

GAETANO SALVEMINI

and

GEORGE LaPIANA

DUELL, SLOAN AND PEARCE

NEW YORK

PRINTED IN THE UNITED STATES OF AMERICA
BY THE VAIL-BALLOU PRESS, INC., BINGHAMTON, N. Y.

TO

Maestro Arturo Toscanini

WHO

IN THE DARKEST HOURS

OF

FASCIST CRIMES

ITALY'S SHAME

AND WORLD MADNESS

UNCOMPROMISINGLY CLUNG

TO THE IDEALS OF MAZZINI AND GARIBALDI

AND WITH UNDYING FAITH

ANTICIPATED

THE DAWN OF THE SECOND ITALIAN RISORGIMENTO

Foreword

A book on contemporary events, especially in time of war runs the risk of becoming out of date from the time it is written and that of its release from the press. We hope that our book will escape this risk both because we have tried to trace in detail some features of recent history which will retain a value for the historians, and because we have added a few pages to cover more recent events.

By the time this book will be out, the invasion of Italy may be in progress; but it will be only the beginning of the hard task of solving the Italian problem. If our book will contribute something towards the right solution of this problem we shall not regret the time and the effort spent in writing it.

We wish first to thank the editors of the periodicals *The New Republic, The Nation, The Protestant, Common Sense, Free World,* and *The New Leader* for their permission to make use in our book of some material which appeared first in their columns. Our thanks go also to Miss Frances Keene who read the final manuscript and prepared it for the press; to Miss Helen Wolf for her assistance in writing several chapters of it, and, last but not least, to Mrs. Josephine Setton to whose invaluable assistance and unbound devotion we owe so much.

Contents

Introduction

IN HIS address to the American people on July 23, 1942, Secretary of State Hull outlined the general principles underlying the American policies for post-war reconstruction and concluded by saying: "In support of such policies an informed public opinion must be developed. This is a task of intensive study, hard thinking, broad vision and leadership, not for government alone, but for parents, teachers and clergymen and all those who, within each nation, provide spiritual, moral and intellectual guidance." Furthermore, Mr. Hull believes that to develop an informed public opinion is a compelling duty which devolves especially "upon those who are in positions of responsibility, public and private."

The writers of this book, American citizens by adoption, having by free choice and moral conviction sworn allegiance to the Constitution of the United States, are thereby materially and spiritually partakers of the great American inheritance of freedom and equal rights; as partakers of such an inheritance we wish to do our part in performing this compelling duty. Before coming to this country we held responsible positions in Italy as writers and educators. Now here, in this United States of ours, we are again writers and educators, again in the ranks of those expected to provide moral and intellectual guidance. It is therefore as teachers as well as appreciative citizens that we answer the call.

Our life and our experiences in Italy provided us with an intimate knowledge of the European, and especially of the Italian, historical background. We are acquainted with the psychology and temper of the various classes of the Italian people, with Fascism, its rise to power, and with the forces in Italy and outside Italy which have sustained it and opposed it.

On the other hand, we have lived long enough in the United States to have identified ourselves with the spirit, the ideals, and the institutions of our adopted country; we have become a part of the intellectual and social framework of American life.

Since we have always believed in freedom and in free political institutions, and since we have never accepted or approved Fascist ideologies and policies in Italy or elsewhere, there is neither in our minds nor in our hearts any conflict between our undivided allegiance, our loyalty, our devotion to America, and our sentimental attachment to Italy—the Italy of liberal traditions, betrayed and destroyed by Fascism.

We shall present to our readers only those facts for which we have satisfactory evidence. We are not connected with any agency of government or public administration, nor do we belong to any specific political or religious group which imposes limitations upon thought and speech. We shall freely express our opinions. We believe that spiritual unity and full cooperation in the war effort, in a country of free citizens and hence of diverse opinions, can be attained only by open and frank discussion of all problems and policies which affect the life of the nation.

And now, having duly presented our credentials and our motives for writing this book, we shall pass on to the special task we have assigned ourselves.

In the post-war reconstruction of Europe, the foundations for which are being laid now, the specific problems of each nation will be but local aspects of the same general problem. It follows that the solution to these individual problems must be dictated primarily by the principles and purposes governing the general plan. The adoption of inconsistent and contradictory methods in the work of national reconstruction, or of wrong or inadequate solutions to the problems of one country, will endanger the whole structure of post-war reorganization, the purpose of which is, above all, to restore and maintain international peace and order.

The absolute need for common working principles which will both solve national problems and insure the success of the general plan for international accord will make the task of reconstruction a very difficult one, and will require more than the best in leadership; it will require also the intelligent support of an enlightened public opinion.

It is our belief that the solution of the Italian problem will be one of the most crucial and most decisive elements in the whole plan of world reorganization. We are not indulging in sentimental bias or in subconscious nationalistic exaggerations when we state that Italy, from a certain point of view, is destined to hold a key position in any European political system. Geographical, political, and religious factors make of Italy a pivotal point in the history of Europe, and hence, to a certain extent, of the world.

As military strategists now fully recognize, the part played by the Fascists in Nazi victories should not be underestimated. American public opinion has been greatly misinformed on this point by the superficial and at times infantile journalistic campaign which seeks to ridicule and caricature, not only Mussolini, but the Italians as a whole. To realize how vital to Hitler the Italian alliance has been, one has only to consider how different the war situation would be for the United Nations, if Italy were on their side. As usual, the sons of darkness were wiser than the sons of light. Before starting their march of destruction, the Nazis secured, first, the alliance and support of Italy as a necessary condition for their victory, and secondly, the alliance and support of Japan, which holds in the Far East a position somehow analogous to that of Italy in Europe.

It is now a matter of history that the first great blunder made by the diplomacy of the democratic nations was that of supporting and acclaiming the advent of the Fascist regime in Italy, and of not realizing that they were thus nursing and encouraging the growth of the germ of a fatal disease, which in time was to threaten their own existence.

We still remember with heartache our sense of dismay when we witnessed the wave of enthusiasm for Fascism and Mussolini that swept this country and flourished especially among the high political, religious, and social classes of America. We still recall how in those days we who tried to open the eyes of the American public as to the real nature and aims of Fascism were looked upon as disgruntled crackpots or, at best, as unrealistic searchers after Utopia.

And we have good reason to believe that even now, more than three years after the outbreak of the present war, there are still considerable sections of American public opinion in which traces of the old myth concerning Fascism still blur the vision of the future. It seems that even in the high political spheres here in America, as well as in England, the fallacy persists that Fascist Italy has made only one great mistake, that of siding with Hitler instead of with the democratic nations. How Fascism could be expected to become an ally of democracy is one of the tragic mysteries of modern democratic diplomacy.

It is obvious that if plans for the reconstruction and reorganization of post-war Italy are built on such premises, the same reactionary forces which brought Fascism into power must again be entrusted with the task of governing the new Italy and of collaborating with the central international organization to preserve democratic freedom, peace and prosperity. How the authors of such a plan for Italy can expect that the elements and forces which patronized Fascism will bend their energies towards the internal pacification of Italy and a sincere collaboration with the international agency is another unfathomable mystery.

Fortunately, there is another section of American public opinion, represented chiefly by many scholars, writers, and political thinkers, who are untrammeled by the prejudices that prevail in conservative and reactionary groups and are not gagged by diplomatic traditions or the niceties of social aristocratic intercourse. These are fully aware of the danger to America inherent in the tendencies and policies of those who represent the other section of public opinion. We count heavily upon their support in the task which we undertake as American citizens in the interest of America.

The United States has now assumed the leadership in this deadly struggle to preserve freedom and civilization, and she will in good measure bear the responsibility for the results. If mistakes and blunders are made as on former occasions, the United States will have to pay a high price for them. No greater mistake could be made than that of patronizing, in Italy or elsewhere, the control of reactionary forces, or of imposing them on a disintegrated country.

The gigantic task of establishing a new international order when victory over the Axis is achieved will require all the wisdom gained from the tragic experiences of the past. It is to be hoped that the sacrifices we make today will help keep our vision clear tomorrow. As far as the United States is concerned, the last twenty-five years have taught us, at enormous cost, that the traditional policy of isolation from European affairs and entanglements works no longer in favor of, but against, our national security and welfare. It is reasonable to assume that the causes and conditions which have forced us to take an active part in this second World War for our own preservation will continue to exist for a long time. It is, therefore, to be hoped that we will not dare to repeat the error of returning to our old isolationism.

History will give full credit to President Roosevelt for having seen clearly that the Nazi war program affected the whole future of the American nation, and for having courageously shaped government policies in view of the necessity for American intervention. After the mistake of the Spanish blockade, President Roosevelt refused to be imposed upon by the opinion of so many Americans who thought that this continent was in no danger and that, no matter what happened to the rest of the world, here life and business could go on as usual. In the teeth of strong and vocal opposition by blind politicians and business men, by pacifists and isolationists, by racial and religious groups, President Roosevelt with foresight and full consciousness of his responsibilities went on with his plans as far as he was allowed within the limits of his constitutional powers. Events have more than justified his policies.

The Lend-Lease plan, which made it possible for America to give financial assistance, first to Britain and later to all the United Nations, without the stigma that accompanied the transactions of the first World War and caused so much criticism and ill feeling; the steps taken to make the United States the arsenal of the democracies; and finally the appearance, after the challenge of Pearl Harbor, of large American military forces, war material, and supplies at all war fronts that could be reached —these are all accomplishments which will be remembered in history as successive steps for the fulfillment of a tremendous task which only the United States could have performed.

We do not know how long the war will last nor whether President Roosevelt will still be at the helm when peace is restored and the infinitely greater task of world political and economic reorganization is begun. But there can be no question that the task will be done with the fullest participation of the United States. In view of the enormous financial support, of the resources in men and materials, of the power and prestige which this nation is contributing to the war effort; and in view of the economic assistance which it will be expected to give to many countries after the war, it is justifiable to assume that the United States will have to take the leadership in the work of reconstruction. In the interest of our national security and the future of American liberty, we must assume a large share of responsibility for the reorganization of the world on the basis of an enduring peace.

Britain will unquestionably share this leadership with the United States. Her power and resources, both spiritual and material, are great. Mr. Winston Churchill, who became Prime Minister when the life of Britian and her Empire hung on a thread and who managed to reorganize British forces in spite of the cruel blows of the Luftwaffe, will pass down into history as the representative of the indomitable spirit and heroic determination of a great people. Their successful resistance when left to carry on the fight alone have earned for the British the admiration and gratitude of all Axis opponents. Her world-wide influence through the British Commonwealth of Nations is a great asset. Britain must be one of the pillars upon which the new world order will stand.

The British policy of the past century was based on the system of the so-called balance of power which, in the British interpretation, meant keeping the nations of continental Europe in a state of unstable equilibrium and rivalry that allowed Britain, by throwing her weight now on one side and now on the other, to play her own game with little risk to herself and be left undisturbed in expanding her Empire. To be sure, a selfish and unscrupulous diplomacy was not the exclusive privilege of England, but certainly this policy contributed more than any other factor to the perpetuation in continental Europe of that state of unrest, suspicion, and jealousy which led the nations to a ruinous competition in armaments and made new wars inevitable.

This system broke down with the first World War, when German military power proved to be stronger than that of Britain and her allies, whose victory was only secured by the armed intervention of the United States. It then seemed obvious that the old system could not be counted on to secure peace, and farsighted statesmen made the first attempt to replace it by a new system of collective guarantees through the League of Nations. Unfortunately, the United States failed to join and went back to its complacent isolationism, while Britain, still more unfortunately, resumed her old game of balance of power.

Annoyed and alarmed by the boisterous claims of a French

hegemony over continental Europe, British diplomacy tried once more the old trick of pitting the new Germany, at that time considered harmless, against Gallic chauvinism; it ostracized Soviet Russia as a power which sooner or later must be driven from European soil; it played ball willingly with Mussolini, then with Hitler, then with Franco in Spain; it did its utmost to shake the foundations of the ill-fated League of Nations.

The old game did not work for long. It got out of hand when Hitler snatched the power of initiative from British diplomacy in blackmailing the other European powers. Since she was unprepared to face a new showdown, Britain shifted to the policy of appeasement. Needless to say, this was precisely the kind of encouragement Hitler needed to feel that the time was ripe for the successful execution of his plans for world domination.

Britain has paid dearly for all these mistakes. She brought herself almost to the brink of ruin. What saved her from a disaster more complete than that she had faced during the first World War was the fact that the United States found it necessary, for its own salvation, to come to her rescue. It seems reasonable enough, after this second terrific experience, to expect England to be convinced that the old game of the balance of power cannot be played again, and that her full and unstinted collaboration in the task of establishing a new system of collective international security is indispensable for her own sake, as well as for the sake of world peace. Since, however, several of the shortsighted men who were responsible for her previous mistakes are still in positions of power, and since there are signs that the old diplomatic tradition is far from dead in some British political circles, the question naturally arises whether or not British collaboration in the post-war period will be hampered by reactionary and imperialistic forces from within. No less disturbing is the question whether the government of the United States will resist such policies or eventually acquiesce to, or worse, cooperate with, them.

We take the view that neither Britain nor the United States can afford to experiment with the peace of Europe and of the world, and that therefore the old balance-of-power policy and imperialism must be abandoned. Hence, the solution to the Italian problem must be approached with a new order in view, based on collective international security and on the maintenance of democratic institutions.

The third power which will have a leading part in the establishment of the new order in the Western World will be Soviet Russia. Whether we like it or not, we must accept the Russian factor in post-war Europe. The resourceful resistance of her armies in the darkest moments of retreat, the brilliance of her victories over highly mechanized German troops, the heroism of her defense of Leningrad and Stalingrad have brought Soviet Russia to the fore as a great military power. The ability and ingenuity she has shown in this war also give assurance that, by exploiting her large natural resources, Russia will soon become a great industrial and economic power.

The rest of Europe must reckon with the fact that the war has brought about a spiritual unification of the Russian people. It has so strengthened the regime of the Federated Soviet Republics that reactionary and conservative political circles in Europe and America must give up any hopes they may have had of Russian disintegration through internal revolution or of radical changes in the Soviet Constitution.

To be sure, the Russia which will emerge out of this war cannot be precisely the same as it was before the German invasion. The cruel experiences of these last two years, the great losses in men and materials, the drastic accommodation of all institutions to the exigencies of military operations and purposes, and, last but not least, the close contacts with the democracies for the common good—all these cannot fail to affect the minds and the emotions of the Russians and their leaders. Changes will occur which, as we hope, will bring the spirit and the letter of the Soviet Constitution nearer to the ideals of democratic freedom and collective security, ideals which are to be the foundations of the new world order.

It is no longer either wise or useful to frown upon the experiments in progressive radicalism which Russia has carried on, violent though the methods of achievement have been. We must not shut our eyes to the fact that large sections of the people of many European countries will look to Russia as a model for those political, social, and economic reforms most beneficial to the masses. The main problem confronting most European countries after the war will be to introduce such reforms without bloodshed and through constitutional measures unhampered by reactionary upheavals.

It will be necessary for the United States, Britain, and other European nations to deal frankly with Russia, if they wish to inspire mutual confidence. Only a real union of nations will achieve the desired goal of peace, order, and social justice in the world. If, instead of exerting ourselves now to create this spirit of mutual confidence and loyalty, we start erecting political, economic, and moral barricades with which to embarrass or even to combat tomorrow our allies of today, Europe will again fall into an abyss of blood and destruction, worse than the one from which we are now struggling to emerge.

We must assume, then, that the cooperation of Soviet Russia will be offered and accepted in peace times, just as it is now during the war. It is with this assumption that we shall approach the problem of Italy.

Keeping in mind this general scheme of things to come, we intend to analyze:

First: the present status of the Italian problem and of the various elements which must be taken into consideration, if we wish to understand its specific aspects and implications.

Second: the principles, policies, and practical measures by which a solution, in our opinion satisfactory, may be reached in accordance with the general scheme of international collective security and peace to be set up when the defeat of the Axis is completed.

In connection with the first point we shall try to describe, from well-established facts and their implications, what kind of plans concerning post-war Italy have been made, or are in the making, in the inner circles of the Foreign Office and the State Department.

One very important problem, and one which cannot be ignored, is whether post-war Italy should retain the monarchy or work out her rehabilitation under a republican form of government; whether the Italian people will be allowed to make a free choice or will be practically coerced into accepting the choice of others. This is not merely a question of form of government. It is also tantamount—as we shall see—to the question whether Fascism shall be wiped out and eradicated from Italian life, or whether it shall remain, disguised in mitigated form.

Since the impression that the Italian people are incapable of self-government and of living peacefully under a democratic or republican constitution is so widespread among Americans, we shall analyze this question in detail. Above all, we shall call the attention of our readers to the fact that the responsibility for the triumph of Fascism in Italy does not rest only upon the Italian people but is shared also by the peoples and governments of the democratic nations. If this be true, as we are sure it is, then the measures to be taken against a prostrate Italy must be dictated by the consciousness of this shared responsibility.

Last but not least, a measure of responsibility for the success and the international prestige gained by Fascism falls upon the Vatican. And as the Vatican contributed, both directly and indirectly, toward making the fortune of Fascism, so it is contributing now to the plans for the future of Italy which are being hatched in our high political spheres. It will not be amiss to throw a little light on this matter.

As for the second point, we intend to deal only with the main issues which will confront the Italian regime after the fall of

Fascism. What we hope to be able to do at present is to indicate the general direction in which the new Italian constitution should set its sails. It would be foolhardy to try to go beyond this aim. The new constitution must express the will of the Italian people, not the imposed will of others, and must be made as time goes on by representatives elected by the people.

We speak as private individuals having no brief or commission of any kind except our love for Italy and our undivided loyalty to the United States.

I. Fascism Without Mussolini

1. Plans in the Making

IN AN address delivered to the American people on February 12, 1943, President Roosevelt went out of his way to reassure the world that the American government and its allies intend to destroy entirely the so-called totalitarian dictatorial regimes:

No nation in the world that is free to make a choice is going to set itself under the Fascist form of government, or the Nazi form of government, or the Japanese war-lord form of government. Such forms are all offspring of seizure of power followed by the abridgment of freedom. Therefore the United Nations can properly say of these forms of government two simple words: NEVER AGAIN!

The President also stated most emphatically:

The world may rest assured that this total war—this sacrifice of lives all over the globe—is not being carried on for the purpose or even the remotest idea of keeping the Quislings or Lavals in power anywhere on this earth.

Why does the world need to be reassured that these are the aims of our total war?

It is evident that several events which have taken place during these last months, together with the apparent direction of the policies of our State Department concerning post-war aims, have created in a large section of the American people growing doubts, suspicions, and fears which can no longer be ignored.

President Roosevelt seemed much annoyed by the criticisms lately directed against the members of the State Department and denounced the critics as being "professional skeptics," "men of little faith," and "pettifoggers" who "are attempting to obscure the essential truths of the war and are seeking to befog the present and the future and the clear purposes and high principles for which the free world now maintains the promise of undimmed victory."

We cannot help thinking that, for once, the pettifoggers have performed a useful service if, by their attempt "to befog the present and the future," they have forced President Roosevelt himself to come out of the clouds which surround our foreign policy and make frank statements concerning the Fascist regimes.

The Administration has been greatly criticized both here and in Britain for the Darlan affair and for the whole policy of government applied in North Africa by the American commander of the expedition. These measures, according to the speakers for the Administration, were justified by military expediency and had the character of temporary arrangements. Information coming from various sources seems to justify at least in part this official statement and to bear out the contention that the services of Darlan and other Vichy men were useful in avoiding more bloodshed in the occupation of French North Africa by American and British troops. Whether or not there was any other way of overcoming the obstacles with which our army was confronted, or whether in coming to terms and accepting the services of Darlan and his followers we paid a much higher price and made more concessions than it was wise to do, are problems which must remain unanswered for the time being and for as long as the American people are kept in the dark about the events that took place behind the curtains in North Africa.

It cannot be denied that the Darlan-Peyrouton affair has had an enormous repercussion, not only in the United States, but among the people of other nations, who were taken aback by the easy yielding to a compromise with Fascism which characterized the first landing of American forces on the shores of the Mediterranean. The North African experiment was taken as representing the pattern and model to be followed elsewhere in the near future. Fuel was added to the fire by a Washington correspondent, Kingsbury Smith, who seems to enjoy the confidence of the State Department and who, in an article published in the *American Mercury* for November, 1942, had already stated clearly that the European nations should expect, not an immediate return to democratic forms of government, but a long transitional period of semi-dictatorships. Later, in February, 1943, this same correspondent, again in the *American Mercury*, told the American public that had been shocked by the Darlan compromise to resign itself to receiving further and greater shocks of the same kind in the progress of the European campaign.

Almost at the same time that Darlan was given leave to retain control of North Africa, the War Department accepted with thanks an offer made by Mr. Otto Hapsburg, the Austrian pretender, to form and lead an Austrian legion to be recruited in the United States among Austrian citizens or American citizens of Austrian descent. It is obvious that the Secretary of War could not have taken such a step without the consent of the President, and it is no less obvious that the recognition of Mr. Otto Hapsburg as the leader of an Austrian legion supposed to fight side by side with American soldiers suggested political implications as to the future of Austria; in other words, it suggested that the American government would back the restoration of the Hapsburg Empire.

It is difficult to imagine that this step could have been justified by military necessity as in the case of Darlan, or even by military precaution, which is the explanation given for our policy of showering with favors and gifts the Falangist regime of Franco in Spain. The War Department obviously did not stop to figure out that there are not enough Austrian men of military age in the United States to make even a meager battalion, much less a legion, unless Mr. Stimson regards as Austrians all the Czechoslovakians, Ruthenians, Poles, Southern Slavs, and Italians who formed a part of the Hapsburg Empire before 1918. It is evident that, apart from being a declaration of policy, the gesture of the War Department had only a symbolic meaning.

Still more equivocal, to put it mildly, has been the attitude of the State Department towards Italy. As far as the American public can judge from what has leaked out about the plans being secretly and discreetly concocted in high circles, our diplomats in Washington are determined to supplant Mussolini with an Italian Darlan or Pétain, either from the civilian or from the military Fascist ranks. If such a plan is carried out, the Savoy monarchy will remain as a guarantee against any radical revolution. A coalition of former leaders, the big business men and clericals supported by the Vatican, would take up the government of the country under the protection of the American and English armies of occupation. Some of the extreme Fascist laws would be abolished, some concessions would be made to save the face of the democracies, and the new regime would, to all appearances, be hailed as a fulfillment of the terms of the Atlantic Charter and the principles so forcibly stated by President Roosevelt.

There is this difference, however, in the handling of the African and the Italian situations. As the prime movers in the African affair, the Americans took the initiative and, as Mr. Eden informed the Commons, thus shouldered the entire responsibility for their collaboration with the men of Vichy. In the Italian affair, on the contrary, British plans had been made long before the State Department gave any hint as to its intentions regarding Italy.

On June 11, 1940, the day after Mussolini embarked upon war against France and England, the *London Times* informed its public that the King of Italy, the Duke of Aosta, and the Crown Prince were not in sympathy with the war policies of Mussolini and had done their best to prevent him from bringing Italy into the fray. By implication, the *Times* made its readers think that these members of the Italian Royal House might be able to do something in the future about removing Italy from the war. This seems also to have been the opinion of the British government because, on December 23, 1940, Prime Minister Churchill, in his address to the Italian people through the British Broadcasting Corporation, told them that "one man and one man alone, against the crown and Royal Family of Italy, against the Pope and all the authority of the Vatican, against the wishes of the Italian people" had ranged Italy in a deadly struggle against the British Empire.

An American newspaperman, R. G. Massock, who was in Italy at that time and had the opportunity to observe directly the reaction of the Italian people to Churchill's speech, wrote in *Italy From Within*, p. 299, that "it was masterful rhetoric, but a complete fiasco." One need not be a towering intellect to realize that "one man and one man alone" could not have forced forty-five million Italians to go to war against the wishes of the Royal family, the army, the Church, and the people themselves. One man alone could not impose his will unless he were backed by a system of government that allowed him to have his way in face of all opposition; and, of course, the leaders and supporters of such a political system are equally responsible for its evil results. The action of "one man" becomes the action of many; the "one man" is the ringleader of the system.

By saddling Mussolini, and not the entire Fascist regime, with the whole responsibility for Italy's war against England, and by urging the Italian people to get rid of "one man and one man alone," Mr. Churchill was telling the great majority of Italians, who never have had, and never will have, any use for Fascism, that what they should do is, merely, to substitute Fascism without Mussolini for Fascism with Mussolini and everything will be fine.

In the same address Mr. Churchill said, speaking of Mussolini, "That he is a great man I do not deny," but he added that this great man became "a criminal" when he declared war on England. Hence, it follows that "surely the time has come when the Italian monarchy and people should have a word to say on these awe-inspiring issues; surely the Italian army should take care of the life and future of Italy." The Italian Fascists who are still loyal to Mussolini certainly appreciated Churchill's admission as to the greatness of the Duce, but they must have wondered by what humorous quirk of fate a great man could turn into a criminal overnight, merely because he declared war on England. In December, 1940, things were not going so well for England on her various battlefields and the Italian Fascists could not help thinking that, after all, the "great man" was right and must be supported by all possible means in the accomplishment of his great work.

The "fiasco" of Churchill's address was soon underlined by the reaction of the Monarchy. Unmoved by the flattery and the appeal of Churchill, the King issued a message to the armed forces urging them to see to it that "no obstacle should halt the rise of Italy." The Crown Prince, too, issued a manifesto to the army ending with the words: "Hail to the King! Hail to the Duce!" The Queen took such pains to identify herself with the German alliance that she adopted the German language and even went so far as to force the Japanese ambassador to speak it also, though the little Nipponese diplomat knew scarcely any German. The wife of the Crown Prince, Marie Jose of Belgium, who was looked upon by some people as an opponent of Fascism because in 1938 in Switzerland she had attended a concert directed by Toscanini, chose precisely a day following Churchill's speech to announce that she had been received as a registered member of the feminine section of the Fascist party (R. G. Massock, *Italy from Within*, pp. 299–300, 389, 390).

For a full appreciation of the policy which the British Foreign Office maintained toward the Italian Monarchy, nothing is more instructive than to observe the antics of the English newspapers as they reflected the views of the diplomatic circles and rather pitifully attempted to keep alive the hope that the Italian Monarchy would, at a given moment, divorce the German master and throw itself into the arms of England.

The King's reaction to Churchill's speech was very disappointing, and hence, in the spring of 1941 the English newspapers published great eulogies of the Duke of Aosta, Viceroy of Ethiopia, who, trapped with his army and cut off from communication with Italy, was finally forced to surrender to the British. The public was told that the Duke of Aosta had always disliked Mussolini and could be trusted and regarded as a friend of England. Much was made of the fact that the Duke had been educated at Eton and as a former Etonian had many friends and connections in the British ruling class.

This news must have surprised the Italians very much, for they knew only too well that the House of Aosta had been closely connected with Fascism from the very beginning. Indeed, it was as a reward for his loyal support that the Duke of Aosta was made Viceroy of Ethiopia by Mussolini.

Very soon, however, it was learned that, while a prisoner of the British in Kenya, the Duke of Aosta was dying of tuberculosis. This was bad luck for the British, to be sure, but the gentlemen of the Foreign Office were undismayed. Their next move was to bring the King down from the attic once more, dust him off, and set him up for a new exhibition. On November 11, 1941, the King's birthday, the British Broadcasting Corporation sent him the good wishes and greetings of the British, just as if the declaration of war on England had not been approved and signed by the King himself. Then, fearing that perhaps the King was too old to be of much future value, the Foreign Office decided to give the Crown Prince a boost. In February, 1942, a dispatch from Lisbon to the *London Daily Telegraph,* reproduced by the American newspapers, urged us to believe that the Crown Prince had turned anti-Fascist and anti-Nazi overnight, nay, that at heart he had always been so, and that, as a result, the Fascist leaders in Italy were exerting every pressure to prevent the old King from abdicating, "for they knew well that should the Prince of Piedmont succeed him, he would immediately issue a call to the people in an endeavor to make peace" (*New York Times,* February 17, 1942).

We wish we could say, at this point, that the solutions of the

Italian problem suggested by the British Foreign Office have been rejected by the diplomats who direct the American State Department. From the beginning, democratic America has looked down upon kings and dictators, and now she has gone to war to preserve for herself and to secure to other people the four freedoms essential to a democratic way of life. It is, therefore, all the more bewildering to find that the policies maintained by the British Tories toward Italy have been more or less adopted by the State Department.

We are not indulging in idle speculation; there is ample evidence that, so far as the Italian problem is concerned, London and Washington see eye to eye, and that they have mapped out the future of Italy in full agreement.

As we shall see more in detail later on, our State Department shared fully the conviction of the British and French governments that Mussolini would remain a non-belligerent and never actually join Hitler on the battlefield. Disappointed in this expectation after June, 1940, they clung to the hope of concluding a separate peace with Mussolini himself. The American press, which reflects more or less the views of our diplomatic circles, was still cherishing this hope in 1942. In fact, we were told by the *Chicago Daily News* on April 25, 1942, that "only by a separate peace . . . can Mussolini hope to save either himself or whatever is left of his regime." And then came the mystery story, printed in the *New York Times*, May 17, 1942, about the group of Fascists who had planned to kidnap Mussolini because they were afraid that he was only moderately pro-German. Most likely, this last humorous invention was the work of a witty Fascist who was making fun of the credulous Anglo-Saxon public.

The military operations in North Africa and the arrangement which left "the Vichy authorities," that is to say, Darlan, in charge of the administration there, immediately raised new hopes that the "Roman atmosphere" might feel the beneficial effect of the Allies' attitude. On November 27, 1942, the *London Daily Mail* remarked:

The last circumstance [Darlan's appointment] is bound to raise secret speculation here [in London] and there [in Rome]. Should things come to the worst, part of the Fascist system might not be perhaps saved by jettisoning Mussolini with his own consent may be and the pro-German section of the party? . . . Should Eisenhower get control of Byzerta more than one Roman dignitary will no doubt examine himself stealthily in the mirror for some resemblance to Admiral Darlan.

The "Roman dignitaries" ready to resemble Darlan are numerous indeed. The Count of Turin, cousin of the King, and then Grandi, so popular with the Cliveden set when he was Mussolini's ambassador to His Majesty's Government, and then Badoglio, and perhaps Federzoni, the chairman of the Italian Academy, as well as several others. Someone has even thought of exhuming the octogenarians Caviglia and Orlando, as if the task to be performed in Italy were merely to establish a Chinese cult of ancestor worship. Graziani, the butcher of Lybia and Addis Ababa, was also a candidate. Even the ill-famed Marshal Cavallero, who after 1928, as manager of the Ansaldo Shipbuilding Company, was involved in a scandal over the construction of warships and who was later Chief of the General Staff during the campaign against Greece, was mentioned as a possible "leader," when he was ousted by Mussolini.

Of course, it was not expected that these leaders would stand alone. They would be supported by some section of the population, or, to be more specific, by the same big business men who financed the Fascist movement in its early days and who have, in Mussolini's shadow, squeezed the last drop of blood from the Italian people during the past twenty years. The magazine *Life* (December 14, 1942) got the following hint from London:

The clear tendency within the Fascist regime is to get rid of Mussolini and the pro-Germans but to preserve the system. Today this is the idea of Italian big industrialists, reportedly led by Ciano, Count Volpi, Senator Pirelli. In other words, a change of pro-German Fascism to pro-Allied Fascism. Leading Fascists are greatly impressed by Darlan's successful switch from Vichy to the Allies.

There is no evidence at all that this "clear tendency" could be discovered "within the regime," but certainly the suggestion made by the Foreign Office must have pleased very much the gentlemen to whom it was addressed: Pirelli, who represents the big industrialists; Volpi, who represents the big financiers; and Ciano, who represents that group of leading Fascist politicians, penniless before the march on Rome but now, by virtue of their plundering, the wealthiest men in Italy. It is most likely, however, that these gentlemen would accept such a kind suggestion as that of the British only after Hitler and Mussolini have surrendered to the United Nations. Then they would be only too glad to substitute pro-Allied Fascism for pro-German Fascism.

2. *Revolution and Separate Peace*

No one has ever insisted that the French, the Belgians, the Dutch, the Norwegians, or the Danes should rise and openly revolt against their Nazi overlords. Only the Italians have been urged to try revolution. This dubious privilege has been awarded them only because a timely Italian revolution would be a godsend from the military point of view. Unfortunately, the suggestion that a Nazi-controlled people revolt is folly. A disorganized and unarmed people cannot rise up against a government which has at its disposal all the implements and complements of war. The collapse of the Second Empire in France in September of 1870, the revolution in Russia in 1917, the Austrian and German revolutions in 1918—all were aftermaths of military defeats. It is only after the armed forces of a government have disintegrated, or only after army chiefs have so thoroughly discredited themselves as to have lost the support of their soldiers, that a serious revolutionary uprising becomes technically possible.

There is nothing that we would like more than to see such another massacre as the Sicilian Vespers, this time directed against the Nazis and Fascists in Sicily. But the daggers and knives which served their purpose in the first Vespers would be inadequate today against totalitarian artillery. Therefore, let us give due credit to Mr. Elmer Davis, Director of the Office of War Information, for his announcement that he does not expect open revolt in Italy. And let us thank him for having put an end to the sinister nonsense of telling Italians four thousand miles away, through commentators snugly tucked away in New York short-wave stations, that they should deliver to us, free of charge, a made-to-order revolution.

The director of the O.W.I. dismissed the idea, not only of an Italian revolution before a Fascist military breakdown takes place, but also of any revolutionary upheaval after such a breakdown has materialized. According to the *New York Sun*, December 7, 1942, he said emphatically: "There is no sign of an active group [in Italy] which could organize real resistance, and we are not encouraging it."

It is obvious that our State Department has not only reached the conclusion that it cannot rely upon a revolution in Italy before British and American armed forces have smashed the Fascist military machine, but it has also lost all interest in any anti-Fascist revolution, since a later revolution would be of no military use. There are headaches enough. According to the "American Plan for a Reorganized World," which was outlined in the *American Mercury* for November, 1942, one of the American aims is to "prevent revolution from developing in the defeated countries."

Such being the plans of our State Department, it is hard to understand why Secretary Berle, in his address of November 14, 1942, should tell the Italians that they must "drive out the traitors and foreigners who have led Italy to the rim of destruction" and remind them that "freedom is not a gift, it is an achievement. You have to attain it yourselves." It is gratifying, nonetheless, to note that someone has at last said "traitors" in the plural and not laid the blame upon "one man and one man alone." Nor can we object to the fact that the Italians have finally been told that their obligation to themselves comes before any they may have to Great Britain and the United States. Although it is patently absurd to incite the Italians to revolt as long as America and Britain are unable to raze the Fascist military structure, it is not absurd to tell them that they will deserve no consideration among self-respecting peoples if they do not win their own liberty by revolting when the Fascist military collapse takes place. But how can the Italians reconcile Mr. Berle's exhortations to revolt with Mr. Davis' statement that no revolt is encouraged?

At any rate, one policy was consistent. "This government," said Elmer Davis on December 6, 1942, "is not broadcasting personal attacks upon King Victor Emmanuel." Mr. Davis might even have added that no one has ever been allowed to take the name of the King of Italy in vain, or to send any message to the Italians unless he confined himself to cursing exclusively "one man and one man alone." Nay more, on June 8, 1942, the Italian listener to American short-wave broadcasts was served a dish of childish historical misstatements in praise of Charles Albert, the great-grandfather of the present incumbent of the Italian throne. The constitution he bestowed upon the Italians in 1848 was so lauded as to make it seem only sensible for the Italians of to-morrow to restore it, although the present King has wholly discarded it.

At the same time, Sir Gerald Campbell, special assistant to Viscount Halifax, British Ambassador to the United States, told us that "although Italy may wish to withdraw from the war, the country has no leader with whom the United Nations might negotiate"; and he expressed the hope that "such a leader will arise" (*New York Herald Tribune*. November 7, 1942).

Sir Gerald no doubt realizes that, while under a free constitution a leader of the opposition is always available, under a dictatorship, any leader, or prospective leader, who threatens opposition, is dispatched to the next world without further ado, as soon as he arises; Matteotti experienced this principle of

Fascist law. Who can foretell what French leader shall arise when Pétain and Laval have been sent to join the shade of Darlan? Does Sir Gerald think that "leaders" of the so-called governments-in-exile really represent the will of their peoples? We suspect that when they return to their countries these "leaders" will have a bad time indeed, unless they return in all humility. The leaders who supplant Mussolini in Italy cannot appear before the collapse of the Fascist regime, and they will arise from among those men who are on the spot. Asking Italy to produce a leader now, because Sir Gerald needs one with whom to negotiate, is a poor joke. If Sir Gerald is seeking his man among those who fought Fascism during the twenty years that the British Foreign Ministers were hurrying to Rome to do business with Mussolini, he knows where to find them. They are either in prison or in exile. Sir Gerald has no such idea in mind, however. He evidently expects to find his man in Italy among the prominent Fascists.

This demand for "leaders" of the type envisaged by Sir Gerald is but an offshoot of Fascist and Nazi thinking—a hankering after the man on horseback, or perhaps a feeling that the common man does not count and that a nation cannot produce leaders when and as they are needed. No, they must be ready-made and placed on the counter with their appropriate price-tags.

"Every road leads to Rome," they say in Italy. And everything we gather about British and American plans concerning Italy leads us to the same conclusion. What the British Foreign Office and the American State Department want to set up in Italy is a Fascist regime without Mussolini in place of the Fascist regime with Mussolini. When they invoke an Italian revolution, they mean a revolution with an eye-dropper, or rather, a respectable coup d'état engineered against the Duce by his prospective successors. The only thing the Italians have to do is to keep quiet and obey their new masters. This is why even Graziani has been mentioned as a possible successor to Mussolini. No man better than he, a sadistic criminal at best, would qualify to prevent or stifle in Italy upheavals which might disturb the siestas of the British Foreign Office and the American State Department.

The Fascist "leaders" with whom Sir Gerald would negotiate would be expected to give him a separate peace. Pétain gave Hitler a separate peace. Therefore, why shouldn't some Italian Fascist "leader" give a separate peace to Mr. Churchill and Mr. Roosevelt?

In April, 1942, England and America were bombarded from Berne, Ankara, Cairo, and even Buenos Aires with news of a possible separate peace between Italy and the United Nations. When the British and American newspapers had been injected with this dope by "influential diplomats" (that is to say, by German and Italian agents), Mussolini went to see Hitler in Austria in order to show that the Axis was stronger than ever. In addition, Italian newspapers and radio stations were instructed to make fun of anyone in Italy who had taken Britain and America seriously. Then, just to liven things up, at the end of May, while Mussolini was demanding territories from Laval, the King and his son, the handsome Umberto, went in person to review troops massed near the French border.

Anyone who is not wholly ignorant of Italian affairs knows that even if the King, the Crown Prince, and such men as Badoglio and Grandi, together with their peers, were by a miracle (it would take a miracle, since none of them is noted for his courage) to be converted overnight into men of independent mind and break away from Hitler and Mussolini, the problem which would confront them could not be readily solved. A dictator like Mussolini cannot be impeached and returned to private life as can the president of a democratic country. He cannot even flee abroad, for no nation would receive him. He must either render his ramparts invulnerable in his own country or be executed. And that's the rub! The Duce is protected on all sides by the secret police. His Achilles' heel is a military conspiracy against him. As the result of such a military coup d'état the whole Fascist party might be disbanded. But a military conspiracy with sufficient force to succeed against the Fascist party could be accomplished only if the army chiefs took the initiative. The question is, will they?

After acting as indispensable accessories to all Mussolini's crimes for twenty years, these army chiefs are now being told that there is still room for them on Mr. Churchill's and Mr. Roosevelt's laps. The more fools they, if, granting they took to the idea of breaking away from Mussolini, they did so before their chief was utterly defeated. As long as there is some chance that he will weather this Cape of Storms under Hitler's umbrella, anyone breaking away from him would run serious immediate risks with no certain future gains. Let them, therefore, wait and see how things turn out. Any time they choose to abandon the sinking ship, they will be received with open arms into our camp. It matters not who the winner may be, the military lords of Italy will come out with both their skins and their positions. They may even be chosen as post-war dictators for Italy. The lot of gangsters has become a comfortable one throughout the world, thanks to the fear of revolution which blinds the leaders of liberty-loving peoples.

Add to the sum of these facts the obvious truth that Italy is no longer an independent nation. Nazi political "advisers," economic "coordinators," military "missions," "comrades-in-arms," railway "executives," "experts" of all kinds, and "agents" of the Gestapo—all control the most vital points, in fact every vital point, in Italy. There are no less than 300,000 German soldiers in Italy. Three hundred thousand Italian workmen are in German factories; these are hostages in Hitler's hands. Italy is no less a German-occupied country than France. France has Pétain and Laval; Italy has her King and her Duce. The day the Italian government wavers in its loyalty to the German alliance will be a grievous one, for it will also be the day on which German "invisible" occupation becomes entirely visible, and will be followed by a well-deserved "purge" in the best Hitlerian style.

Last but not least, what do the British Foreign Office and the American State Department offer to the King, the Crown Prince, and their cohorts, if they should decide to break away from Hitler? In its issue of November 7, 1942, the London *New Statesman and Nation* deplored the grimly typical plans of "certain influential circles" in Britain which maintain that, when the Allies have won the war, the logical procedure for Britain is to create a new balance of power in the Mediterranean by "strengthening" some of the smaller Allied nations and by "weakening" or even breaking up Italy. Observed the *New Statesman and Nation* wisely, "Listening to some of these plans for European reconstruction takes one back to the peacemakers who used to carve up Europe in the eighteenth century."

If one wants to get a glimpse of what those eighteenth-century ideas were, one has but to read an editorial in the London *Nineteenth Century and After*, November, 1942:

No exceptional insight is needed to see what British foreign policy ought to be—the policy indicated by the words *balance of power*. . . . The purpose of Allied operations against Italy should be a separate peace on the most moderate terms possible. She must of course be disarmed, she must withdraw from the Balkans and cede Istria (with Trieste, Fiume and Pola) to Yugoslavia. She must restore the Greek Islands to Greece. She must surrender the island of Pantelleria *for strategic reasons*. She has already lost Abyssinia. The future of Libya and Cyrenaica must be determined, above all, by the demands of *British Mediterranean strategy*. . . . She should not be made to suffer any undue humiliation or exactions. . . . It is true that if Italy wanted to make a separate peace, the Germans would not let her. Nevertheless, the certainty of peace on moderate terms will make a rift between Berlin and Rome. . . . The equilibrium of Europe and the security of the Mediterranean demand a strong Yugoslavia disposing of naval bases and a fleet that will give her the command of the Adriatic. . . . Yugoslavia and Greece should receive at last a considerable part of the Italian fleet and air force under terms of peace and should be enabled to draw on the Italian shipbuilding industry, at least for a period, so that the foundation of Balkan sea-power, *as auxiliary to the British sea-power* may be laid [*italics ours*].

The Italians would be expected to feel grateful for these "most moderate terms" and happy that Britain has not asked for more.

Such ideas are not fostered only in England. The *New York Times,* in one of its leading articles for December 1, 1942, pointed out that a problem exists which "would concern the borders of Italy, especially those that have been in dispute with Yugoslavia." If the *New York Times* had told us that there is to the east of Gorizia, Trieste, and Istria a compact population of about 250,000 Slavs who should be left free to go with Yugoslavia, and that this would in no way harm Italian national integrity, it would have been stating the issue. But the equivocal phrasing of its statement strongly suggests that in America, too, something malodorous is being cooked up in the kitchen.

If one needs further indoctrination, he can meditate on what Commander King-Hall, an influential British M.P., wrote in the London weekly *Picture Post* of November 21, 1942. He stated that if Italy breaks away from Hitler, "the United Nations will respect the territorial integrity *of the mainland of Italy. Italy's frontiers will be as in 1914* [*italics ours*]." By "mainland" Commander King-Hall seems to mean the Italian peninsula exclusive of the islands of Sicily and Sardinia. And by saying that the "frontiers will be as in 1914" he implies that not only the compactly Slavic territory with a population of about 250,000 in the hinterland of Gorizia, Trieste, and Istria would be severed from Italy, but also Trentino, Gorizia, Trieste, and Istria. Such would be the reward of the Italians, if they broke away from Hitler. Commander King-Hall does not say what the Italians may expect, if they do not comply with his summons to join the United Nations. We can guess: utter dismemberment.

The motives underlying this plan are obvious. The wise men of the British Foreign Office, whatever their intention as to setting up a system of "collective security" in Europe, wish to secure for the British Navy and the Air Force full control of the Mediterranean. Owing to the development of submarine and air warfare, the small island of Malta is no longer suitable for such

a purpose. Sicily and Sardinia, however, would be excellent situations for air and naval bases. The British Admiralty (the "influential circles" of the *New Statesman*) covets them.

To be sure, section one of the Atlantic Charter told us that
Britain and the United States "seek no aggrandizement, territorial or otherwise." But Great Britain will never seek that aggrandizement. If it happens, it will be the other United Nations
which will force Britain to take over Sicily and Sardinia, and
Britain, though unwilling, will bow to their demands. Territorial aggrandizement is usually called "responsibility" by the
British.

It is also true that section two of the Atlantic Charter states
that the United Nations "desire to see no territorial changes
that do not accord with the freely expressed wishes of the peoples
concerned." But plebiscites could be easily manufactured in the
Europe of tomorrow, where the starving populations will be
forced to reply upon British and American relief.

It would hurt Italian feelings to see Sicily and Sardinia in
British hands. However, the Italians might be kept so busy by
their eastern neighbors that they would not have time to mourn.
In 1915 Sir Edward Grey allotted to Italy Slavic Dalmatia and
German South Tyrol. Why, then, shouldn't Mr. Anthony Eden
allot Trentino to Mr. Otto Hapsburg and Trieste and Istria either
to Otto or to Yugoslavia, according to circumstances? Some such
distribution will be necessary for the realization of the British
diplomatic dream, which is to restore the old balance-of-power
policy; for it is only by the juggling of racial minorities, now
to one side of a boundary, now to the other, that this game can
be successfully played.

From these observations, it becomes possible for us to understand how General Simovich, then Premier of the Yugoslav
Government-in-Exile, could list in his radio address of June 27,
1941, Istria, Trieste, Gorizia, among the national territories
claimed by Yugoslavia. A group of American citizens and resi-

dents of Italian origin lodged a protest with Viscount Halifax against the statement in which the general made these claims. Lord Halifax answered in the following words: "I am glad to be able to state that the Yugoslav President of the Council was stating his own views for which His Majesty's Government accepts no responsibility." The Viscount did not say that "His Majesty's Government had never promised nor would ever promise Gorizia, nor Trieste, nor Istria to any Yugoslav Government." He merely said that the British government did not accept responsibility for the fact that Simovich had such views. Yet it might, on its own account, have views identical with those of General Simovich. General Simovich's radio address could not have been broadcast without the sanction of the Foreign Office, since not one single word is broadcast from London, unless it has been authorized by the proper officials. General Simovich's views were something more than his own personal views.

A striking difference is to be observed between the apparent proposed treatment of France and that of Italy in British and American declarations of settlements after the war. If by "Italy" and "France" one means the Italian and French peoples, neither is responsible for the blunders and crimes of their political and military leaders. At the most, both are responsible to the same extent for blindly allowing their leaders to do what they did. If, on the other hand, by "Italy" and "France" one means the Italian and French governments, it is not clear why Pétain should be regarded as less criminal or less contemptible than Mussolini and the King of Italy. Nevertheless, the French are consistently told that France will be restored to her previous position; the Italians are never told what future they are to expect. The significance of such silence is obvious. A strong France is needed for the British Foreign Office to carry on in Europe its traditional policy of balance of power; whereas a dismembered Italy would permit the British Admiralty to seize control of the Mediterranean route.

An American journalist, Mr. Chinigo, who was in Italy up to the end of the year 1941 was asked by popular leaders and even by officials who were Fascists only by necessity:

"What sort of a post-war world is America planning? What will be the fate of the Italian people as a national unit in America's plans? Will we be made to suffer for a course we were bludgeoned into pursuing?" . . . These men who have already chosen the black leaders whom they will pluck from being on the day of Italy's national vendetta ask that America give them the answers now (*Boston Daily Record*, February 3, 1942).

Another American newspaperman, Mr. Herbert Matthews, who lived in Italy up to the spring of 1942, wrote in the *New York Times Magazine* for December 6, 1942:

If an invasion of Italy is to be attempted the careful psychological planning that is necessary should include clear-cut guarantees to the Italians that neither Britain nor any other nation is going to slice up their country after the war. There is a certain fear among Italians that Britain might ask for Sicily and Sardinia as bases when the war is over. By radio and other means, including the underground, assurances of the integrity of their territory should be made known to the Italians. . . . It is a question of showing the Italians that a triumphant Germany will make Italy one more vassal state in Europe and that a triumphant United States will make Italy a free and intact nation.

But the men of the British Foreign Office and the British Ministry of Information seem to think that the most suitable psychological preparation for an invasion of Italy includes the pledge to Italian Fascists and anti-Fascists alike that their country will be broken up or at least mutilated.

Mussolini has not yet given any signal of alarm of the danger which threatens Italian national integrity. It would be foolhardy for him to call attention to the dangerous pass to which he has brought the Italian nation. But when he is up to his neck, he will not fail to use this point to rally the Italians to the defense of their national unity against "Anglo-Saxon Imperialism."

It is hard to believe that there are in Italy, even among the most stupid and corrupt Fascist politicians, people willing to break away from Hitler in order to pave the way for the mutilation of their own country. Even if such people can be found, how do the American and English governments think they can carry on the affairs of Italy in her name and sign treaties and agreements binding on the Italian people? Under such conditions, those leaders could remain in power only so long as they were protected by foreign guns—not one minute longer.

Thus, the most likely assumption is that Mussolini's associates, civil and military, will stick to Mussolini as long as they can. Only on the day when the Nazi-Fascist military strength collapses, being assured of their good British and American Fascist-minded friends' support, would they stage a "fake" revolution to remain masters of Italy.

3. Propaganda

After General Wavell's blitzkrieg in Libya in the spring of 1941, there were great opportunities for the democratic re-education of the Italian prisoners in the Near East. Many of these prisoners, not only privates but officers as well, were fed up with Mussolini. They applauded anti-Fascist speakers at improvised meetings. The idea spread among them that an anti-Fascist legion should be formed. In the beginning, British local authorities favored this plan, and segregated the anti-Fascist prisoners from the Fascists. A thousand privates and ninety-two officers including a colonel had already been gathered together. At this point, however, following orders from London, the British once more grouped together Fascist and anti-Fascist soldiers, under the control of Fascist officers and Fascist chaplains.

The idea that a legion of anti-Fascist volunteers be raised among the Italian war prisoners was not peculiar to the war prisoners in Egypt. In its issue for May 17, 1941, the London *New Statesman* published the following item:

What are we doing with our Italian prisoners of war, who now number more nearly 200,000 than 150,000 men? They are thoroughly disillusioned with the Fascist regime, but most of them are political illiterates. Has it occurred to our military authorities that we might help them to educate themselves? The more intelligent of them would welcome books to while away their long captivity. An Italian friend of mine, one of the ablest adversaries of Fascism since its early days, makes a suggestion which I should like to commend to White-hall. It is that we should reprint for their use, of course in Italian, a few outstanding books which could recall to them the free tradi-tions of their motherland. . . . This might begin the process of re-education. Probably it is too optimistic to look to these prisoners as part of a Free Italian or Garibaldian Legion, but we might find some very useful political material if the intention is some day to promote a democratic revival in Italy. The priests in whose care they now are will not turn their minds in that direction.

Most likely, a few months of well-planned intellectual and moral preparation would have yielded a sufficient number of men to form an Italian anti-Fascist legion. It would not have been expected that they would bring victory to the United Na-tions. They would have been utilized in military operations with the aim of creating around them prestige as the result of bravery and sacrifice and of promoting unrest against the Fascist regime in Italy. On the day the Fascist regime in Italy collapses, a few thousand well-equipped and well-disciplined men could act as rallying points for wider military organizations and form the skeleton of the forces for the defense of the new political regime. He who holds the more important cities in a country like Italy, endowed as they are with a centralized civil service, will hold the entire country. This will be especially true, if the population is fed and finds work, thanks to friendly relations between the provisional government and the victorious powers. That small army of Italians, by their contribution to the war of liberation, would make the support of foreign armies unnecessary to the new regime. Machiavelli teaches that unarmed prophets are doomed. On the other hand, if the men of the new regime were to rely on foreign armed help, they would be discredited and it would be impossible for them to confront, with the necessary moral prestige, the daily difficulties attendant on every new government.

But nothing was ever done along those lines. The souls of the Italian war prisoners were entrusted to the care of an Apostolic Delegate who, in the fall of 1941, took a large group of those who were in Palestine to visit the holy places at the expense of the Pope. The *Osservatore Romano,* the Vatican newspaper, on November 18, 1941, rejoiced at such "an initiative, certainly without precedent among prisoners of any war."

Naturally we have no objections to the spiritual comfort that prisoners of war may find in religion and in the ministrations of priests; but anyone who knows how generally the Italian clergy, especially that part of it doing missionary work in foreign countries, has been won over to Fascism, would hardly expect these priests suddenly to become teachers of democracy to the prisoners entrusted to their care.

Mr. Herbert Matthews found the following situation in India:

Politically, the Italian prisoners are all most cautious: some are rabid Fascisti or act that way, but most of them are indifferent, although they are careful not to antagonize the Fascist-minded. A few admit to being anti-Fascists. The commandant said they were "terrified" of anything which smacked of propaganda. They will not listen to the radio, are afraid to read newspapers and whenever anything is done for them they are suspicious (*New York Times,* October 24, 1942).

Those "few" prisoners who admit that they are anti-Fascist must be plucky and stubborn men indeed, if they are prepared to challenge, not only their own Fascist supervisors, but the British overlords as well.

The British government gave the Geneva Convention, which pledges the governments not to carry on any political propaganda among war prisoners, as the reason why no liberal education was allowed. At a time when all conventions have been discarded, this worship of the Geneva Convention, which by the way does not mention political propaganda, deserves unbounded admiration. Do the British think that what the Fascist officers and chaplains who are in control of the prisoners say and do is not political propaganda? The above-quoted *New York Times* correspondent also wrote: "We could not visit or talk to individual prisoners because that is forbidden by the Geneva convention." The prisoners have, however, at their disposal the Rome radio, which supposedly does not carry political propaganda. On the other hand, the Geneva Convention was ignored when the Yugoslav soldiers who were in the Italian army in Libya, and who were made prisoners by the British, were allowed to be reorganized under the Yugoslav flag.

In the London *Daily Mail*, November 11, 1942, one reads:

> People who are in touch with Italian prisoners of war find that the men often have no more idea of the elementary institutions of democracy than they have of the laws of the Medes and the Persians. Some of the prisoners working on the land in this country were surprised at the prosperous conditions of British farmers. It was hoped that this would open their eyes to the blessings of democracy. Instead their naive conclusion has been: So Mussolini was right after all when he told us that the British had got hold of all the riches of the world and left nothing for us poor Italians.

Why should they think otherwise? In the course of two years nobody was allowed to tell them that they were mistaken. This would not only have run counter to the dictates of the Geneva Convention, it might also cause trouble in Italy when the war is over. The Italian war prisoners are to be kept on Fascist ice so that when they return to Italy, they will help maintain "law and order" in the face of "Bolshevism." At the time of writing thousands of Italian war prisoners are being brought to America. Will they be as insulated as those in the hands of the British?

While nothing was being done to create among Italian prisoners a democratic frame of mind which might be put to use in Italy during the period of post-war reconstruction, the British Ministry of Information was chanting in all possible keys the anthem of Italian cowardice.

No reasonably intelligent person laughed at the Polish catastrophe in 1939, the British failure in Norway, and the Dutch, Belgian, and French disasters in 1940, nor at the tragedies of Yugoslavia, Pearl Harbor, Singapore, Java, the Philippines, and Tobruk in 1941 and 1942. When soldiers have to fight against superior armament, or against the obtuseness of their own chiefs, especially if the two go hand in hand, disaster is inevitable. In the case of the Italians in Greece during 1940 and 1941, and in Libya in 1941, as with the French in 1940, inferior armament and bad leadership made a beatable combination. Add to this the fact that the Italians were not fighting a war of self-defense on their own soil, as were the French. They were sent to attack Greece, a small, harmless country from which they had nothing to fear. Then they found themselves fighting in the Libyan desert —the most wretched spot in the world—a spot from which no Italian peasant could ever hope to earn a living by the direst sweat of his brow. On the battlefields of Greece and Libya the Italians "found that right to strike of which Fascist legislation had deprived them in peacetime." Yet, from June, 1940, Pantelleria Island and the Greek Dodecanese in the Eastern Mediterranean were successfully defended, not like Malta, by Britishers against Italians, but by Italians against Britishers. It was 12,000 Italians, not 12,000 Britishers who, abandoned by God and man, without an air force, without anti-aircraft defense, without tanks, with their uniforms in rags, improvised barbed wire out of bundles of thorns, grew vegetables on every available piece of ground in order to have food, and resisted 193 days before surrendering in the plateau of Gondar in Ethiopia. If the defenders of Gondar had been British, the British Ministry of Information would have exalted their heroism to the sky, as they had done for the defenders of Tobruk. If the British Ministry were not run by narrow-minded men, it would not have ignored the daring, desperate attempts made by young Italians to force the defenses of Gibralter and Malta. They would have described them, giving credit where credit was due, but advising them to put their readiness for sacrifice at the service of a better cause. However, the British Ministry of Information had decided that all Italians are cowards, and cowards they must remain.

Intelligent men are generous. It is the stupid man who is not generous, and he pays for his stupidity. When Mussolini embarked on his ill-fated war in June, 1940, there was a universal current of hostility against him in Italy. All those who were in Italy at that time, and have since come away, agree that the days of the collapse of France and the entrance of Italy into the war were days of national mourning in Italy. In street cars, trains, cafes, everyone was silent. The Italian people, generally expansive and talkative, could find no means other than gloomy silence by which to protest against the policies of their dictator. The British Ministry of Information should have taken advantage of such a situation and driven a wedge between the Fascist regime on the one hand and the Italian soldiers and people on the other. They should have told both the soldiers and the civilians that it was sheer folly to die in the service of a criminal and blundering dictator; that by refusing to fight in a dishonest and badly prepared war under the leadership of incompetent generals, they were giving evidence of common sense and foresight; that they would show even greater common sense and foresight by revolting against their military chiefs, making short work of them and marching on Rome to do away with the dictator and his associates. Instead of this, the British Ministry of Information laughed at the cowardice of the Italians.

Mussolini seized upon this blunder and used it to his own advantage. He succeeded in stirring up anger, hatred, and an urge for revenge, especially among officers of the Italian navy, which was not as inefficient as our Colonel Blimps believed, and in the air force, which was reorganized and re-equipped under German leadership.

While there has never been any chance of successful upheavals among the civilian population in Italy, there was bitter discontent in the army, navy, and air force, as a result of graft and mismanagement on the part of the military chiefs. This field for political warfare might have yielded portentous fruits, had it been intelligently handled. The navy would have been particularly fertile ground. Friendship and admiration for Britain have long been traditional in it. Moreover, it had never fallen under Nazi control and it possessed a greater amount of autonomy than the army and the air force. But the eagles of the British Ministry of Information made a special point of using the navy as a butt for their jokes and slanders.

The London *Evening Standard* for November 12, 1942, printed from Montreal, Canada, a Canadian pilot's experiences in Malta:

The Italians come in fairly low, but the Nazis always arrive flying pretty high and go in for hit-and-run tactics. The Italians always stay longer and seem to have more all-round courage.

The correspondent added that the pilot "surprised interviewers by rating Italian fliers who attacked Malta above the Germans, both for courage and skill." Of course he "surprised interviewers." Had not the British Ministry of Information filled the world with stories of Italian cowardice?

In his address of December, 1942, Mr. Churchill ought to have said to the Italians: "We are sorry that we have to bomb you, but war is war. We were bombed by the German and Italian air forces in 1940. We now have to answer in kind. The responsibility for our common suffering is not ours, who did everything possible to avoid the war; it lies with Hitler and his partner Mussolini. As long as this war lasts, we have no choice but to go on bombing Germany and Italy." Instead, Mr. Churchill said: "If you do not surrender we shall reduce you to dust." If the Italians surrender, they are branded as cowards; if they do not, they are to be reduced to dust.

A better knowledge of the human spirit, even if it is not British, would have been of great service to Mr. Churchill. At the time of the Ethiopian rape in 1935–1936, his Tory predecessors had already rendered Mussolini the great service of pushing practically all the Italians into his army by the tragic farce of the so-called sanctions. It seems that Mr. Churchill is now willing to repeat the same mistake on a larger scale, for he is doing his best to force the Italians to close their ranks around Mussolini with a moral unity which did not exist before 1941.

An Englishman who has a thorough knowledge of Italian history and mentality has written as follows:

Italy as a nation has never been ridiculous. The history of the Italian people has been one long tragedy, not least the tragedy of being called "pleasure-loving" by supercilious English people. The truth is that the history of Europe is far more vivid, and has been far more vital, to Italians than to other peoples, precisely because European history is peculiarly the history of Italy. It is Italians, more than any other people, who have suffered from the faults and ambitions not only of their own compatriots, but in a much larger degree from those of foreigners. The Fascist urge of self-assertiveness is not to be patronizingly brushed aside as "faintly ridiculous." It is an explosion of a repression. It is the expression of a feeling of injustice. It is the psychological reaction to the conviction that Italy has for too long been marked out for spoliation by the foreigner. Fascism is the exaggerated expression of that sentiment. That is why Fascism has turned despoiler. Such a revulsion produces distortion, but the distortion is a grim one. It may still prove a tragedy for the rest of the world, as well as for Italy (Hambloch, *Italy Militant*. London, Gollancz, 1941, pp. 246–247).

The British plan of mutilating a Fascist-Italy-without-Mussolini could not be carried out against American public opinion. The contempt for Italian cowardice, therefore, had to be fostered in America also. On January 8, 1942, the *New York Times* gave the story of twenty British airmen, who, unarmed, took 250 Italian prisoners. What had really happened was that nineteen British airmen, who had been shot down in the Mediterranean, landed unarmed in Libya, carrying one of their gunners, who was seriously wounded. They were met by an isolated patrol of fifty or sixty Italians. The latter intimated to the Britons that they were prisoners. The British contended that it was the Italians who were the prisoners, since the territory was in British hands. Had they been fanatical wild beasts, the Italians would have killed the Britons and the story would have come to an end then and there. But they were sensible fellows. Why kill unarmed and inoffensive persons? Besides, if it was actually true that the territory was in the hands of the Britons, the Italian nuclei who had been left behind, had to choose between dying of hunger and thirst in the desert and surrendering. Thus Italians and Britishers agreed that they would march together to the next post. If the Britons were really there, the Italians would admit they were prisoners; if the Italians were there, the rôle of prisoners would fall to the Britons. The latter won the bet. The story, a story of common sense and humanity, was presented by the *New York Times* as a document of English heroism and Italian cowardice, under the caption "Twenty Britons Talk Way Through Italian Lines; Downed Fliers, Unarmed, Take 250 Captives."

Often in news originating in Greece and Yugoslavia we have read that the Italian soldier, as a rule, does not behave as cruelly as the Nazi soldier. When they can, they try to alleviate the misery of the population. Anyone who knows the Italian people is not surprised at this. The Italian kills too often when blinded by rage, but ordinarily is incapable of cold and calculated brutality, what the Germans call *Schadenfreude*. There are in Italy, as in all countries, criminals. These have formed the skeleton of the Fascist party and command the troops of occupation in Greece, Albania, and Yugoslavia. Let us hope that on the day of reckoning the Italian people themselves will do justice to these criminals, unless the British Foreign Office and the American State Department intervene to hinder spontaneous popular movements. Meanwhile, in Greece and the other occupied countries, the Fascist leaders have not succeeded in making of the ordinary Italian a cruel fiend.

It is obvious that this behavior on the part of the Italian soldier does not please the Fascists and the Nazis. It is to their interest to stir up the Italian soldier against the populations of the occupied countries. The most effective way is to tell him that his humanity and his aversion to acts of terrorism do not provoke gratitude but are construed as evidence of cowardice.

Now let us read the *New York Times* of October 22, 1942, and learn that Greek soldiers in Egypt told the *Times* correspondent that the Greeks hate the Germans more than they do the Italians, because the former have proven "the most brutal of the occupying forces"; but they "hold the Italians in complete contempt," because when the Italians clash with the Greeks, they "run like a bunch of rabbits." To be sure, the Italians "are ameliorating their conduct" in Greece, but this is because they "are more intelligent than the others; they see farther; they see that they've lost the war" and behave well "in the hope of being let off more easily when our time for revenge comes."

There is no reason to suppose that the correspondent of the *New York Times* did not have the conversation he reported. It is not an easy task to avoid identifying a people with their own government, and after what Mussolini has done to Greece, the Greeks have plenty of reason to hate the Italians; and the best way to hate one's foe is to feel contempt for him. But before the correspondence reached New York, it had to go through the local military censorship of Cairo and the central political censorship of London. Thus, the responsibility for it belongs to those same British authorities who have engineered the campaign about Italian cowardice. Then comes the responsibility of the paper's New York staff, which should have known that the correspondence would most likely be relayed from New York to Argentina, from there to Italy, and from Italy to the Italian soldiers in Greece and Libya. The reaction is not difficult to guess, given the fact that the Italians are men and not angels. Moreover, the dispatch was published on the very eve of the British offensive against Rommel in Egypt, and Rommel needed the soldiers of the eleven Italian divisions on the Egyptian front at fighting pitch. Last but not least, the citizens of Italian extraction in this country are giving 400,000 men to the American armed forces. Fostering an inferiority complex among those fighting men and wounding the sentiments of a large section of the American population could not displease Mussolini. Mussolini in his propaganda always manages to kill many birds with one stone.

There are, however, people in England who have begun to realize the evil consequences attendant upon these blunders. In the London *Daily Mail* for October 27, 1942, one may read:

Ridicule a man and you make him an enemy. So it is with nations. Surely, the Italians ran away at Caporetto, but they also stood firm on the Piave before the Allies came to their aid. Most armies retreat some time or other. No, while the R.A.F. brings home to Italians in Italy the destructive side of modern war and the Eighth Army batters their sons in Africa, it is important to reconsider our psychological approach to the Italian people. Italy is giving and has given Germany great help in this war. On her account large British naval forces have been tied to the Mediterranean when they have been required elsewhere. She has forced our merchantmen to take the long Cape route and has given Rommel a supply line to Africa and thus forced us to keep large forces in Africa for the defence of Egypt and the Suez.

Is it too much to hope that this kind of advice will be heeded in America? Up to the present, our wise men in Washington have followed blindly in the footsteps of the British Ministry of Information as regards the methods and purposes of propaganda among the Italians.

Knowing that a revolution cannot break out in Italy today, and yet demanding a revolution so as to be able to indict the Italians who do not deliver the required revolution—and then discounting and discouraging any revolution as a result of Nazi and Fascist breakdown—and then clamoring for leaders who either cannot come to the fore now or could only be picked up from among the members of the royal family and Fascist chieftains—and then planning eighteenth-century dismemberments —and then opposing any work of military organization and democratic re-education among Italian war prisoners—and then spreading methodical scorn of Italian cowardice—everything hangs together. There is method in this stupidity.

Unfortunately, it is not the wise men of London and Washington who pay for this stupidity. It is British and American youth.

II. Monarchy or Republic?

1. The House of Savoy and Fascism

So FAR as the British Tories and some of the spokesmen for Washington are concerned, Mussolini must go, but not the House of Savoy. Whatever happens, the British-American diplomats will support the Monarchy, because, in their opinion, the Monarchy still retains the confidence of the large majority of the Italian people. Furthermore, they believe that the Monarchy is essential to a well-ordered Italian political regime and that Italy is not yet ripe for a republican constitution.

To our way of thinking, this contention is altogether wrong and wholly unjustified by all the evidence at our disposal. In order to clarify our position at this point, let us begin by stating some well-known facts which cannot be disputed by even the most ardent supporters of the monarchy for Italy.

First of all, it is undeniable that when, on October 28, 1922, the King refused to sign the decree of martial law submitted to him by the Cabinet and thus prevented the government's using the army to suppress the Fascist rebellion, whatever his intentions might have been, he thereby assumed personally the whole responsibility for the consequences of his refusal. When the next day he called Mussolini to form a new cabinet, well knowing that the Fascist party had only a very small representation in the Parliament and in the country as a whole, he again assumed personally the whole responsibility for his choice made, as it was, contrary to the usual parliamentary procedure. When in the fall of 1924, after the Matteotti murder, he rejected the appeal of a large section of Parliament and of the rank and file of the Italian people to oust Mussolini and return to normal constitutional practice, he again acted on his own responsibility. Last but not least, when he accepted and ratified with his signature all the laws and decrees which abolished the constitution for all practical purposes and established the dictatorship, he did so from choice. If he had desired to do so, he could have refused his signature to the decrees which changed the character of the Italian government, just as he had, in 1922, refused to sign the decree of martial law drawn up by a legally constituted cabinet.

It is not important at present to determine whether or not the King, in his acceptance of the Fascist regime, violated either the spirit or the letter of the Constitution and broke his oath to the nation. The important fact is that the Monarchy and Fascism combined in a common cause and have remained closely associated for twenty years. The Monarchy accepted and officially sanctioned the Fascist program of submitting the whole life of the nation to the absolute control of the Fascist party, at the same time abolishing all other political groups and all constitutional liberties. The Monarchy cooperated actively in the Fascist program of territorial expansion and conquest by military might at the expense of weaker nations. The Monarchy profited by such conquests, made though they were in open violation of international obligations previously assumed by Italy, and it further added to its coat of arms and to its titles the Imperial Crown of Ethiopia and the Royal Crown of Albania.

It is no less evident that the Monarchy failed to function as a stabilizing force in the political life of Italy and became instead the instrument and servant, first of a small minority which seized power by violence and against the will of the majority, and later of a tyrannical dictatorship ruling by decrees which bore the signature of the King. It likewise failed to perform its duty of preserving peace in the system of international relations.

Mussolini and the Fascist spokesmen and historians have repeatedly expressed their gratitude for the support and cooperation received from the Monarchy throughout the period of Fascist rule. Sympathizers with Fascism the world over have expressed at one time or another their admiration for the wisdom of the King in abetting Mussolini and his government. Lastly, the Vatican bestowed lavish praises on the King for having given way before the "man sent by Providence" who made Italy's peace with God.

It thus seems that there is unanimous agreement among Fascists and anti-Fascists, liberals and radicals, Catholics and Protestants that Fascism is indebted to the King and the King to Fascism, and that, since there has been close collaboration between the two, a goodly share of the responsibility belongs to the King. However, although both the friends and enemies of Fascism in Italy and elsewhere acknowledged the high degree of support the King has given Fascism, the former regarded the royal support of Fascism as a wise and honorable venture, while the latter regarded it as a betrayal of the best interests of Italy.

Of course, after Mussolini's "stab in the back" of France, and even more after the United States was dragged into the war against the Axis, the prevailing view in this country has been that Fascism is evil and the Duce contemptible. Former admirers of the Duce have become his detractors; American newspapermen who used to write winning articles from Rome on the accomplishments of the government are now back home after expulsion from Italy, writing vigorous articles and books in an attempt to reveal the machinations which went on behind the scenes. Certain Catholic bishops and clergymen who used to bless Mussolini's name, now wax very eloquent in reminding us from the pulpit and from the press that the Pope condemned Fascist ideologies long ago. Even the collective letter of the American Episcopate in 1942 has recognized that this is a war for the preservation of liberty and religion. Many of these clergymen thought before Pearl Harbor that it was not our business to interfere in the struggle against Nazism and Fascism. Now they have seen the light.

But if we are now agreed in believing that Fascism is a plague and that Mussolini's downfall is greatly to be desired, we should also agree that, not only Mussolini, but all other abettors of the Fascist regime, should be eliminated. By what process of logic many persons separate the cause of Mussolini and Fascism from that of the Monarchy and all other servants of Fascism is beyond comprehension. But so they do, and obviously it is not by force of logic that they may be convinced of their mistake; they will change their minds only when they see the tragic result of this mistake, and then, unfortunately too late, they will recant.

Mr. Walter Lippmann, the widely read American columnist, stated in his article for November 21, 1942 (*New York Herald Tribune*), that "when Mussolini and his henchmen are disposed of, there will remain in Italy the vestiges of legitimate and historic authority by means of which the transition to the new Italy can be made. For if there is not, it will be difficult in the chaos of Italian defeat to find Italian authority able to speak for Italy." At the head of these vestiges of legitimate and historic authority Mr. Lippmann lists the Monarchy. The Monarchy is the institution which will have the authority to speak for the new Italy. By a rapid change of mask the King, who for twenty years through his speeches from the throne has been the voice of the Fascist dictatorship, will become the voice of the new Italy. The past will be forgotten as far as the Monarchy is concerned; the title of legitimacy puts the King above all moral law—above even the dictates of common sense.

More than a century ago, in the days of Prince Metternich, the word "legitimate" had a clear-cut meaning. A political regime was legitimate if there was behind it an historical tradition. The legitimate King of France was, in 1814, Louis XVIII, descendant of Henry IV, who had died in 1610. When Louis XVIII died without a son, his brother, Charles X, was his legitimate successor, and today the Comte de Paris is the legitimate heir of Henry IV and Charles X.

Guglielmo Ferrero gave the word "legitimate" quite a different meaning. A political regime, according to him, was legitimate if it was freely supported by such a large body of opinion that no attempt to overthrow it by force would have any chance of success, and therefore it needed very little force to carry on against its opponents. On the other hand, a political regime was illegitimate or no more than quasi-legitimate, if it could not rely on the consent of a body of opinion sufficient to give it a firm foundation, and therefore was compelled to rule by fear or deception. Ferrero's legitimacy was "popular" and not "historic," although in his opinion the perfection of legitimacy would exist where tradition and popular consent were one. This is why, in Ferrero's opinion, the British Constitution, enjoying both advantages, embodies the most satisfactory form of legitimacy. Ferrero did not think that in Europe today historical tradition could suffice as a basis for legitimacy without spontaneous popular consent.

When he speaks of "vestiges of legitimate and *historic* authority," Mr. Lippmann is obviously thinking of legitimacy in the Metternichian sense.

What are these "vestiges" in the Italy of today?

The House of Savoy is no doubt legitimate in the Metternichian sense. To be sure, between 1859 and 1870 it made use of the illegitimate means of revolution to unseat all the other legitimate dynasties in Italy. Queen Victoria looked upon the first King of United Italy, Victor Emmanuel II, as the secretary of an American trade union would look upon a strikebreaker or a scab. But, one after the other, all the other sovereigns of Europe acknowledged the accomplished fact. The last of them was Pope Pius XI, who in 1929 renounced all claims outside Vatican City and got in return seven hundred fifty million Italian lire in cash and one billion lire in Italian government bonds. Thus, the

House of Savoy is now wholly legitimate in the Metternichian sense of the word.

According to Metternich, if a king has had historical legitimacy bestowed upon him by God, and if his divine right is acknowledged by other legitimate sovereigns, he is always right and his subjects must carry out his infallible orders. Emperor Ferdinand I, at the time of Metternich (1835–1848), was the legitimate sovereign of the Austrian Empire, though he spent his days catching flies and counting the coaches which passed under the windows of his palace. Today Mr. Otto Hapsburg is the legitimate successor of Ferdinand I.

Ferrero was of the opinion that the House of Savoy in Italy was never invested with legitimate authority, since it was never based on a sufficiently wide body of opinion and therefore had to resort to violent repression or shrewd deception in order to remain in the saddle against vast currents of popular will. According to Ferrero, the Savoy regime, before the advent of Fascism was but quasi-legitimate, a kind of cross between historical and pseudo-democratic legitimacy. After the Fascist regime set in, there no longer remained any vestiges either of traditional or of democratic legitimacy.

According to Mr. Lippmann's doctrine of historic legitimacy, Ferrero was wrong. A follower of the Metternichian doctrine has only to take notice of historic tradition and bow before it. The flaw in this doctrine is that it works only in quiet times, and not in moments of stress when a king is meant to do something more than catch flies. Even then, however, the remedy is at hand. The "legitimist" entourage of the incapable or unsuccessful king, legitimacy or no legitimacy, induces him to abdicate. So Emperor Ferdinand abdicated in 1848, and King Charles Albert, the great-grandfather of the present King of Italy, abdicated in 1849. One has to come to the United States —a country whose political institutions arose from an "illegitimate" revolution—to find uncompromising worshippers of historic legitimacy who support the present King of Italy, or at least his prospective successor, even in the midst of a catastrophic breakdown of traditional values all over the world.

The mistake made by Mr. Lippmann in advocating a primary rôle for the Monarchy in the Italy of tomorrow was precisely to build his argument upon the principle of legitimacy. Mr. Lippmann overlooked the important fact that between the pre-Fascist Monarchy, which had a definite place in the liberal constitution, and the Monarchy of the Fascist regime there is, to be sure, a dynastic, but not a political continuity. The Fascist Monarchy was a new creation with a different nature and a different function. Just as the Fascist so-called Parliament was not and did not profess to be a continuation of the extinct democratic Parliament, so the Monarchy went through a similar process of extinction and then of revival in different form. The new Fascist Parliament became merely an audience for Mussolini's speeches and the new Monarchy became only a rubber stamp for the Duce's decrees. All claims of political legitimacy were lost in this process because the historical continuity was broken. The allegiance of the nation to the Monarchy, based on a definite contract represented by the constitution, was severed. It cannot be renewed without the consent of the people.

2. Does Italy Need a King?

Are the Italian people disposed once more to entrust the Monarchy with the guardianship of their reconquered liberty and to let the Monarchy speak for the new Italy?

It is admitted by all, whether friends or enemies of the House of Savoy, that by becoming the vassal of Mussolini and the servant of Fascism, the Italian Monarchy has lost its prestige. The endless jokes, which made the rounds in Italy and were so gleefully reproduced in the American press, about the diminutive King holding the bag for the Duce, reflect the low level reached by the Monarchy in the eyes of the Italian people. It is true that now the American newspapers, while multiplying with subtle ingenuity the jokes about Mussolini and fleeing Italian soldiers, have ceased altogether to practice their wit on the Italian King. But as far as the Italians are concerned, there is no reason to believe that they have changed their minds about the King and his authority. Nothing has happened lately to encourage such a change. If anything, the resentment and disgust of the Italian masses must have reached a more acute stage under the weight of all the calamities and misery of this last period. Military defeats, loss of the colonial empire, German control of the administration, of the police, and of the economic life of the country, privations and suffering beyond endurance, and finally, the bombing of cities and the expectation of worse—these are bitter fruits of the Fascist regime that the Italian people can see.

It is inconceivable that this people, crushed by the most disastrous humiliations and now forced to fight and die for the victory of arrogant Nazi masters whom they hate, can still be counted on to have faith in the Monarchy and to expect from it salvation and guidance. A monarchy is not like a political party in a democratic country. A party may fall into disrepute and lose its prestige because of the venality or the mistakes of its leaders but, by changing men and programs, it may regain prestige and power and eventually atone for its past errors. Neither is it like the old absolute monarchies in which the king could do no wrong. A constitutional monarchy is supposed to be the untarnished symbol of the law, above all political parties and groups. Once a constitutional king has betrayed his sacred duty, once the ideal has been desecrated by gangsters in the gaudy uniforms of state ministers, marshals, generals, and whatnot, once the symbol has become a tragic caricature, the butt of jokes and epigrams, it cannot be restored to its previous state of honor and respect. Its prestige is gone forever.

The position of the House of Savoy in the Italian Risorgimento is due, in great part, to the fact that when the revolution of 1848–

1849 was crushed by the military intervention of Austria, this was the only Italian dynasty which did not abolish the free constitution of the little Kingdom of Piedmont. The Bourbons of Naples and Sicily, as well as all other Italian princes, forgetting the solemn oath which they had taken to maintain a constitutional government, were glad to re-establish the old absolutism and to send their state ministers to the gallows, to prison, or into exile.

The record of the House of Savoy in its long history, to be sure, was not such as to inspire great confidence in its faithfulness to promises and alliances. But King Victor Emmanuel II, though inclined to follow the example of the other Italian princes, did not abolish the constitutional regime. Court historians then created the legend that after the crushing defeat of the Piedmontese army at Novara by the Austrians and the abdication of Charles Albert, the young King Victor Emmanuel stood fearless before the Austrian Marshal Radetzsky and, spurning threats and allurements, saved the constitution. Legend or no legend, Victor Emmanuel got the credit and was nicknamed the *Re Galantuomo,* "the honest king," while the Bourbon of Naples went down in history as the *Re Spergiuro,* or "the perjurer king." A few years later the Bourbons and all other Italian princes were swept away, but Victor Emmanuel became King of a united Italy.

King Victor Emmanuel III reversed the policy of his grandfather. Led by fear, by force of circumstances, and by the bad advice of the generals and admirals of his entourage, he yielded to a threat of violence and surrendered the government to the Fascist mob. The Monarchy became the accomplice of Fascism and virtually signed its own abdication.

Courtiers and also some foreign agencies in England and America have tried, for their particular purposes, to create a modest but legendary saga around King Victor Emmanuel. Not being able to say that he "stood fearless before Mussolini and saved Italy" and thus make him appear a figure of heroic size, they have attempted to picture him as a pathetic figure, a victim, not of his own, but of others' mistakes.

And so the legend that the King is and has always been anti-Fascist at heart was spread abroad. It is said that he remained faithful to his duty as a constitutional monarch, that it was not he who abolished the constitution or who made possible its abolition, since the laws establishing the dictatorship were passed by the representatives of the people, and as a result he was deprived of all power and therefore of all responsibility. They forget to mention that those laws were passed by a Parliament from which all opposition groups had been expelled by force and deprived of their mandate, and that the King still had the right and the duty to refuse his signature, if he had had the courage to face the consequences.

Realizing that this line of defense made little impression, the non-Italian champions of the Monarchy abandoned the King as too old and senile to be rejuvenated and turned their attention to the Crown Prince. They described the handsome but brainless heir presumptive of the throne as the most fervent enemy of Fascism, ably seconded by his Belgian wife, a promising hero ready at the right moment to attack the Fascist dragon, sword in hand, and to purge the earth of the Fascist plague.

To be sure, the Prince had more than one reason to hate Fascism and the Duce; they had demoted him from Crown Prince to Prince of Piedmont and had subordinated his right to succeed his father to the approval of the Fascist Grand Council. By this measure, the Duce held both father and son at his mercy, bound hand and foot to the Fascist chariot. As G. A. Borgese has remarked with a delightful sense of humor: "What he [the King] thoroughly disliked was the idea that his son might be dispossessed of the job; perhaps realizing in his subconscious that the young man could never possibly fit in any other employment" (*Goliath*, p. 237). Mussolini now held the knife by the handle, and he could count on the complete passivity of the King. He could even take the liberty of playing practical jokes on His

Majesty, as when he, the Duce, made both the King and himself "First Marshals of the Empire," as if a single "First Marshal" would not have sufficed to destroy the Empire.

As for the Crown Prince, or rather, the Prince of Piedmont, knowing that his future depends upon his good behavior, he has done his best to appear the most docile and devoted of the Duce's subjects and has never let any occasion go by, birthdays and funerals, victories and triumphs, great speeches and the like, without immediately sending to the omnipotent Duce a telegram of congratulation or of condolence or of unlimited confidence and extravagant praise. A collection of those telegrams, already published by newspapers, ought to be reprinted in handy form for the edification of the American State Department.

The Italian people are very well informed about the King and his son. The Fascist press has been zealous in emphasizing the deeds of the royal family in favor of the Fascist regime, and has registered in detail all manifestations of its unbounded devotion to Mussolini. The Italian people have still, even after twenty years of Fascist domination, a great deal of common sense and decency left. They know very well that even the humblest man, if he has a bit of self-respect and cherishes a good reputation would never in his private life and in his affairs endure such humiliations and debase himself to such a point as have these degenerate scions of Savoy. In these matters the common people go straight to the point and make no distinction between those who are high and those who are low. Even if they cannot speak for fear of the police and the spies, their minds and their hearts know the truth and they cannot but feel disgust for the crown and a sense of shame for the Italian nation.

Most of the American correspondents who were in Italy in 1940 and 1941 noticed how low the Monarchy had fallen in the estimation of all Italian classes. S. R. Davis of the *Christian Science Monitor*, J. T. Whitaker of the *Chicago Daily News*, H. L. Matthews of the *New York Times*, the Packards of the United Press, R. G. Massock of the Associated Press—agree that "the royal family is as bankrupt politically as Mussolini," that "the House of Savoy has lost greatly in prestige," that "important middle and upper middle class groups are now bitterly attacking Victor Emmanuel," that "the King has lost the respect and probably earned the contempt of his people," that "both Americans and English vastly overestimate the personal standing and influence of the royal family in Italy," that "the royal family is now definitely committed to Fascism and must continue to support the Duce," that "the Crown is in contempt among many Italians," that "the Court has identified itself so closely with the German alliance that it is idle to try to wean them away from Germany." If all this is true, as we believe it is, and if the British Foreign Office and the State Department are determined that Italy have a king at all costs, they will have to find him in some other royal family than the House of Savoy.

Lacking imagination, they do not seem to have thought of this solution to the problem. There are now scattered in the four corners of the world more than a dozen royal families left jobless by the war of 1914–18 and by the present war. It should be easy to find among them a king for Italy to establish a new dynasty and replace the Savoy family. There are still the descendants of the Bourbons of Naples and a large brood of Austrian archdukes. With one of them on the throne of Italy, the historical nemesis would be complete, all traces of the Risorgimento would be erased forever, and a brand-new Italian kingdom could take its place in the new balance of power conceived by the reactionaries for the post-war peace.

In the history of political institutions the so-called constitutional monarchy, in which the king reigns but does not govern, is but a stage in the transition from the absolutism inherent in the notion of a monarchy to the republican form of government, which is the classical form of a democracy. To be sure, in a period of transition a constitutional monarchy may prove useful as a stabilizing element in a regime of free institutions lacking a long tradition and a well-developed system of checks and balances so essential to a democratic government. But like all institutions which represent a transitional compromise, the constitutional monarchy becomes in time unnecessary for the working of a democratic government, and if it is not eliminated, remains as a parasitic survival in the body politic. As most parasites become incubators and carriers of poisonous germs, so the monarchy, when it reaches this stage, may easily turn into a menace to democratic institutions. It may become a docile instrument of reactionary forces to re-establish by violence a regime of absolutism which might thus appear clothed in a legitimate title, having received the investiture from the monarchy. The classical example of how a degenerate, parasitic monarchy may be used as a shield and a stepping stone by a reactionary dictatorship has been provided by Fascist Italy.

A simple consideration born of facts should suffice to dispel the illusions of those who still believe (or feign to believe) that the Monarchy is and will be either necessary or useful to the Italy of tomorrow. Had Italy been a democratic republic in October, 1922, instead of a kingdom, and had there been a president with limited constitutional powers elected by the people, instead of weak-willed Victor Emmanuel, would the decision of the Cabinet to proclaim martial law and put down the Fascist upheaval by force have been turned down? And would Mussolini have been called upon to form a new government?

It is well known that the first reaction of the King to the Fascist attempt was in favor of the Cabinet's decision. The Fascist rabble was neither numerous nor well equipped and, according to the competent opinion of General Badoglio, then in Rome, it would have disbanded at the appearance of the army. But at the suggestion of other military advisers, who were in the Fascist conspiracy, the King changed his mind. He was made to fear an attempt to supplant him and his family by his cousin, the Duke of Aosta, who was waiting nearby at Perugia. The fear of having to face a dynastic conflict, remote and perhaps fantastic as it was, was enough to make him forget everything else.

If, however, the supreme authority of the country had been a president, who would not have had any dynastic interests to protect, the situation would have been different. A president neither could nor would have hesitated a moment to approve the decision of a Cabinet which represented the majority of the Parliament and the majority of the Italian people. With a president in the place of Victor Emmanuel, the Fascist upheaval would either have been avoided or easily suppressed, and Mussolini, instead of taking the train to Rome from Milan where he was waiting out of danger, would have rushed to seek safety beyond the nearby frontier. Italy, and perhaps the world, would have been spared the present tragedy.

But Italy is not the only example of such a tragic experience in the political life of a nation. For more than half a century the same process took place again and again in the small kingdoms of the Balkans. Constitutional monarchies there served periodically as springboards for the seizure of power by reactionary groups with a program of nationalistic imperialism, of hatred and ruthless oppression of racial minorities, and thus provided the spark for several European wars. The Fascist idea of so using the Monarchy has not even the merit of originality; it was merely one of the means by which Fascism "balkanized" Italy.

The champions of monarchical institutions usually point to England as providing the evidence of the benefits, the practical value, and eventually the lasting character of a constitutional monarchy. This is not the place to analyze the reasons why this system has become traditional in England, but it is not without significance that there was once an English king who tried to curb the traditional powers of the political representative bodies and lost his head on the block. It is also important to remark that in modern times the English Monarchy has identified itself with the British Empire and has become, not only the symbol, but the juridical and constitutional link of the British Commonwealth of Nations.

But Italy is not England; there is not an Italian commonwealth of nations. In Italy, the Monarchy has not only lost its prestige by its servile submission to the dictatorship, as we have already said, but it has allowed Fascism the opportunity to give the Italian people most convincing evidence that a king is nothing but a superfluous organ in the body politic. The Fascists, a small minority which seized power by force, needed the Monarchy only because they needed to acquire the appearance of legitimacy by governing with its consent.

The new regime which will supersede Fascism in Italy will not need the Monarchy in order to be and to appear legitimate, because a democratic regime of free institutions receives its mandate, and therefore its legitimacy, from the people and from no other source.

3. The Political Unpreparedness of the Italians

The main argument advanced by the champions of the Savoy Monarchy is that the Italian people as a whole are politically immature and incapable of handling successfully the delicate machinery of a democratic and republican regime. We are told that Italy had a regime of free institutions under a constitutional monarchy for over fifty years; it never worked well, and then at the first impact of a small force of Fascists, it disintegrated like a house of cards. Democracy had no deep roots in the Italian soil, no long tradition, and no grip on the Italian consciousness. You cannot build a republic on such foundations; a constitutional monarchy with a system of restricted free institutions of such character as to prevent new dictatorial attempts is what Italy will need for a long period. Otherwise, she will fall prey to bloody internal revolutions and chaos, during which extreme communist groups will conquer the power and endanger the stability of the whole European peace. This, so the legend has it, is the lesson that the Fascist experiment has taught Italy.

An analysis of these points will show how unwarranted such conclusions are in the light of history and of common sense.

The history of Italy from 1870 to the first World War is not brilliant in glorious deeds, military power, or territorial expansion of much importance. It is the modest history of a country which, having finally secured its political unification after centuries of division and foreign domination, worked hard and with perseverance to build up all the necessary instruments of a new national state and to develop the economic and intellectual life of the nation.

It is not necessary here to enumerate in detail the achievements of free Italy during those fifty years of her new existence as a united and independent nation. They are minutely described in many historical works written not only by Italians but also by French, German, and English historians, which can be easily consulted by our readers. One of the more recent of these histories is that of Benedetto Croce, available in an English translation.

In 1896, a year of serious difficulties and troubles for Italy, Abbott Lawrence Lowell, then Professor of Government at Harvard University, passed the following judgment on modern Italy:

The Italian statesmen have had great obstacles to encounter. They found the country divided into a number of separate provinces, each of them with its own peculiar habits and traditions, and some of them socially disorganized. They found it defenseless and poor, and for the most part well-nigh devoid of railroads or telegraphs. They have welded these provinces together in a single nation, to which they have given a uniform administration and enlightened codes of law. . . . They have created a large army and a powerful fleet, and they have covered the land with a network of railroads and telegraphs. What wonder if it should appear that amidst all this labor some things had been left undone, and others had been done imperfectly; if it should prove that in establishing a free government among a people with a defective political training, some institutions had been set up which are inconsistent with each other, or ill adapted to the condition of the country. The nation has not yet worked out her problems, but she has two great advantages: her people are patient and sensible in politics, and have proven themselves willing to bear the immense cost of national regeneration; and she has a number of men, both among scholars and in active public life, who are fully sensible of her difficulties, and are trying earnestly to solve them. (*Governments and Parties in Twentieth Century Europe,* Boston, 1898, pp. 229–230).

G. Volpe, the official historian of the Fascist regime, in his book *L'Italia in Cammino* (*Italy on the March*) (Milan, 1927, p. 59), writes:

There were in Italy ferments of activity, forces of renovation and urge for constructive work. Twenty years had not gone by between the transfer of the capital to Rome (1871) when the wonderful energies, the hard work, the capacity for renovation shown by the Italian people and its response to the stimuli of the surrounding world, gave results visible to all careful observers. Political unity and the action of the government urged, helped and transformed all these energies into real values.

The reader will find in the pages of this Fascist historian a summary account of the achievements of the free regime: the balancing of the budget, construction of roads and railways, reclamation of lands, creation of industries and expansion of commerce, establishment of public schools and scientific institutions, provisions for the care of the historical and artistic treasures of Italy, social legislation for the protection of labor and for the welfare of the working classes.

It would be easy to reproach pre-Fascist politicians with all kinds of mistakes and misdeeds, ill-advised undertakings, unused opportunities, waste and extravagance. Not all the problems that confronted the country were solved. Not always were the solutions adopted the best nor the methods employed the most efficient. Could all problems have been solved in so short a time? Has there ever been in history any country which solved all its problems in half a century and without blunders? If one judges the handiwork of the pre-Fascist politicians by the standard of some flawless ideal—the method of the political reformer —there is no politician who would not be sent to hell. But if one adopts the method of the historian, that is, if one compares, as far as Italy is concerned, the starting point in 1871 with the point of arrival, the first World War, and the poverty of national resources with the wealth of other countries, one cannot fail to conclude that no country in Europe had made such strides in so short a time.

Those who are familiar with the early history of the United States, which possessed unlimited resources, can understand and sympathize with the efforts, the industry, and the good will, as well as with the conflicts, the mistakes, and the shortcomings, of the Italian free regime after the Risorgimento.

The task of blurring that picture and of superimposing upon it a distorted view, a caricature, of men and events in that period was assumed, not by foreigners to Italy, but by Italians, the leaders, the propagandists, and the official historians of Fascism. To be sure, they had had some predecessors in the work of denigration and vituperation of the new Italy. The newspapers, periodicals, and books of the reactionary clerical groups had made generous use of the regime of freedom to ridicule Italian liberals and their free institutions, to attribute to them evil intentions, to magnify mistakes and to forecast ruin and desolation. The daily *Unità Cattolica* of Florence and the Jesuit *Civiltà Cattolica* of Rome were among the worst offenders in this endless campaign, but, after all, nobody paid much attention to them, and they were barely seen outside the sacristies and some clerical institutions.

However, when the Fascists took this leaf from the book of the clericals, and of the Jesuits in particular, they carried on the campaign in an intensive fashion in newspapers, periodicals, and books, in speeches and interviews designed especially for foreign countries. It became a commonplace with Fascist propagandists in the United States to speak of pre-Fascist Italy as "a dunghill"—a Mussolinian word—and of the "debased, stupid, criminal" politicians, who had misruled and exploited the country for half a century.

The coincidence between the clerical and the Fascist disparagement of the Italian free state was due primarily to the fact that both clerics and Fascists had a common hatred of liberalism and democratic institutions, though they had different purposes and aims. To the Fascists, the alleged debasement of Italian political institutions was to be the justification for what they emphatically called the "Fascist revolution," which had destroyed liberty. They could boast more easily of the Fascist achievements, magnifying everything that was done by the new regime, even taking credit for everything that had been done before. They even took unto themselves Mazzini, Garibaldi, and Cavour as forerunners of Fascism and, submitting the whole history of the Risorgimento to a strange travesty, they affirmed that Mussolini had taken over their work where they had stopped; the period between was only a dark blot on the history of Italy, to be cursed and forgotten forever.

This propaganda was very effective, especially in the United States. It was above all acceptable to the Catholics, who were well prepared to believe this version of Italian history, since American Catholic books followed the same line of historical misrepresentation as their Italian clerical guides. They had read in the *Catholic Encyclopaedia* that "the idea of Italian unity arose towards the end of the eighteenth century," and that "this idea was taken up and was vigorously pressed by the enemies of Christianity who held that if, under the pretext of the unification of Italy, his temporal power should be wrested from the Pope, the Church of Christ would of necessity come to an end" (Vol. VIII, p. 234). This pious gem of historical interpretation we owe to the Italian Jesuit, Tacchi-Venturi, who wrote the history of Italy for the American *Catholic Encyclopaedia,* and who became in time one of Mussolini's most influential advisers.

The unification of Italy, having been the work of anti-clericals bent upon destroying the Church, could not but produce criminal statesmen using criminal means. Hence Garibaldi was, according to the *Catholic Encyclopaedia*, a highway robber, Cavour an immoral cheat, and Mazzini a leader of a gang of assassins and a mad dreamer. But finally Mussolini arrived, and he saved the Church from the Italian gangsters. This was the picture of Italy and of her pre-Fascist history that the average American Catholic had, and perhaps still has, in his mind.

The depreciation of pre-Fascist Italy by the Fascist propagandists both at home and abroad was soon followed and sometimes incongruously accompanied by an equally forceful campaign of exaltation of the virtues, the grandeur, and the genius of the Italian people. Before Hitler had appeared to proclaim the dogma of the Germanic race, the Fascists had gone far enough in preaching the superiority and the great destiny of the Italian nation, which had produced Mussolini and with him a new political and social order soon to be adopted by all other nations of the world under Italian leadership. The Italian people, whose supposed inactivity and ignorance unfitted them even for self-rule before the advent of the Duce—now that they were entirely without liberty, their necks beneath the axe of Fascism —had sprung, Minerva-like, full grown from the head of the Duce, the greatest people on earth, to devise the political patterns for the rest of the world to live by!

This was the origin of the legend of the political immaturity of the Italian people, a legend that is now exploited, not only by clerics, but by some American champions of democracy, who for various reasons wish to reduce the Italian people almost to the level of incompetents.

In 1920 Lord Bryce, in his book *Modern Democracies*, had no qualms about listing Italy among the countries where a democratic regime was working. Of course, he did not fail to notice that there were weak spots in the Italian political constitution and practice; but weaknesses and defects can be found in all democracies, and Lord Bryce did not hesitate to expose also those of the English and of the American systems and traditions. Lord Bryce never had any suspicion that some peoples were fit, and others unfit, for liberty; much less did he suspect that Italy was to be ranked in the latter class. Italy, in Lord Bryce's analysis of modern democracies, was certainly not at the top, but neither was she at the bottom.

One of the observations that were made by some writers on Italy in pre-Fascist days was that the percentage of registered voters who cast their ballots on election day was rather low. And it is a fact that this percentage fluctuated between fifty-five and sixty per cent of the whole electoral body. But to infer from this fact that the large majority of the Italian population was either indifferent to politics or too ignorant to know how to exercise their right to vote is entirely unwarranted. First of all, the important fact must be considered that thousands and thousands of Italian voters were workers who, at election times, were earning their livelihood as emigrants in Austria, Germany, France, Switzerland, in the various Mediterranean regions, as well as in North and South America.

In the second place, there exist no people under the sun who possess such a perfect education for democracy that everybody, without exception, goes to the polls on election day. The figures of the percentage of voters who exercise their right have no absolute but only a relative value. From this relative point of view, Italy does not compare unfavorably with other nations. In Italy in 1913 the percentage of voters was 60.4 per cent and in 1919, 56.6 per cent. In the United States in the 1932 presidential elections, 57 per cent of the voters cast their ballots; in 1936, 62 per cent, and in 1940, 65 per cent.

After the advent of Fascism and under the initial influence of its propaganda, the political backwardness of the Italian people became a dogma . . . a dogma of English and American reactionaries. Even a serious and fair-minded historian like G. M. Trevelyan, in discussing "Historical Causes of the Present State of Affairs in Italy" (Lecture at the University of Oxford, October 31, 1923, London, Milford, 1923), could affirm that the Italians are incapable of observing constitutional methods in government:

People sometimes ask me, why [in October, 1922] could the Italians have not effected the change of government that they desired by means of a general election? . . . I reply by pointing the inquirer to their [the Italians'] social and political history, which has unfitted them for expressing themselves by means of a general election. It is really very difficult for thirty or forty millions of people to get the government they desire by means of a general election, unless they are to the manner born. We [English] have this obscure inherited instinct. The Italians have it not. . . . How then do the Italians naturally express their wishes?

Mr. Trevelyan's answer is simple. In the Middle Ages, he says, when the Italian cities wished to change their government, they "did not do so by a general election, but by a row in the piazza. The citizens gathered together and clubbed some unpopular person, or pulled down his house." And so they did in 1922. The March on Rome was but a repetition of the old method, "a series of rows in the piazza culminating in a great national row in the piazza. . . . When the soul, the mind, or the passions of the Italian people require to have vent, they find it in a row in the piazza."

This overlooks a great many pertinent facts.

In 1183, thirty-two years before the birth of Magna Charta, the Italians wrested from Emperor Frederick Barbarossa the Treaty of Constance, which granted self-government to all the cities of northern Italy; the English Magna Charta contained the rights and privileges of only a handful of feudal barons. What was the English "obscure instinct" doing in 1183? Why did it awaken only in 1215? During the thirteenth century, while England's "instinct" was taking its first insecure steps towards the representation of the merchants in Parliament, the lower middle classes in northern and central Italy were trying to gain control of their city governments and abolished serfdom among the peasantry.

They did not succeed in establishing a parliamentary regime. There were many "rows in the piazza" everywhere. But were not the Wars of the Roses fought in the streets and fields of England? Italian social struggles led to despotic institutions. Tyrants arose everywhere in Italy. But was Henry VIII a constitutional king before whom Italian tyrants had any reason to feel humble? Was the revolution of 1648 anything other than a "grand row"? And was the revolution of 1688 brought about by a parliamentary election? English "obscure instinct" has worked rather badly, even as far as later times are concerned. The Chartist upheaval was a "row" in the streets and not a contest by ballot.

Bees, ants, and newborn babies perform their instinctive functions, which are perfectly adapted to their aims. This has not been the case with English "instinct." The English people have had to win its democratic institutions during centuries of conscious moral and intellectual effort, trial and error, success and failure, ups and downs, friction and often tremendous waste.

Nowadays, many Americans think along the same line as Mr. Trevelyan. In a letter to one of the writers of this book, an American who had been in Italy, stated:

Parliamentary government had broken down before the Duce appeared . . . and indeed the Italian government, so long as it was strong, was always a veiled dictatorship, whether Cavour or Crispi or Giolitti happened to be at the helm. It's a very old story, as the history of Rome would attest. It almost seems as if parliamentarism— which is the essence of the "Democratic Republic," as the English-speaking peoples understand it—were alien to the Latin nature.

We quote from *The Nation* (March 27, 1943) the answer to these remarks:

When one writes, "The Italian government, so long as it was strong, has always been a veiled dictatorship, whether Cavour or

Crispi or Giolitti happened to be at the helm," one should define the meaning of the word "dictatorship." If one means that in Italy the Prime Minister shaped the country's policies, the statement is correct. But in this sense Roosevelt's America also is a "dictatorship." Bernard Shaw's basic argument in favor of Hitler and Mussolini was always that Great Britain no less than Italy and Germany was a "dictatorship." In fact, in Great Britain the Prime Minister, when backed by a solid parliamentary majority, controls domestic and foreign policies.

However, when one puts together in the same dictatorial box Cavour and Mussolini, Roosevelt and Hitler, Churchill and Stalin, one must distinguish again between a "dictatorship number one" in which anyone criticizing and opposing the men in power is dispatched to jail or to the next world, and a "dictatorship number two" in which the right to criticize and oppose the men in power is granted to the citizens.

"Dictatorship number two" in former times was termed a "free regime. . . ."

A "free" regime permits habeas corpus, freedom of the press, of association, of assembly, trade-union freedom, religious freedom, freedom of teaching, elective local government, parliamentary institutions, etc. These institutions did exist in Italy. They do not exist now. They make the difference between a "free" and a "dictatorial" regime.

Parliament, one of the institutions of a "free" regime, was working rather poorly in Italy. But what were parliamentary institutions in England before the Act of 1832? . . . To be sure, we do not forget that British national elections in 1924, 1931, and 1935 were won by the Conservative Party through three swindles—the Zinovieff letter in 1924, the put-up scare about the Post Office savings in 1931, and the fraudulent promise to stand by the League of Nations in the Italo-Ethiopian dispute in 1935. Such swindles, however, are part and parcel of that process of trial and error through which mankind has to pass in its endeavor to grow less imperfect.

Is political freedom a particular privilege bestowed by the Almighty God upon the Britons and those in America who claim to have British blood in their veins even if it is Irish or German, and even if not all immigrants originating in England belonged to precisely the same moral breed as the Pilgrim Fathers?

There is a brutal German Nazi doctrine of the Nordic race, and there is another doctrine of race soaked with suave Anglo-Saxon cant: "You are unworthy of reaching our heights; we are endowed with a parliamentary nature, a parliamentary genius; you have to be content with dictatorships." The notions of "nature," "genius," "instinct" spring from the assumption of something primitive, permanent, and unchangeable—"race."

After all, these theories have not even the distinction of novelty; they were worked out long ago. German philosophers and historians of the nineteenth century fancied that each people has been endowed with deep-seated instincts of its own which control its development and explain its history. Everybody knew that in the Italy of the Middle Ages the Guelphs and the Ghibellines used to murder each other in the streets, for which reason Romeo and Juliet could not marry and came to a pitiful end. Everybody knew also that in the Renaissance Caesar Borgia and many other tyrants had been in control of the Italian people. The case of England was just the opposite, for everybody knew that she had received Magna Charta in 1215. Thus, Italian folk spirit, *Volksgeist,* was tyrannical, while English *Volksgeist* was parliamentarian. Liberal German historians, who admired English free institutions, announced that the thirst for liberty was an essential feature of Teutonic-English instinct. Why the Teutonic liberal *Volksgeist* performed its wonders in a country like England, inhabited by a crossbreed of Celts and Teutons, instead of developing in Germany, where the Teutonic race had remained (so they said) untainted in its *Volksgeist,* nobody ever bothered to explain. Now that Germany has become a totalitarian country, German professors will find out that the pure Aryan *Volksgeist* is not parliamentarian but totalitarian.

The longer the history of a people, the more numerous and manifold are the forms of *Volksgeist* which can be traced in it. Who more faithfully embodied Italian "natural character" or "obscure instinct," Julius Caesar or Caligula, Saint Francis of Assisi or Casanova, Dante or Pietro Aretino, Manzoni or D'Annunzio, Toscanini or Mussolini? What is there in common between the instincts of the English in the time of the Saxon Kings and in the time of David Lloyd George? The English national character, when Henry VIII married six wives, one after the other, was not the same as that which forced Edward VIII to abdicate because he wanted to marry a woman who had had already no more than two husbands. If there were a breakdown of democracy in the United States, it would be easy to find proofs of North American Fascist *Volksgeist* in the Ku Klux Klan, Huey Long, the Black Legion, company unions, Father Coughlin, the lynching of Negroes, etc., etc.

We are far from disputing the fact that at given moments each group of mankind presents given features of its own, not only physical, but also psychological. What we do dispute is that an historical development can be explained by "instinct" or *Volksgeist* of "national character." Any lazy mind, as soon as there is a hole somewhere in its knowledge of causes, can stop that hole by one of these words. We must not delude ourselves into believing that we have solved an historical problem when we have only cloaked our ignorance in a tautological fallacy not seldom springing from nationalistic self-complacency.

III. The Responsibility of the Italian People

1. The Struggle against Fascism

THOSE who speak today of the political immaturity of the Italians base their arguments mainly on the fact that twenty years ago free institutions died in Italy and were replaced by a dictatorship. This is undeniable. But, we are told, it is also undeniable, that the Italian people proved incapable of preventing the Fascist revolution; moreover, they have endured Mussolini's absolute regime for twenty years. Every nation has the government it deserves, and evidently the Italians have not deserved better than a ruthless dictatorship. Consequently, these same Italians will, in the near future, need a government of restricted liberties and strong coercion to secure peace and order in Italy and to prevent her from disturbing both European and world peace. So the argument runs.

We shall not try to dodge this question of responsibility; if anything, we welcome this opportunity to summarize the historical evidence concerning the measure of responsibility in the Fascist tragedy that really belongs to the Italian people.

We cannot, of course, pause here to trace historically the origins of Fascism and its rise to power. Indeed, it is not necessary, since this task has been done again and again in many languages by reliable historians. It is important, however, to note at this time that the myth of Fascism's having saved Italy from Bolshevism has been exploded by historians of all ranks, be they anti-Fascist or Fascist, Protestant or Catholic, Italian or non-Italian. Those who persist in repeating the slogans formulated by Fascism in its infancy are lamentably lacking either in good faith or in intelligence.

The original Fascio founded by Mussolini was a small, ultra-revolutionary group composed of desperadoes who advocated a Leftist, anti-capitalist, anti-religious revolution. But the real Fascism, which came into existence in 1921, when the danger of a revolution, if it had ever existed, was certainly over, consisted in a reactionary movement subsidized by large landowners, bankers, and industrialists, who hired Fascist bands which they proceeded to swell with their own followers. This Fascism was not the creation of Mussolini, who had opposed the transformation of the Party until he found himself alone and hastened to assume leadership of it again.

Against this Fascism the Italian people carried on a long and bloody struggle. What Italy went through in that period from the fall of 1920 to the fall of 1926 was really a civil war in which the Italian people were betrayed: by the wealthy class which created the new Fascism; by the army generals and officers who supplied Fascist bands with weapons, ammunition, and trucks; by the Giolitti government which allowed the Fascists to carry on their so-called punitive expeditions under the disguised protection of the police and with impunity from the courts; and, finally, by the Monarchy which in the end abandoned the country to the Fascists as a conquered territory.

Fascism was still a small minority at this time, a minority which could and should have been defeated had there been a clear understanding of its implications and its possibilities for evil. We must remember that in the life of the new Italy this was a maiden experience and there had as yet been no precedents established from which to judge the results of Fascist domination. During the economic and social crisis that immediately followed the war, the disorders, strikes, and excesses perpetrated by the disappointed working classes in Italy were not much worse than those which took place in other European countries. At the beginning of 1921, Italy was gradually returning to normal conditions. The social revolution which had been feared did not take place only because the rank and file of the Italian people did not want it; what they wanted was that at least some of the promises made so lavishly to the working classes during the war be kept, and that the exploitation of labor be stopped, not only by words and ambiguous laws, but in reality and for good. On this point the Socialists and the Catholic Populists were in full accord, even though their labor unions were often at loggerheads. The failure to carry on a revolution when it would have met with little or no resistance was in itself evidence of the common sense of the mass of the Italian people. Likewise, the counter-attack launched by the upper groups, which hired the Fascist desperadoes when the crisis was over, was evidence of the antisocial and reactionary mentality which the small wealthy class of Italy shared with like classes in other countries.

A strange combination of muddy thinking and cheap Machiavellianism got hold of the various groups: the ultra-revolutionary Fascists sold themselves to the capitalists and reversed their program; the capitalists thought that the time had come to make the masses pay for the scare they had suffered and played ball with the Fascist hoodlums; the Nationalists, a noisy crowd of pseudo-intellectuals who had regarded the Fascists with utter contempt, now shook hands with them and joined in the fray; and, last but not least, the politicians who were in the government cast a benevolent eye upon these paladins of reaction and let the military chiefs, the police, and the courts more or less openly assist the Fascists in their criminal exploits. They all cherished the illusion—they were all quite sure—that they could use Fascism, each for his own purpose, and that, having squeezed the lemon, they could then discard it without more ado.

When Mussolini seized power, not a few Italians thought that, although the procedure had been illegal, the man could and would put an end to civil war, and that his government, despite its sin of origin, would gradually establish peace, and then maintain law and order by constitutional means. Mussolini himself, by forming a coalition cabinet and by announcing that the era of violence and mob rule was over, quickened such hopes and was given powers to carry out his promises.

But peace and justice were not Mussolini's objectives, much less those of the Fascist chieftains who now expected to gather the full fruits of victory and were hardly disposed to share them with others or to go "back to normalcy." By the creation of the Fascist militia and the grant of powers to Fascist officials over and above those of the regular government functionaries, the political balance was tipped, and civil war began all over again. The illusions of those who had expected Fascism to disappear in its own victory, or to be transmuted by some political alchemy into a constitutional regime, were quickly dispelled when Mussolini announced that Fascism was a standing revolution that was always in motion and would never stop.

Now resistance to Fascism was much more difficult, since it had at its disposal the whole machinery of government and the militia. Yet the resistance did not cease. For four years more Mussolini failed to conquer the Italian people. The murder of Matteotti, had it not been for the faintheartedness of the leaders of the opposition and for the treachery of the King, would have marked the end of Fascism. Then came the undisguised dictatorship and the Italian people were thoroughly enslaved.

The fact is that it took Fascism six years to conquer Italy: six years of unequal struggle between a power which had at its disposal all the resources of the government, the police, the militia, and the Monarchy on the one hand, and, on the other, a reluctant people whose labor organizations had been wiped out, whose leaders had either betrayed them by going over to the enemy, or had been murdered, forced to flee, or merely rendered helpless by the sweep of events. Six years of struggle which would have ended in the victory of the people, if Fascism, besides having the support of such groups and classes in Italy as we have here described, had not been protected and aided also by powerful forces outside Italy. Here we come to a most important feature of the history of that period.

2. *The Voice of America*

The impression created abroad by the Fascist success varied according to classes and countries. Socialists and radicals in France, Germany, England, and other countries sneered, half amused, half disdainful, at the spectacle of that strange revolution which appeared to them so farcical. "Only among the Italians can such things happen, a people of organ grinders, mandolin players, and yelling tenors. But *chez nous . . . bei uns . . . it can't happen here!*"

Conservatives of all hues and all countries were delighted; Mussolini had slain the red dragon; Italy was saved and the danger that communism would further expand was over. It seems that the two countries in which Mussolini and his Fascism achieved the greatest success in publicity and popularity were England and the United States. At first, the publics of both these countries were highly amused at the performance going on in Italy. The Fascist revolution appeared to them a kind of magnified grand opera which presented Mussolini as the tenor hero who saves the fair contralto, Civilization, from the vile embrace of Caliban, the wicked revolutionary basso. They applauded vigorously the posturings of Mussolini and hissed no less vigorously at Caliban.

Yet it was not long before certain more serious-minded people began to realize that Fascism was more than a one-night stand. In England the government saw that Fascism and Mussolini could be used conveniently to foster English interests in Europe and elsewhere. In America the government, a Republican administration at that time, had no special political interests of its own to protect by catering to Fascism, but the bigwigs of the party, the standpat reactionaries of the old guard, were in full sympathy with "the restoration of order" and the defeat of "communism" in Italy. Moreover, there were in the United States large and powerful groups which had interests to foster and so became vociferous admirers of Fascism. Side by side with the Italian propagandists who had flocked to this country, they assumed the task of acquainting America with the great benefits that Fascism was bestowing upon the whole world. Bankers who had opened their coffers to the Fascist government and to the Fascist administrations of several large Italian cities; business men, both Italian and American, who were heavily interested in importations from or exportations to Italy; lawyers, judges, professors, and intellectuals who had Italian connections, either through institutions, groups, or important individuals, or who were decorated by the Fascist government with cheap knighthoods; politicians who were anxious to secure votes from Italian groups and associations in this country; and finally, the representatives of the Catholic Church, both ecclesiastics and laymen: thus reads the list of Americans then ready to sing the praises of Mussolini and Fascism on all occasions. We need hardly mention the nice old ladies who were traveling in Italy and finding that trains ran on time, or the pretty young girl students who were delighted by the chivalrous love-making of youthful Fascist Romeos. The ever-growing chorus of Mussolini's worshippers in this country became so noisy that anyone who spoke ill of Fascism and the Duce was thought to have taken leave of his senses.

A few examples of this praise of the Duce and Fascism in the American press, ludicrous in the light of subsequent events, will not be amiss at this point. The reader can judge for himself the number of recruits to Fascism which such eulogies as these must have gained for the Duce.

Let us begin with the bankers. Here are a few quotations from an address given by Mr. Otto H. Kahn, head of a great banking house, before the faculty and students of Wesleyan University, November 15, 1923:

> The credit for having brought about this great change in Italy and without bloodshed [!] belongs to a great man, beloved and revered in his own country, a self-made man, setting out with nothing but the genius of his brain. To him not only his own country but the world at large owes a debt of gratitude.
>
> Mussolini was far from fomenting class hatred or utilizing class animosities or divergencies for political purposes.
>
> He is neither a demagogue nor a reactionary. He is neither a chauvinist nor a bull in the china shop of Europe. He is no enemy of liberty. He is no dictator in the generally understood sense of the word.
>
> Mussolini is far too wise and rightminded a man to lead his people into hazardous foreign adventures.
>
> His government is following the policy of taking the state out of business as much as possible and of avoiding bureaucratic or political interference with the delicate machinery of trade, commerce and finance.
>
> Mussolini is particularly desirous for close and active cooperation with the United States. I feel certain that American capital invested in Italy will find safety, encouragement, opportunity and reward.

It is to be noticed that Mr. Kahn was picturing Mussolini as a champion of liberty and an angel of peace precisely a few months after the Corfu affair, the first exploit of the Duce in international brigandage. Of this episode Mr. Kahn said:

The incident of the bombardment of Corfu is infinitely deplorable, but this bombardment was neither planned nor desired by the Italian government and I know that its results were most profoundly regretted by it.

Mr. Kahn, though he spoke in his own name, was known to represent a group of financial powers in America. The Italians felt that his voice was the voice of American gold. His address, printed by the "Italy-America Society" of New York in both English and Italian, had a wide circulation in Italy as well as in this country. This society brought together the pro-Fascist American aristocracy and Italo-American notables of New York and other cities.

Side by side with Mr. Kahn went Dr. Nicholas Murray Butler, President of Columbia University and Nobel Prize winner for peace. For years Dr. Butler, who had received the highest decorations bestowed by the Fascist government, boasted of his warm friendship for Mussolini. Dr. Butler announced to "an amazed world" that "the Italian national vigour was being reborn with the advent of Fascism"; that "it was safe to predict that just as Cromwell made modern England, so Mussolini would make modern Italy"; that "Fascism is a form of government of the very first order of excellence"; that "we should look to Italy to show us what its experience and insight have to teach in the crisis confronting the twentieth century." Dr. Butler was proud to say that "he had a notion that Rome might again become the capital of the Western world" because "Italy had now intelligent and eager leadership and, accordingly, interesting things might happen in the next few years."

Is it any wonder that the Italian people who read these compliments by Dr. Butler, educational light of America, thought that American educators as a group had become admirers and disciples of Mussolini? It is still less to be wondered at that these panegyrics should encourage the Duce and his cohorts to still bolder ventures. If the Fascists had not thought of it themselves, Dr. Butler's prophecy that "Rome should become the capital of the Western world" must have aroused their enthusiasm to fever-pitch. What could such a phrase suggest except that they must conquer the Western world and establish Fascism, that "form of government of the very first excellence," everywhere it could be done?

Consistent with his premises, Dr. Butler allowed the Casa Italiana of Columbia University to become a center of Fascist activities and Fascist propaganda. Professor Giuseppe Prezzolini, a convert to Fascism, was made director of the Casa Italiana, which became also the headquarters of the Italy-America Society and other Fascist transmission belts.

No less sympathetic to Fascism than these representatives of high finance and culture were some of the members of the American diplomatic service. Richard Washburn Child, who was sent as American Ambassador to Italy by the Harding administration, outstripped all other American worshippers of Mussolini. In his book *A Diplomat Looks at Europe* (1925) he drew such an idealized picture of Fascist Italy and a demigod called Mussolini that he made even the Fascists laugh. A few years later, in 1928, Mr. Child once more lent his pen and his reputation by appearing as the editor of a so-called *Autobiography of Mussolini*, alleged to have been brought forth by the Duce and put into English by Mr. Child. Actually, as Mussolini himself stated afterwards in his memoir of his deceased brother, Arnaldo (*Vita di Arnaldo,* 1932), the book was written by Mr. Child on the strength of some material, mostly sheer invention, furnished him by Mussolini and his brother. This *Autobiography* was in reality, then, a literary fraud which Mussolini, with the active connivance of Mr. Child, put over on the English-speaking world.

As to the contents of this *Autobiography,* it is enough to say that Mussolini did not dare to have it published in Italian. But the Fascist newspapers in Italy loudly heralded its appearance and quoted from it such laudatory passages as were suitable to convey to the Italian public an idea of how great was the esteem in which Mussolini was held by American diplomats and even by the American government itself. Of course, the Italian public knew nothing of Mr. Child and the Harding administration.

In the wake of American financiers, college presidents, and diplomats followed "experts" in economics, historians, philologians, and archaeologists. Political scientists, economists, and sociologists, who had from the beginning found much to admire in the Fascist system of government, or who had discovered that Mussolini had on his advent to power performed the miracle of balancing the state budget overnight, became altogether lyrical when Fascist propaganda launched the myth of the "corporative state." They flocked to Italy to see for themselves the organization and the workings of the Fascist corporative state. They flooded the world with articles, essays, pamphlets, and books. They told the American public as early as 1931 that the corporative state was, to use the words of Professor P. M. Brown of Princeton University, "the most amazing creation of Fascism for the solution of the thorny problem of the relations between capital and labour"; and that it was "an extraordinary achievement worthy of the closest study and admiration."

Yet, strange as it may seem, it was only in November, 1934, that the so-called corporations were inaugurated and, as the *New York Times* (November 10) announced, that "the wheels of Mussolini's new Corporative State started turning." When the wheels started turning, it soon became apparent that they were turning to no purpose, and it was not long before everyone realized that the corporative state never existed in Fascist Italy. It was a sham. As an English scholar who could see behind the empty words said: "The term corporative has been used, if not invented, to rouse a sense of wonder in the people, to keep them guessing and to contrive, out of the sheer mystification of an unusual word, at once to hide the compulsion on which the dictatorship finally depends, and to suggest that a miraculous work of universal benevolence is in the course of performance" (Finer, *Mussolini's Italy*, p. 499).

At any rate, the homage paid by supposedly authoritative foreign scientists to Fascist Italy as the inventor of a model political and social order could not fail to flatter the Italians. They knew, to be sure, that the corporations established were not in fact what they purported to be in theory. But since foreign observers spoke so highly of them and described them in such attractive colors, many Italians were led to think that the corporations, though not as yet working as planned, nevertheless marked the beginning of a great new development devised by Italian genius. Was not Mussolini telling them that the Italian people under Fascism had become the greatest nation on earth? Were not the voices of more than one representative of the American people heard saying, under the dome of the Capitol at Washington, that "America needed a Mussolini"? Mussolini must be right. The ever-growing chorus of admiration for the Duce and Fascism sung by foreign powers had its effect: many Italians became convinced that Mussolini was mapping out a glorious future for them.

A deeper and more lasting impression was made on Italian minds by the fact that from the beginning of Fascism the joyful chorus that celebrated the merits of the new regime was joined by the robust and pious voices of the Catholic clergy and laymen the world over. Among them the myth of Fascism trampling under its feet the Bolshevik monster had become a kind of dogma. As soon as Mussolini, shortly after his advent to power, began his courtship of the Vatican, the enthusiasm of the American Catholics for the Duce and his Fascists increased by leaps and bounds.

The favorable disposition of the Catholic clergy towards Mussolini showed itself first in America and was more unanimous here than in Italy. In Italy the Vatican had to move warily, for large numbers of the lower clergy were still suffering heavily from Fascist violence, and only at the end of 1926 were the last traces of clerical resistance to Fascism wiped out. In America there had been no struggle, and enthusiasm flowed unhampered by memories of bloodshed. It waxed greater when Pius XI, on December 20, 1926, stated that Mussolini had been sent by Divine Providence. It reached a high pitch at the time of the Lateran agreement, and finally it reached its climax when Mussolini sent the Fascist legions on the Spanish "crusade" and was so highly commended and complimented by the Pope himself.

Here are only a few illustrations of the type of statement made by church dignitaries in this country in the cause of Fascism.

In 1924, Cardinal O'Connell of Boston, while the civil war was going on in Italy, stated that

Italy was in process of undergoing a marvelous transformation since Benito Mussolini had seized the reins of government. . . . I have never in my life witnessed a change so impressing. I see perfect order, cleanliness, work, industrial development (*Progresso Italo-Americano,* January 3, 1924).

In 1926, Cardinal O'Connell accepted a high Fascist decoration and, in his address of thanks to Mussolini's representative, he stated:

Mussolini is a genius in the field of government, given to Italy by God to help the nation continue her rapid ascent towards the most glorious destiny (*Il Carroccio* XXXIV, p. 553).

As late as the fall of 1934 Cardinal O'Connell was still regarding Mussolini as "the miracle man." According to His Eminence, Mussolini had shown "great forbearance and magnanimity" after King Alexander of Serbia had been assassinated in Marseilles by agents who had enjoyed the protection of the Duce.

In 1925, the Archbishop of Chicago, Cardinal Mundelein, back from a visit to Rome, made the following statement in a newspaper interview: "Mussolini is a great big man, the man of the time."

At the inauguration of an Italian parochial school in his diocese in October, 1926, Cardinal Dougherty, the Archbishop of Philadelphia, spoke "exalting religion and Fascist Italy" and applauded vigorously when one of his priests, who spoke after him, "in a brilliant discourse, referred to the admirable work of the Duce and the Fascist government" (*Giovinezza,* October 28, 1926).

Cardinal Hayes of New York was the special object of Mussolini's affection, since the Duce four times presented His Eminence with decorations—each higher than the one preceding —all of which the Cardinal accepted with high praise for the Duce (*Il Carroccio,* XIX, p. 353; XXIII, pp. 350, 563; XXX, p. 139).

We need not descend to mere archbishops and bishops, many of whom received, at one time or another, decorations from the Fascist government as a sign of appreciation for their cooperation in creating a halo of greatness and almost of holiness around the head of the Duce and for their fostering among American Catholics and non-Catholics the cause of Italian Fascism.

Much less do we need to descend to the level of priests, friars, monks, and nuns, or to the Jesuits of the weekly *America,* or to the editors of two or three hundred Catholic diocesan bulletins, newspapers, periodicals, and whatnot. Neither is there any need to do more than mention Father Coughlin and his followers, or the many others who, under the cloak of Catholicism, bespoke an American Mussolini who would bring the blessings of Fascism to this country. A collection of the books, articles, essays, sermons, addresses, and utterances of bishops, priests, sacristans, and Catholic laymen which saw the light during that period, would form a good-sized library and stand as a strange but significant monument to the intellectual blindness caused by fanatic devotion and by a reactionary, organized ecclesiasticism. We shall deal with the relations between the Vatican and the Fascist regime in the next chapter. At present we are interested only in the important part that the support given to Fascism by representatives of the Catholic Church in America had in strengthening the hold of the Fascist regime on the Italian people.

3. The Voice of England

The history of the English government during the period between the great wars is not such as to fill a sensitive Englishman with pride.

We are fully aware that the times were difficult, that the English people were strained and would not stand for any action which would bring a threat of war, and that social unrest among the working classes was assuming serious proportions. We agree also that French chauvinism did not make the task of reorganizing a new Europe out of the debris left by the war any easier, and that the clash of the various nationalisms, especially in the newly created independent states, made Europe seem like a madhouse. But even when all the extenuating circumstances are granted, the fact remains that the English cabinets proved unusually incompetent and used the powerful influence of England more in the wrong than in the right direction. The most pungent critics of those English policies have been the English themselves and we need not improve upon their scathing indictment of the men responsible for those policies.

One of the most fatal mistakes made by the English government was that of abetting and helping Mussolini's Fascist regime. With a complete lack of foresight they looked upon Fascism as an element of stability rather than of disintegration in post-war Europe. Mr. Kahn's opinion notwithstanding, the Corfu affair, not to mention the nationalistic boastings and threats with which Mussolini's speeches were filled, would have been more than enough to suggest that the change of government which had taken place in Italy and the anti-democratic program of Fascism constituted a new danger for all Europe.

English politicians and diplomats were sure that no matter who ruled Italy, they could count upon his being a pliable instrument of English policies. Had it not been so in the last war? Among English diplomats the old idea still prevailed that a certain friction between Italy and France was to be maintained as a measure for continental equilibrium. Mussolini with his francophobia, which he had borrowed from the Italian Nationalists, was the man who fitted precisely into the English scheme of European politics. He must be cajoled gently along the path marked by English interests. After all, Italy needed the support and friendship of England, while England had no other use for Italy than that of employing her occasionally as a cat's-paw to reach for certain goals that could not be conveniently realized in other ways.

In the chain of events which permitted Mussolini to strengthen his dictatorship, England played a conspicuous part. Prime Minister Baldwin and Foreign Minister Curzon helped Mussolini, in 1923, to save his face after his criminal attack on Corfu. At the time of the crisis brought about by the Matteotti murder, while Italy was seething with indignation and Fascism was on the verge of ruin, the English foreign minister, Sir Austen Chamberlain in December, 1924, made the move of paying an official visit to the Duce. It was the first time that such a dignitary of the English government had ever condescended to pay such a compliment to Italy. The English minister rushed ostentatiously to shake the hand of the Duce which was at that moment, in the opinion of the Italians, wet with Matteotti's blood. It was at that meeting that the Geneva Protocol was thrown to the wolves.

In December, 1925, Sir Austen went again to Rome and assured Mussolini that, as far as England was concerned, he could have a free hand in dealing with Ethiopia. At that moment, antiFascist pogroms were taking place everywhere in Italy. In August, 1926, Sir Austen met Mussolini in Leghorn and gave him a free hand in Albania, while the anti-Fascists were putting up their last resistance in a forlorn battle.

To be sure, there was a reason why the head of England's

Foreign Office took a hand in salvaging Mussolini in 1924 and kept so closely in touch with his activities in the years that followed. Just at that moment, England was having a serious row with Turkey over the Mosul oil wells. Young Turkey, having recently defeated the Greek army, was in no mood to yield to British demands. Hence, the suave Sir Austen used Mussolini as a threat to the Turks, by reviving Italy's old claims to Adana and persuading the Duce to mobilize the Italian fleet. Under this menace the Turkish government hastened, in 1926, to make an agreement with England.

This was only the beginning of the British courtship of the Duce. We do not need to rehearse what is history: how in December, 1933, Prime Minister Ramsay MacDonald and Foreign Minister Sir John Simon went to Italy to pay their respects to the Dictator and to concoct with him the famous Four Power Pact which would have put France at the mercy of Hitler; how in April, 1935, the same two men went to Stresa, *not* to discuss the Ethiopian affair, although everybody knew that Mussolini was preparing to attack that country, a member of the League of Nations. The present foreign minister, Mr. Eden, acted during the Ethiopian war as chairman of the committee on sanctions, the purpose of which was *not* to impose any sanction that might have stopped Mussolini's war. It was again Mr. Eden who in 1937 accepted Mussolini's promise not to modify the status quo in the Mediterranean area. But in the Adriatic, that is to say in Albania, he allowed the Duce a free hand. Finally in January, 1939, after Munich, while the Italian Fascists were clamoring for Nice, Savoy, Corsica, Tunis, and more, Prime Minister Neville Chamberlain, accompanied by his foreign minister, Lord Halifax, went to Rome "with his umbrella on his arm, as a commercial traveller of the British Empire, anxious to sell the Duce a proposal to maintain the European *status quo*" (R. G. Massock, *Italy from Within*, p. 119). It was too late. Mussolini had already sold out to Hitler.

So long as Mussolini acted as England's cutthroat, he enjoyed great popularity in conservative British circles. To show their appreciation they took to their bosoms Mussolini's representative in London, Dino Grandi, the man who in 1921 could write that "there was nothing that he dreaded more than to be considered a Fascist," but who very soon became one of the Duce's most devoted bootlickers and rose from the sidewalks of Bologna to become a count and Fascist foreign minister. When Mussolini had to satisfy his daughter Edda's ambition, Grandi made room for the Duce's son-in-law, Ciano, also decorated with a comital crown, but Grandi got the next best office, the London embassy. What a wonderful time Grandi had in England!

As a member of the Non-Intervention Committee for the Spanish war, Grandi not only lied with a brazen face about the Fascist help given to the rebels, but in a fit of noble indignation protested in strong language against the wound inflicted upon the honor of Fascist Italy by the Russian representative who denounced, with facts and figures, Fascist intervention in Spain. Naturally, the English members on the committee could not entertain any doubt that, having to choose between the Italian count and the Russian comrade, they could trust the former as a gentlemen of their own ilk and hold the other in contempt as a proletarian liar.

In like manner, the English politicians and intellectuals who extolled Mussolini and Fascism to the sky in books, essays, and articles beyond the number produced in any other country, formed an army of no small size.

There was a cavalry made up of such knights as Sir Percival Phillips, Sir Frank Fox, Sir Leo Chiozza Money, Sir Charles Petrie, Sir Charles Marriot, Sir Ernest Benn, Sir Philip Gibbs. There was an infantry led by Major Barnes, Major Yeats-Brown, Mr. Heathcote, Mr. McClure-Smith, Mr. Goad, Mr. Munro, Mr. Paul Einzig. And there was an artillery composed of newspapers and reviews—the *Daily Mail,* the *Daily Telegraph,* the *Morning Post* (which shared the same Italian service as Mussolini's newspaper *Popolo d'Italia*), the *Observer,* the

Spectator, the *Saturday Review,* the *Nineteenth Century and After,* the *Financial News.*

The *London Times* occasionally published some mild criticisms of Mussolini artfully submerged in an ocean of praise, but it made amends by printing articles which expressed unstinted admiration for the benefits of Fascism.

Among the English Catholics, Mussolini was almost canonized. A Mr. T. K. Haydon in a book entitled *Fascism and Providence,* published by the leading Catholic firm of Sheed and Ward (London, 1937), expounded the theory that Fascism was the result of special divine intervention, and though he believed that God had planned its rise as part of a natural order, he did not altogether exclude the possibility that "God had sent an angel to whisper in the ear of Benito Mussolini."

Even men like Mr. Churchill, the man destined to play such a leading part in the present war and to append his name to the Atlantic Charter, shared with his friends of the English aristocracy a deep appreciation of Mussolini and Fascism. In an interview granted in January, 1927, Mr. Churchill, never a man to be satisfied with half measures, stated, "If I were an Italian, I would don the Fascist Black Shirt." In 1931 he voiced his admiration of "the monumental work of Mussolini" and affirmed that "the best years which Spain has known had been those lived under the dictatorship of Primo de Rivera." Still later, in *Collier's Magazine* for September, 1938, Mr. Churchill extolled Mussolini far above Washington and Cromwell and praised the Italian King for having recognized and accepted Fascism. Even as late as December, 1940, he could tell the Italians that Mussolini was "a great man."

What the English Tories thought of Italian Fascism in general and of Mussolini in particular during that whole period can be gathered more fully from the pamphlet *The British Case,* written by Lord Lloyd with an introduction by Lord Halifax (then head of the Foreign Office) in December, 1939, more than a year after Munich and three months after the outbreak of the present war—at a time when the ugly features and criminal exploits of Fascism could no longer be ignored by even the dumb animals in the courtyard. We give here a short extract from that pamphlet by a man who is now the official spokesman of the English Cabinet in the House of Lords and was sponsored by Lord Halifax, present British Ambassador to Washington. Never have we seen a more shameful distortion of history or a more complete lack of knowledge than appear in the following excerpt. It must be read with care.

Above all the Italian genius has developed, in the characteristic Fascist institutions, a highly authoritarian regime which however threatens neither religion nor economic freedom nor the security of other European nations. The Italian system is founded on two rocks: first, the separation of Church and State and the supremacy of the Church in matters not only of faith but of morals; second, the rights of labor. The political machinery of Fascism is indeed built on trade unionism while that of the German State is built up on the ruins of the German labor movement. The Italian State, *like that of Spain and Portugal,* is neither socialist nor capitalist, but syndicalist; but all these regimes assert what every Christian regime must assert and what Nazism and Communism alike deny, the antecedence of the family over the state. Finally, the structure of the state in Italy, Spain, Portugal and Greece is based upon an independent and self-supporting industrial system. So far from the regimes of these countries arrogating to themselves the almost limitless responsibilities of industry and a slave owner's control over labour, they have conferred on labour and industry jointly new responsibilities in law as well as in fact and have to this extent not increased but actually diminished the powers of the central government. In Italy, the economic Corporations, severally and collectively, discharge nine tenths of the work of the modern state and these Corporations, representative of the employees, the management and the share-holders, are the supreme executive authority in all non-political affairs. . . . There is much in the non-political character of Italian Fascism which would be wholly distasteful to the English but *there is much in the Italian Labour Charter which we should, and do, admire* [*italics ours*].

When, as here, ignorance, stupidity, and insincerity reach the sublime, they should, and do, command our admiration.

4. The Benefits of the Dictatorship

For almost twenty years American and English newspapers published glowing descriptions of the wonderful accomplishments of the Fascist regime. Not a few of the American correspondents in Rome seemed to have lost themselves. Especially ardent were the ever-increasing ranks of impressionable women reporters, who visited Rome, to be entranced by the Duce.

Even now, former admirers of Mussolini, though they may have changed their minds about the character of the man and his place in history, have kept to the habit of reminding us how Mussolini brought order and discipline out of chaos, drained swamps, built roads, erected monumental structures, improved agriculture, increased the population, restored religion, won a colonial empire, and made the name of Italy respected and feared throughout the world.

This insistence on Mussolini's former accomplishments before he turned international criminal by declaring war on England and America, is not constantly voiced to freshen the nostalgic memory of a lost love; it often serves the more useful purpose of providing evidence that the Italian people, not being capable of governing themselves, need a wise dictator, such as Mussolini was before he came under the bad influence of Hitler.

It would be an unnecessary digression for us to analyze each of these accomplishments in detail and show that many of them were far from beneficial to Italy. The cost of others was scarcely commensurate with their aims and results, and some were no more than showpieces designed to impress foreigners with the grandeur of the regime. Useful works were carried on, to be sure, and some developments of real value to the people were begun. Any regime that has lasted for twenty years, bad as it may be, is bound in the natural course of events to do some things that are not bad. Tyrants, absolute kings, and dictators have always been great builders of monuments which they hoped would remain forever as witnesses of their glory. But we know that such works have often been erected by squeezing the last penny from the poor, that some of them were not done in the best interests of the nation.

In the Fascist regime, part of the expenditures for public works was not met from current income; the contracts provided payments by installments extending, on the average, over ten-year periods, though sometimes such payments extended over more than fifty years. The financial pledges thus incurred did not appear on the records of the national debt, and by this method a sum of over three billion and a half dollars was omitted from the public debt in the budget. By 1933 this hidden debt amounted to seventy-five billion lire. F. A. Repaci stated in *La Finanza Italiana, 1913–1932*, pp. 310–31, "Certainly in the decade which followed, this hidden debt rose to frightening proportions. If we calculate the entire hidden debt incurred by the Dictatorship from 1922 to 1943 at one hundred billion lire we may be sure we are not exaggerating." When the Fascist government seized power in 1922, the national debt amounted to ninety-three billion lire; it now stands at six hundred billion lire, which is six times the yearly income of the entire population of Italy.

The accomplishments of a regime must, after all, be measured, not by palaces, stadiums, roads, and military barracks thrown up in a few years by the reckless spending of the people's resources. They are rather to be judged by the result obtained in improving the political, economic, social, and cultural life of a nation. Need we do more than summarize the achievement of Mussolini and the Fascists? Italy no longer has political existence as an independent nation; she has become a mere appanage to Nazi Germany. Economically, Italy has reached almost the lowest level in her whole history. Socially, Italy has seen the reestablishment of a system of feudal barons—the Fascist leaders—who have gathered in their hands wealth and power in abundance, while the rest of the people has lost all freedom and been reduced to starvation rations. Culturally, Fascist Italy has lived on the gains made by the previous generation, but has produced nothing of its own that is worthy of mention.

Those who still assert that the present misery of Italy comes of Mussolini's fatal mistake in going to war as Germany's ally, but that his work previous to this blunder had been all constructive and to the benefit of Italy, are either ignorant of the fact or choose to forget that Mussolini's whole policy from the very beginning of his regime was directed toward what he liked to call the *Impero Romano,* which in the last analysis had to be conquered by force of arms. War was thus glorified as an instrument of civilization. In war lay progress. Youth was to be warlike. Might and right were identical. The people of Italy were regimented under the strictest compulsion and forced to bear a burden of military expenses quite beyond their resources. When the moment finally came for action, after the ephemeral conquest of Ethiopia, and after the rape of Albania, which was already under Italy's political and economic control, that empty shell of empire collapsed, revealing criminal inefficiency, gross negligence, and poor generalship in the military organization built up by Mussolini through so many years and at such cost to Italy.

All that Mussolini's megalomania and the promises of Fascism have come to mean for Italy is, unhappily, heaps of ruins of modern cities to add to those of ancient times, military defeat and loss of prestige, economic exhaustion, frightful losses of men and material, profound discouragement, and awful suffering. Italy has become a vassal state of Germany. The lovely streets of Italian towns now resound with the heavy tread of Prussian boots. The glory of Fascism has passed away.

How can the petty achievements of Fascism, with its puppet statesmen, compensate for the ruin of modern Italy? Italy has paid, and may have to go on paying, a fearful price for having been the cradle of Fascism and for having failed to stamp it out before it stifled the country's liberty and free institutions. England, the United States, and the whole world are paying a heavy price in blood and destruction for helping Mussolini first to secure a firm hold on Italy and then to wreck the League of Nations, to nurture Nazism in its infancy and to embark upon his inglorious career as an empire-builder.

Though hypothetical "if's" count little in history, it is reasonable to think that without the precedent of Fascism the Nazi venture might not have taken place. If it had taken place, however, and had led to war, we may be sure that a free, democratic Italy would not have made common cause with Nazi Germany. Already, from earliest times, experience has taught that *"quidquid delirant reges plectuntur Achivi"* (Whatever wrongs the great commit the people have to suffer for).

Have the bankers, educators, diplomats, bishops, and all the others who exalted Mussolini now learned that lesson? Surely we are justified in doubting it as long as they hark back to accomplishments of the Fascist regime.

Thus the moral and political responsibility for the triumph of Fascism in Italy is not confined to the Italian people and their leaders; it is a responsibility shared in part by the people and the leaders of many countries. Why, then, must the blame be cast only on the Italian people? Why, then, must the Italian people alone be held guilty for the tragic consequences of mistakes made by so many? Why must the Italian people alone be considered incapable of living under democratic institutions?

It is with a sense of deep regret that we have found it necessary, in presenting Italy's case, to rehash all this past history and recall to memory the misjudgments and mistakes of financiers, diplomats, statesmen, intellectuals, churchmen, and others who, by their words or their actions, contributed to the solidifying of the Fascist regime in Italy and to the spread of its influence to other countries. Some of these men are no longer living; and perhaps some of those who are have had a change of heart regarding the Duce. It were a far easier thing to let this unpleasant past lie in its grave. Unfortunately, it is an unquiet grave from which still rise the ghosts of old errors and false notions not yet dispelled even by the tragedy of the present war.

IV. The Vatican

We preserve and shall preserve both memory
and perennial gratitude for what has been done
in Italy for the benefit of religion, even though
not less and perhaps greater was the benefit derived by the party and the regime.
—Pius XI, Encyclical *Non abbiamo bisogno.*

1. The Vatican and Fascism

IF ANYONE ventures today to suggest that the Vatican in any
sense supported the Fascist regime, every Catholic voice in America is raised in formidable protest. Diocesan bulletins and Catholic journals wax indignant and heap abuse upon the head of
the accuser. It is much like stirring up a hornets' nest.

The Catholic answer is that Pope Pius XI, as well as his successor, Pius XII, condemned in encyclicals and other messages
the principles of totalitarianism, statolatry, and racial privileges
—principles that constitute the very essence of Nazism and Fascism.

As far as it goes, the answer is quite true. It is no less true that
Pius XII has urged all peoples and governments to respect treaties and agreements and to abstain from war; during the present
conflict, he has asked repeatedly that they put an end to it. Pius
XI protested against the persecution of the Jews. Pius XII deplored the invasion of neutral countries like Belgium and Holland; he protested against the German atrocities in Poland and
elsewhere, and he even refrained from recognizing as a crusade
the war against Bolshevik Russia. Last but not least, he suggested
as a basis for peace and reconstruction in a war-torn world a program that has several points in common with the Atlantic Charter.

We do not dispute these facts. But it is equally indisputable that the Vatican established friendly relations with the Fascist regime from its very beginning and later concluded with it the Lateran agreements, through which the approval of the Church secured for the Duce and his government national and international prestige which would have been otherwise unattainable. When Pius XI expressed his opinion that Mussolini "was the man sent by Providence," the Catholics of the world accepted the papal verdict and, placing Mussolini's name in the special niche reserved for the great benefactors of Christianity, they burned before it the incense of their admiration and gratitude. These facts are written with equal clarity on the other side of the ledger.

No historian, whether of the present or of the future, will be able to understand and explain fully the many Fascist successes in international affairs without taking into account the friendly relations between the Vatican and the Fascist dictatorship. Fascism exploited to the utmost this friendly disposition of the Vatican, furthering its program of expansion and conquest.

At this point the apologists of the Vatican, who cannot now speak as well of Mussolini and Fascist Italy as they did in the past, feel duty-bound to explain that the Pope, in accepting Mussolini's friendly advances and in concluding with him the Lateran Treaty and Concordat, was moved, not by political, but by religious motives. The Church, they say, is at all times willing to accept any form of government which respects the rights and liberties necessary for the spiritual mission of its ecclesiastical institutions. Aiming only at the religious welfare of the people, the Pope, as Pius XI said, is willing to bargain even with the devil for the sake of saving a soul.

We grant, with due reservation, that the purposes and intentions of the Pope in dealing with Fascist Italy were essentially religious. But whatever the Pope's intention, the fact remains that the Lateran agreements had also a political content and political implications. They led to the establishment of close relations between the Fascist State and the Vatican, not only of a diplomatic and administrative nature, but financial as well, for a considerable share of the income of the Vatican is dependent upon the State treasury of the Fascist regime. The Lateran Treaty was not merely a treaty of peace between two formerly hostile powers; it was also a treaty of alliance between them, though the alliance was restricted to certain specific purposes. Whether the Pope's intentions were religious and spiritual, whether he was justified in making such a deal, and whether he was right or wrong in choosing the moment he did to settle the Roman question—these are all considerations which in no way alter the fact that the Vatican, by its political action, bestowed its blessing on the Fascist regime, increased Mussolini's prestige, and contributed greatly to the strengthening of Fascism, both in Italy and abroad.

Now that it is clearly understood how responsible Fascism is for the present world calamity, everyone agrees that any contribution to the rise and growth of Fascism and its devouring policies was, to say the least, a mistake. It was a mistake for the British government to back Mussolini; it was a mistake for American bankers to supply Mussolini with funds; it was a mistake for American educators to praise Mussolini and Fascism; it was a mistake for the diplomats of America and of other countries to flatter Mussolini by assuring him that his government was to be a model for the governments of the world. It was no less a mistake for the Vatican to have contributed so much to the prestige and the strength of the Fascist regime both at home and abroad. As it is true for all others, be they men or institutions, so it is true for the Vatican that mistakes carry with them a certain amount of material and moral responsibility.

It would not be necessary to dwell further on this point, were it not for the fact that Catholic apologists deny that the Holy See has ever incurred any responsibility in dealing with Fascism. Others who are neither ignorant of the history of the relations between the Vatican and Fascism, nor compelled by a lack of

good faith to contest the facts, explain the philo-Fascist policies
of the Holy See by assuming that it was the victim of Fascist deception. It is, however, very difficult to excuse the Vatican on
these grounds.

The Vatican was, so to speak, in the midst of the fray and it
knew the character of the men and the nature of the events which
led to Mussolini's dictatorship. It could not have had any illusions about the methods employed by the Fascist government
and the spirit which motivated its policies. During the civil war
of 1921–26, all the organizations, all the social and economic
institutions, unions, cooperatives, and clubs which the Italian
Catholics had built in previous years, and which had become the
bastion of the Populist Party, suffered heavily at the hands of the
Fascists. Not a few priests connected with those institutions had
been beaten, treated with castor oil, or, in some instances, brutally murdered. Fascism, far from showing any affection or respect for religion and the Church, appeared at that time a great
menace to them, and certainly the past of its leader, Mussolini,
was not very encouraging. The Jesuit periodical *Civiltà Cattolica*, which chronicled minutely and faithfully all the work
of destruction and violence wrought against Catholic institutions and the clergy by the Fascists during the civil war, both
before and after the March on Rome, did not conceal its serious
apprehensions for the future of the Church under Fascist domination.

And yet it was before the March on Rome that Pope Pius XI
rendered a great service to Fascism. The long and tragic crisis
of the Italian Parliament, of which Fascism had taken full advantage, could and should have been brought to an end by a
coalition of the liberal democrats, the Catholic Populists and the
Socialist Reformists. Together they could have formed a government capable of controlling the situation and of repressing
the acts of violence perpetrated both by the Revolutionary Socialists and Communists, and by the small Fascist minority. The
Socialist Reformists had broken away from the rest of the So-

cialist party and were now more than willing to collaborate with other progressive groups. Their program was far from any extreme radicalism, since they advocated social and political reform, to be carried on not by revolution but by gradual and constitutional procedure.

The program of the Populists was very similar to that of the Reformists, as far as social and economic legislation was concerned. Divergent points of view concerning religious policies were such as could be ironed out. At any rate, Don Sturzo, the leader of the Populist Party could have been trusted to conclude an alliance without detriment to the rights and liberties of the Catholic Church in Italy, as well as those of the Vatican in the international sphere.

A circular letter from the Vatican to the Italian hierarchy (October 2, 1922) bid the clergy not to identify themselves with the Populists and to assume a neutral attitude in the political conflict. Such an order issued at that moment could not fail to be interpreted as a repudiation of the Populist Party by the Church.

On January 20, 1923, Cardinal Gasparri, the Pope's Secretary of State, had a secret interview with Mussolini. The Bank of Rome, which was controlled by Catholics and to which Italian Catholics, Vatican prelates, and the Holy See in part entrusted their funds, faced imminent bankruptcy. Mussolini pledged himself to save the bank by the intervention of the State. He kept his word and bankruptcy was avoided at the cost, it was said, of one and one half billion lire, which, needless to add, came out of Italian taxpayers.

Mussolini knew that in destroying the parliamentarian regime and the free institutions he could count on the support of Pius XI, who had no use for democracy. When Don Sturzo, at the Congress of the Populist Party in Turin in April, 1923, burned his bridges and tried to range his forces on the side of the irreconcilable opposition to Fascism, the Vatican again came to the rescue: Don Sturzo resigned the leadership of the Party. In his book *Italy and Fascismo* (New York, 1926, p. 137), Don

Sturzo, speaking of himself in the third person, thus describes his resignation:

> The personal pressure of the Government and of its friends was heavy and continuous; at the critical moment the man who was believed by Fascisti and philo-Fascisti alike to be the pivot of the situation, the convinced adversary of Mussolini, left the leadership of his party because of obscure Fascists threats of armed reprisals against the Church. . . .

One does not need to be a master of divination to decipher this rather cryptic statement. The threats of reprisals against the Church, to have been effective, must have been made to that high ecclesiastical authority which alone had the power to act.

Still later, at the time of the crisis brought on by the Matteotti murder, the Vatican cooperated in the salvage of Mussolini by administering the death blow to the Populist Party, whose representatives, together with the Socialists, had withdrawn from the Lower House and asked the King for the dismissal of Mussolini. But at that very moment Pope Pius XI came forward with a warning to Catholics that any alliance with the Socialists, even with those of the Right wing, was forbidden by the Catholic moral law which condemns collaboration with evil. By this intervention Pius XI sabotaged all negotiations for the coalition and opened wide the door to the Fascist *coup d'état*. It is significant that coalitions of Rightist Socialists and Catholics had taken place in Belgium and in Germany and that the Pope had not felt it necessary to remind them that no cooperation with evil is admitted by Catholic morals. Events have proved that by his action Pope Pius was in fact cooperating with a much greater evil, that is to say, with Fascism.

By order of the Vatican, all priests were obliged to resign from the party and give up all the administrative and political positions which they held in the Catholic organizations. This meant the final disintegration of the Populist Party, which was dependent upon those organizations, and these in their turn were, especially in the rural districts, under the control of priests.

We do not need to rehearse here the mutual compliments

which the Vatican and the Duce exchanged periodically during
the first three years of the dictatorship, from 1926 to 1928, or
to mention the little scraps which came now and then to cloud
the sky of that Fascist-clerical honeymoon. But we cannot pass
over in silence two remarkable statements made late in 1926.
The first belongs to Cardinal Merry del Val, who on October 31,
while he was presiding as a Pontifical Legate at the celebration
of the centennial of St. Francis in Assisi said:

> My thanks also go to him [Mussolini] who holds in his hands the
> reins of the government in Italy, who with a clear insight into reality
> has wished and wishes Religion to be respected, honored, practised.
> Visibly protected by God, he has wisely improved the fortunes of the
> Nation, increasing its prestige throughout the world.

The amazing thing was that just at that time Mussolini, the man
"protected by God" and so zealous in the cause of the Catholic
religion, had let loose his Blackshirts in the hunting out and
bludgeoning of the members of the Catholic Action all over
Italy. It was to protest against this persecution that Pius XI, in
a famous address of December, 1926, after some bittersweet remarks on the policy of Mussolini towards the Catholic Action,
uttered the second statement, his historical phrase that Mussolini was "the man sent by Providence."

In October, 1926, when negotiations for what were to be
the agreements of 1929 were started, the Vatican already knew
the fundamental points of Fascist ideology, its doctrine of statolatry, its totalitarianism, and its claim that it was responsible
only to itself for the moral justification of its actions, or, in the
words of the Fascist philosophers, that the State had not only a
political but also a moral personality (*lo Stato etico*) of its own
and that this ethical essence of the State was supreme, absolute,
and independent of the ethics of individuals or of any organization, be it religious or not. The principle "nothing against the
State, nothing above the State, nothing outside the State" had
been proclaimed most solemnly by Mussolini himself.

Pius XI did not have to wait until June, 1931, when he found
himself involved in an open quarrel with Mussolini over the

interpretation of the Lateran agreement, to discover what Fascism was. But it was only then that he finally decided, in his Encyclical *Non abbiamo bisogno,* "to point out and condemn all those things in their program and activities which we have found to be contrary to Catholic doctrine and practice and therefore irreconcilable with the name and profession of Catholicism." This Encyclical, although it saved the face of the Vatican as far as the doctrinal issue was concerned, nevertheless bore sad testimony to the muddy and hopeless situation in which the Pope had placed the Church by his entanglement with Fascism. Pius XI had gone so far in accepting favors and gifts from Mussolini and the Fascist regime that now he could be accused of ingratitude by Mussolini. The Pope answered that he recognized and was grateful for the benefits received, but that the bestowing of benefits had been mutual and Mussolini had perhaps got the best of the bargain:

We preserve and shall preserve memory and perennial gratitude for what has been done in Italy for the benefit of religion, even though not less and perhaps greater was the benefit derived by the [Fascist] party and the [Fascist] regime.

American Catholics who become angry and indignant when somebody says that the Vatican favored Fascism, would do well to ponder over this passage of that Encyclical which they quote so often as evidence of the anti-Fascism of Pius XI. Was it not St. Augustine who said "Rome has spoken, the question is settled?" And they ought to ponder, too, over the remark which the Pope added:

Recent events lead us seriously to doubt whether these previous benevolences and favours were actuated by sincere love and zeal for religion, or whether they were not rather due to pure calculation and to an ulterior purpose of domination.

Strange that the Pope had to confess such blindness to the purposes of Fascist benevolence and that only "recent events" had led him to "doubt" Mussolini's intentions! In the light of the history of the last decade we now know for sure that the "doubts" of Pius XI were more than justified and, therefore, that his statements were a frank confession that he had favored and supported the Fascist party and the Fascist regime. He had made a sad mistake. The Pope admitted that he had gone too far in his benevolence toward the regime:

We have always refrained from formal and explicit condemnations [of Fascism]; we have come to such a point as to believe possible and to favor compromises which seemed inadmissible to others.

Still more strange are the conclusions reached in the same Encyclical from those premises the Pope had so forcefully stated concerning the unchristian, immoral, and pagan principles and practices of Fascism. What worried Pius XI most was precisely the fact that Fascism was not merely a philosophy of life and of government; it was a philosophy in action, carried out in practice in a totalitarian way as befitted a totalitarian state. Fascism was not merely an abstract theory but a concrete reality, embodied in the Fascist party and in the Fascist regime. The Fascist principles were "already in great measure put into effect to the exclusive advantage of a party and a regime based on an ideology which clearly resolves itself into a pagan worship of the State."

Such being the case, one should expect that the condemnation of Fascism implied by necessary extension the condemnation of the Fascist party and the Fascist regime. All his predecessors, for more than a century, had, for instance, condemned the principles and practices of Freemasonry and under penalty of excommunication had at the same time forbidden all Catholics to become members of any lodge of Freemasons. But the subtle system of logic which prevails at the Vatican was accommodating when dealing with Fascism. Pius XI, after his solemn condemnation of Fascist principles and practices, took pains to explain in the same Encyclical that "we have not meant to condemn the [Fascist] party and the [Fascist] regime as such." As a consequence, the collaboration of the Catholic Church in Italy with Fascism not only continued but was greatly intensified from that time on. By what subtle scholastic distinction His Holiness could separate the Fascist party and the Fascist regime from the principles which they practiced, and thus absolve the former while condemning the latter, has never been explained.

Still more pitiful was the Pope's solution to the question of the Fascist oath of allegiance to Mussolini, obligatory for all who applied for membership in the Fascist party, for all holders of public offices, teachers, and professional men. Many Catholics whose consciences rebelled against the implications of that oath of personal allegiance to the Duce ("to believe, to obey, to fight") had inquired of the Holy See whether the oath did not violate the principles of Christian morals and whether they could take it. Pius XI told them that the Fascist oath which pledged the taker to doctrines and activities condemned by the Church was unlawful for Catholics. This meant that to take the Fascist oath was a sin. But the Pope also suggested the way to cheat the devil by taking the oath without sinning. A Catholic could take the oath "before God and his conscience" simply by adding to it the mental and therefore silent reservation "excepting the laws of God and of the Church." Excellent casuistry, but rather puzzling when suggested by the Supreme Guardian of Morals and the Infallible Vicar of Christ on earth.

Pius XI went further. A royal decree of August 26, 1931, summoned all university professors to sign an oath in which they had to swear to "educate active and valiant citizens devoted to the country and to the Fascist regime." Those professors who, because of their moral integrity, had up to that time resisted all pressure to sell themselves and their educational mission to Fascism were put in the tragic position of either forfeiting their self-respect, their consciences, and their prestige with the students, or of being reduced to poverty and cut off from their scientific activities. The Vatican might at least have kept quiet. But on December 4, 1931, the Vatican paper, Osservatore Romano, published an editorial, the author of which pretended to believe that in the formula of the oath the words "Fascist regime" meant not the "Fascist regime," but "government of the

State," a State which might also be non-Fascist. He pretended also not to understand that the formula of the oath pledged the professors to teach that Fascist doctrine which the Pope had condemned as incompatible with Catholic doctrine and morals. As a consequence Catholic teachers were advised to take the oath.

The open, enthusiastic support given to the Ethiopian war by the whole Italian clergy, high and low, by bishops and friars and by the Jesuits, is well known, just as it is well known that Pius XI himself, after some sibylline utterances about just and unjust war, in his address of May 12, 1936, when the crushing of Abyssinia by poison gas was a *fait accompli,* felt the need of partaking "the triumphant joy of an entire great and good people over a peace which, it is hoped and intended, will be an effective contribution and prelude to the true peace in Europe and the world."

Even the Catholic historian who in 1941 wrote *Church and State in Fascist Italy,* Professor D. A. Binchy, and who through a maze of scholastic distinctions and subdistinctions weaves his interpretation of Vatican connections with Fascism and exonerates the Vatican completely, at this point gave up the task and stated:

> The notion that the military triumph of a country which had been formally proclaimed a law breaker and an aggressor by the vote of over fifty nations was a hopeful prelude to true peace in Europe and the world, was not likely to carry conviction. The repercussion of this unfortunate phrase largely nullified the genuine effort made by the Vatican to maintain its neutrality in an extremely difficult situation. . . . For once the forceful personality of Pius XI had betrayed him into taking a false step on the treacherous path of international politics and his very natural love for Italy went perilously near to compromising the tradition of rigid impartiality established by those great universalist Popes Leo XIII and Benedict XV (p. 651).

A great fuss was made in 1938 by the Catholic press the world over, especially in this country, in connection with Pius XI's condemnation of Fascist anti-semitic legislation. The Pope even wrote a letter about it to Victor Emmanuel, who answered po-

litely that the matter would be considered, which meant he
could do nothing, and another letter to Mussolini, who did not
even answer. The Popes have always disapproved of open persecutions and pogroms of Jews. But let us not forget that the Catholic Church and the Vatican have never approved of the principle
and practice of giving Jews, wherever they live, equal rights with
the Christians among whom they live. The thought of the high
ecclesiastical circles on the Jewish question was clearly expressed
in a long series of articles which appeared in *Civiltà Cattolica* of
Rome. This periodical, edited by the Jesuits, many of whom are
professors at the Pontifical Gregorian University where the boys
of the American College in Rome receive their instruction and
their ecclesiastical training, has no official character. But since
its chief editor is appointed by the Pope, it usually reflects closely
the official trend of thought in high Vatican circles. According
to *Civiltà Cattolica* (October 3, 1936):

Two facts which appear contradictory are to be found together
among the Jews scattered in the modern world: their control of
moneys and their preponderance in Socialism and Communism.

The Jews, therefore, not all of them but many of them, "constitute a serious and permanent danger to society." What is the
remedy? Their assimilation by the Christian population would
be the ideal solution, but the Jews refuse to be assimilated. Zionism could offer an escape, but it is impractical. There remains
the old "ghetto," but the good-hearted Jesuit writer could not
stand the thought of it and suggested instead "even to-day a way
ought to be found to render the Jews innocuous, as the Church
succeeded in doing in the Middle Ages, with means more suitable to modern conditions and without persecutions (p. 45)."

The question of Zionism was discussed at length in the issue
of June 5, 1937. It described all the obstacles which make this
solution inadvisable and remarked that the Jews, "foxy profiteers, penetrate into all international organizations and especially in two of them, Freemasonry and the League of Na-

tions." The article concluded by advocating again that "a suitable way ought to be found to change their wicked mentality (p. 423)." In the issue of June 19, 1937, the delicate subject of the conversion of the Jews to Christianity was explored and rather discouraging statistics were given. Only 1132 baptisms of Jews had been found in the Rome registers for the century from 1836 to 1936, and the largest number in a single year was a paltry 46 in 1936. Returning to the same subject in the issue of July 3, 1937, *Civiltà Cattolica* analyzed the methods of converting the Jews followed in various countries, such as in England and in America by Catholics and Protestants, and warned them not to make "a common cause with the promoters of anti-semitism and to avoid anything that might cause offense or humiliation to the Jews." At the same time, however, it stated that "it is necessary to limit relations between Christians and Jews, so as to remove any danger for the Christians and [without having recourse to anti-semitism], to raise a barrier against the twofold perturbing Jewish preponderance, the materialistic-financial and the revolutionary preponderance."

Zionism was again taken up in the April 2, 1938 issue, especially the Palestinian Jewish settlements, which, according to the writer, had been a great mistake in British policy. The best solution would be to force the Jews to evacuate Palestine again. This time *Civiltà Cattolica* suggested more clearly its own solution of the general Jewish problem. It could be no other "than that traditionally adopted by the Popes," that is to say, "Charity without persecution and prudence with suitable provisions, such as a form of segregation and identification suited to the time, or in a word, the kind of hospitality and civil relations such as are used with foreigners (p. 77)." Another more outspoken article of July 16, 1938, dealt with the Jews in Hungary, giving some statistics on their predominance in the life of the country and finding the Hungarian laws of 1922 restricting Jewish activities fully justified.

The Fascist newspapers were filled with delight by these

articles; they reprinted or summarized them and even exhumed other old and more aggressive anti-Jewish articles published by *Civiltà Cattolica* twenty and thirty years ago. The fiery anti-clerical Fascist leader, Farinacci, was the happiest of all. In his newspaper *Regime Fascista* (August 30, 1938), he summarized a vitriolic anti-Jewish article published by *Civiltà Cattolica* in the fall of 1890 and humbly remarked: "We must confess that Fascism, in its proposals and its execution of them, is milder than the rigid *Civiltà Cattolica*." He lavished his praise on the "loyal, courageous battle of the wise and irreprehensible Jesuits," and finally stated: "Modern states and societies, even the healthier and bolder nations of Europe such as Germany and Italy, have much to learn from the Fathers of the Society of Jesus." These compliments, from such a source and with such implications as they suggested, irked the good Fathers, who, however, had no other remark to make than that those articles "half-a-century old, referred to social conditions and to doctrinal controversies very different from those of today."

The protest of Pius XI against the anti-semitic laws concerned primarily the Fascist prohibition of intermarriage even in the case of converted Jews. This was a direct violation of the Concordat of 1920. In his address of December 24, 1938, the Pope complained of this and other violations of the concordat, but he added that it was not a matter about which he intended to make any fuss:

We say loudly that after God, our appreciation and thanks go to the very high Persons. We mean the very noble sovereign and his incomparable minister, to whom is due if the so important and beneficial work [the Lateran agreements of 1929] could be crowned with a good ending and happy success. . . . The thought of starting a controversy is far from us.

Confronted with these and many other facts, omitted here for the sake of brevity, which bear witness to the ultra philo-Fascist policies of the Vatican, Catholic apologists take refuge in the theory that the Church deals with all forms of government, good and bad, without passing judgment upon them, in order to profit from all opportunities offered to carry on its spiritual mission. Between two evils, that of dealing with even an unchristian or pagan government and that of letting the Catholic religion and the Church suffer disabilities or persecution, the Church chooses the former as the lesser evil.

Furthermore, it is one thing to hold and teach the loftiest doctrines and another thing to apply them to concrete and specific cases conditioned by the circumstances of time and place. We cherish lofty ideals, believe in them, do our best to see them realized; but in practice we are forced to compromise. So does the Church. This theory was developed and cast in a scientific-theological form by the Jesuits of *Civiltà Cattolica*, who called it the theory of the *thesis* and the *hypothesis*. The thesis is that the Church at all times and under all circumstances teaches the immutable, sacred doctrine and moral principles which are contained in the divine law and divine revelation. On this point the Church does not admit of any hesitation or any compromise. But the practical application of these principles, and especially of the moral principles, depends primarily on the hypothesis or supposition that both men and circumstances in a given society at a given time are likely to stand at such a high level. Since this never, or very seldom, occurs in this miserable world of ours, the hypothesis does not hold. The Church is forced to set aside the principles which remain inviolate in their sacred shrine, and adopt other and lower criteria of action. Thus, for instance, the doctrines and practices of Fascism were in opposition to the thesis and had to be condemned by the Church. But the Fascist party and the Fascist regime were the hypothesis. Hence, the Church could compromise and come to terms with them. This is a typical Jesuit elaboration and systematization of a theory which, though starting from sound common sense degenerates through sophistry into a kind of sluggish casuistry in which intellectual honesty and moral integrity are finally lost sight of altogether.

A few timely considerations on this point will not be amiss. Does the principle of indifference to the forms of government mean that the Church does not care whether there is or is not any moral question underlying the form? Does it mean that in practice the Church says indiscriminately to each and every political force in the world something like this?: "You get the power; once you have attained it, no matter who you are, how you got there, or what you do, we will deal with you, provided you agree to recognize and protect the rights, liberties and privileges of the Catholic Church."

Don Luigi Sturzo, the founder and leader of the Catholic party of Populists, and an excellent and unimpeachably orthodox theologian, in his article "Politique et théologie morale" published in the *Nouvelle Revue Théologique* (Paris, September–October, 1938), reminds Catholic moralists of the elementary truth that "in concrete reality there is no form without content," and in the case of governments, "it is the content that gives value to the form." The content is necessarily not only political, but ethical, and as such, it affects one way or another the consciences and conduct of those who are governed. Therefore, "it is not sufficient to condemn the principles on which a modern state rests." The essential point to remember is that *"one of the most absolute duties of Christian morals is to avoid cooperation with evil."* The moral problem with which the Church is confronted is precisely whether, in dealing with a government whose principles are condemned as pagan or anti-Christian, the Church by the practical arrangements which it makes with such a government does not tacitly cooperate with evil.

This problem, remarks Don Sturzo, does not arise in governments having liberal, democratic constitutions "in which all citizens are free to support a program which they judge to be the best for the good of the country and to belong to any party which best fits their mentality." In such regimes every individual can cooperate in seeking the common good; he is free to support policies and measures which agree with his principles and to oppose those which conflict with them. Such is not the case in totalitarian regimes, where "political non-conformism, both theoretical and practical, or even a moral reservation, however small it may be, not only would not be permitted, but would be considered as a crime against the country or against authority. . . . The essential character of totalitarianism is such that the citizen finds it impossible to remain outside the system, since totalitarian politics penetrate the whole life: family, culture, religion, business, external activities." We must face the question: "To what degree is it possible for a Catholic to collaborate with a totalitarian state? Collaboration implies the freedom to disagree and withdraw. Is this possible and at what price?" Of course, there is no doubt about the answer to this question. Collaboration is impossible because the price to be paid is the throwing overboard of the fundamental principles of Christian morals.

Don Sturzo is a pious clergyman and he is too loyal to the Papacy to apply these principles and conclusions directly and openly to the pontifical agreements with the Fascist and Nazi regimes. He limits his remarks to the havoc that this collaboration has caused in the Catholic conscience and the deplorable confusion, to the point of aberration, among the clergy and among writers on Catholic moral theology. He quotes various typical instances of such aberrations, as that of the Austrian Father R. P. Brettle, O.F.M., who a few days after the occupation of his country by Hitler wrote these "amazing" words: "During this change of regime many people have asked me how I, as a pastor of souls, could reconcile with the love of Christ the fact that the Jews will everywhere be ousted from their jobs and replaced by non-Jews. I have answered that the idea of this replacement has always existed in the plan of Divine Providence. Nobody invited the Jews to come to the various European countries. The Jewish question had not yet been solved. Now our Führer, Chancellor of the Reich, is solving it in a radical way, but one which will mean liberation for both parties."

Don Sturzo further observes that preachers and moralists now speak willingly of the cult of the nation, of races and classes, of obedience to the State, and similar things. He refers to a book, *Landschreiben katholischer Deutschen an ihre Volks und Glaubensgenossen* (published by the Catholic firm of Aschendorf, Munster, 1935), by Kuno Brombacher and Emil Ritter, who in the name of a group of Catholic theologians try to prove that Nazism and Catholicism can be reconciled.

Turning to Italy, Don Sturzo remarks: "They say that Italy under Fascism is in a favorable moral and religious condition. One should beware of a situation in which favors and persecutions depend only upon the will of one man. When favors abound, moral conscience weakens and there will be no resistance when the time to resist comes. I could give a long list of abuses of power [of the Fascist regime] against which nobody [among the Catholics] has opposed the principle of a moral limit [of political power]." He observes, too, that when the militarization of children was ordered, by which children six years old are registered as Sons of the She-Wolf and receive Fascist education, there was no criticism, no protest, no reservation. The totalitarian regime teaches the people to accept the cult of violence, of might over right, to hate any opponent without regard for his personal rights and his life. This evil spirit has been unchained in the world by the totalitarian governments; at the beginning it was met with a very feeble opposition by the Catholics, and very soon that opposition ceased altogether.

Don Sturzo, continuing his enumeration of these evils and his denunciation of Catholic moralists who have approved them either openly or at least by their silence, comes to this conclusion: "We have been accustomed to defend moral and social values in a regime of democracy and independent thinking; now we must accustom ourselves to doing our best in totalitarian regimes, even though we must return to the catacombs, and even at the risk of being classified as traitors, and as enemies of the state, of the nation, of the race, of our class, and of humanity."

We may be allowed to go a step further than Don Sturzo and apply these principles and conclusions to the policies of the Vatican. We say to the policies, not to the vague speeches and homiletic effusions in which moral principles and moral values are theoretically stated and defended. Actions count more than words in this tragic crisis of world dimensions. It seems clear to us that a great many provisions of the Lateran agreements (both the Treaty and the Concordat) imply and make obligatory extensive collaboration between the Church and the Fascist state. For instance, what is the meaning of the oath of allegiance to the state that all Italian bishops and parish priests are duty bound to take? An oath of allegiance to a totalitarian state becomes in fact a totalitarian oath implying acceptance of all authorities, laws, and policies of the state, as well as the duty of abstaining from all words and actions contrary to the tenets of the state.

The cooperation of church and state is fully assured by the provision that all appointments made by the Holy See to bishoprics and major benefices, as well as those to minor benefices made by the bishops, may be rejected by the Fascist government "for political reasons," that is to say, all clergyman so appointed must be chosen from among those who have professed Fascism and are devoted to the Fascist authorities. A clergy so chosen and placed in the key positions of the Church, and paid either entirely or in part from state funds, could not fail to become one of the strongest supports of the Fascist totalitarian state.

This active cooperation of the Church in Italy with a regime which the Holy See denounced as pagan and immoral in its theories and practices and therefore evil, was made possible—nay, was imposed upon Italian Catholics—by the Treaty and the Concordat negotiated and concluded by the Vatican. If the principles and the moral laws so well analyzed by Don Sturzo are valid, as we think they are, there is no justification for the policy of the Vatican towards the Fascist regime, just as there is no justification for either the approval or the silence of the Catholic moralists as regards the evil practices which Don Sturzo has rightly denounced.

Pius XI was obsessed by his fear of communism and by his distrust of democracy to the point of considering Fascism as a lesser evil. He was also convinced that Fascism had come to stay and that a return to free institutions was not to be expected in Italy for at least several generations. History has proved him wrong. Fascism was, not only from the political, but from the moral and religious point of view, the greatest evil that ever afflicted Italy. It was the first decisive step towards the immense world tragedy of our time. Fascism, like all dictatorships of its kind, like all regimes of violence and brute force, by which a small minority subdues and exploits a whole nation, was not and could not be a permanent system either in Italy or elsewhere. In papal Rome it used to be said that the Papacy thinks in terms of eternity, and that its policies are dictated by a far-sighted view of the future. This characteristic of the papal policies was contrasted with those of the worldly politicians, who think only of coming elections, and who seek to assure their success by watching the windcock, their only moral guide. Pope Pius XI, however, cannot be ranked among the farsighted popes, at least as far as his policies towards Fascism and Nazism are concerned. He mistook the spirit of darkness for "a man sent by Providence" to help the cause of religion and the Church, and he thought that the heavy and bloody clouds of Fascism were solid ramparts upon which he and the Church could lean for support.

Neither the historian nor the moralist can absolve the Vatican of its responsibility in this tragic episode of the history of Italy and of the world. Theoretical condemnations, as Don Sturzo tells us, are not enough when the authority which condemns at the same time cooperates and causes the people to cooperate with the evil that is condemned.

2. The Vatican and President Roosevelt

In December, 1939, President Roosevelt departed from the policy of his predecessors, who had officially ignored the Vatican since 1867, and established a diplomatic connection with the Holy See by sending Mr. Myron Taylor as his personal ambassador to the Pope. What kind of negotiations have been going on, and what kind of agreements have been reached through Mr. Taylor's shuttling back and forth between Washington and Rome are impenetrable mysteries. The secrecy which envelops these activities reminds one of Mussolini's negotiations for the Italian Concordat. There is, however, not the slightest suspicion that President Roosevelt is planning to make a concordat with the Holy See, at least not at the present time.

Since the "high contracting parties" have not taken the American people into their confidence, and since it is likely that the mystery will be fully revealed only when the archives of Hyde Park are opened to the public, the historian of today can only attempt an explanation by piecing together every bit of evidence he can gather from reliable sources.

It is obvious that Mr. Taylor's diplomatic task has to do with international politics, in which both the Holy See and Washington have an interest. Why did the Vatican feel the need of discussing its international plans and problems with the President of the United States? And why did the President of the United States, a country largely Protestant which draws a sharp line of separation between church and state, feel the necessity of discussing American international problems with the Vatican? As far as the Vatican is concerned, enough is known of its policies to understand the purposes of its moves on the political chessboard.

We must begin by recalling the famous Article 24 of the Lateran Treaty of February, 1929, which reads:

The Holy See in relation to the sovereignty which belongs to itself also in the international field, declares that it wishes to remain and will remain extraneous to all temporal conflicts among other States and to all international Congresses held for such objects unless the contending parties make concordant appeal to its mission of peace; [the Holy See] reserving, however, in any case, [its right] to make effective use of its moral and spiritual power. As a consequence of this declaration Vatican City will always and in every case be considered neutral and inviolable territory.

This article was not imposed or suggested by Mussolini but was desired by Pius XI. Since Napoleonic times, the Vatican has adhered to a policy of neutrality. Such a policy was followed by Benedict XV during the first World War. Now that Pius XI was making a solemn renunciation of all claims of the Holy See to its former Pontifical States, there was still less reason why the Vatican should desire to be involved in the political conflicts of Europe. To remain in the serene atmosphere of neutrality seemed the best way of protecting the Church and its interests.

Back in 1927 and 1928, when Pius was negotiating the Lateran agreement, the outlook of the international situation in Europe was not discouraging. To be sure, there were clouds in the sky, but no open conflict seemed likely to occur for a long time to come. The danger from Bolshevism, which the Holy See regarded with such apprehension, had been conjured up. Italy was Fascist. It was not to be feared in either England or France. Germany with Hindenburg seemed safe for the time being. The democracies were losing ground, and the prevailing point of view was that they would be displaced, not by Communism, but by conservative and reactionary forces. Looking at the map of Europe, Pius XI could feel sure that in spite of the unrest and the convulsions which were shaking the political world, no wars were to be expected and no substantial changes in the existing situation. Meanwhile, the Vatican, anchored as it was to the concordats which it had concluded with most European states, could remain aloof, at least officially, from international politics, while gathering the fruits of those agreements to which the treaty and the concordat with the Fascist regime were soon to be added.

This policy of neutrality, however, did not mean that the Holy See intended to remain in isolation and to be only a passive and disinterested spectator. Hence, the important clause in which the Holy See reserved the right to express its judgment on conflicts involving moral principles or ecclesiastical and religious interests, was incorporated in the article. Since the Holy See is not a military or economic power and its intervention in a conflict could have only moral value, and since there can hardly be a conflict of nations which does not raise a moral problem of right and wrong, or which does not affect ecclesiastical institutions and religious interests, it would seem that the Vatican, by this reservation, rendered void of all significance its preceding declaration of absolute neutrality. In fact, such a reservation left the Pope free to wield his only weapon, the weapon of his moral judgment, and thereby to exercise a political influence over the Catholics of the world.

On the other hand, Mussolini, although well aware of the implications of this clause, did not and could not raise any objection to the freedom of the Holy See in matters of religion and morals. Had he demurred on this point, the Treaty could not have been concluded. But he, too, had his mental reservations while signing the agreement; he reserved to himself the right to interpret the article in his own way.

According to Mussolini's interpretation of it, Article 24 of the Treaty was parallel to Article 43 of the Concordat, which forbade the Italian clergy, from the bishops to the lowliest friar, to belong to any political party or to engage in any political activity. This meant, of course, that only political activities and opinions contrary to those of Fascism were forbidden, and that pro-Fascist activities and ideas were not only acceptable but required. The Church in Italy was expected to do its full duty in the service of the Fascist State, and the Vatican, as the central organ of the Church, was expected to do likewise in a larger sphere.

The long and bitter conflict which followed the signing of the

Lateran agreements was ostensibly over a few points in the Concordat; actually it was a test case involving the fundamental issue of interpretation. In other words, which party had the authority to interpret the whole agreement and to impose that interpretation upon the other party as final? The struggle centered upon two main points: the Fascist control over the Italian Church, and the right of the Pope to freedom of expression on moral and religious principles in matters connected with political institutions and affairs.

After many verbal fireworks the Vatican, under the threat of Fascist reprisal, had no other choice but to surrender as far as the "fascistization" of the Italian Church was concerned. It was not that the Pope was averse to the support of the Fascist regime by the Church, since he himself had done so much to bring about this support. He could not agree, however, to the curtailment of certain ecclesiastical activities, which he considered to be religious, but which Mussolini branded as political. Neither could the Pope approve of the Fascist attempt to absorb the Church in Italy into the Fascist system. Pius XI failed to win his point; he had already gone too far in his compromise with Fascism and there was no turning back.

As to the question of the pontifical right to freedom of expression, Pius delayed settling it as long as he could, but when Fascist pressure became unbearable, he affirmed this right energetically, not by mere words but by action. He showed Mussolini in no uncertain terms that he still could and would speak freely by publishing the encyclical *Non abbiamo bisogno*. It is important to remember that the Pope, fearing his encyclical would be boycotted by the postal and telegraph offices of the Fascist regime, sent it by special envoy to France to be published. The Holy See had maneuvered itself into such a critical position that it had to resort to subterfuge in order to speak to the world.

As a consequence of this experience, the Vatican fully realized that the clause in Article 24 of the Treaty was a dead letter as far as Fascism was concerned, and that only with difficulty and at the risk of conflict and reprisal could the Pope express himself freely where Fascism and Fascist interests were directly or indirectly involved. From that time on Pius XI used his right of free expression most sparingly and with the utmost caution. On the other hand, Mussolini ignored the papal encyclical and used more adroitly than ever the means of coercion at his disposal. The conflict thus came to an end, at least as far as the external relations of the two parties were concerned, and their collaboration in matters of interest to them both went back to normalcy.

In the following five or six years the European picture changed more rapidly and more ominously than Pius had thought possible. The advent of the Nazi regime in Germany seemed, at first, to bode little good for the Church. The German bishops, who had had time and opportunity to acquire a first-hand knowledge of Nazi ideas and purposes, looked with distrust and fear upon Hitler and his followers. But such was not the opinion of Cardinal Pacelli, the Pope's Secretary of State, who after having spent fourteen years in Germany as Apostolic Nuncio was supposed to be closely acquainted with the German situation. In fact, negotiations for a concordat were soon launched and an agreement was concluded with a speed very unusual in the annals of Vatican diplomacy. The unhappy results of that concordat are well known.

By the fall of 1936 it had become clear that the peace of Europe was not going to last long. The assassination of Dollfuss, the Ethiopian war, the march on the Rhine, and finally the Spanish rebellion which started in July, 1936, were ominous signs of the new crisis impending. What worried the Vatican most was the trend of affairs in the Spanish Republic, in which the Pope saw the spectre of Bolshevism projecting its shadow over the Mediterranean. It is now a matter of history that the plot of the rebellion was hatched with the connivance of Mussolini whose air force appeared on the scene during the first days of the revolt, and that the Pope did not stint his blessings of the rebels and of the dictators, who had taken upon themselves the task of securing the defeat of the Republic.

To be sure, Hitler and Mussolini did not fight in Spain for the sake of the Church or to please the Pope; their purposes were far from religious. Nonetheless, they both, especially Mussolini, earned the deep gratitude of the Vatican and the American Catholic clergy, which was mobilized to influence public opinion in favor of the rebels. This mobilization of the American clergy had a further purpose. It was obvious that the Spanish Loyalists could expect only the worst from the Tories of the English government. Their hopes of help from France were cruelly disappointed; the French government, in a state of perpetual crisis, was following in the wake of England in its international policies. Only from Soviet Russia could the Spanish government buy the arms and ammunition so sorely needed to crush the rebels and their allies. But Russia was far away, the means of communication difficult, and the deliveries few and far between. There was, however, another market more easily accessible and better furnished—the United States of America.

It was, then, a matter of vital importance to the Vatican as well as to the dictators to prevent the opening of this market to the Spanish Loyalists. Since neither Hitler nor Mussolini could at that moment bring any pressure to bear on Washington, or even solicit directly the support of our State Department, the task of performing this deed was left to the Vatican. By using to the full the influence of the Catholic Church in American politics, and by unleashing the loudest and most unscrupulous propaganda in the Catholic press, the pulpit, the schools, and, as we shall see, by appealing directly to President Roosevelt, the Vatican performed its task with more success than it perhaps had hoped for.

The Vatican had for a long time cherished the idea of establishing official connections with the government of the United States. It seemed a disgrace that a nation in which the Catholic

Church has such a large following and is so wealthy and powerful should not have diplomatic relations with the central government of the Church. But the principle of separation between Church and State and, even more, the anti-papal traditions still strong among the Protestant majority of the United States had always appeared unsurmountable obstacles to the fulfillment of the Vatican's desire. In the fall of 1936, apart from the Spanish affair, there were other important reasons why the Vatican should make a new effort to secure the friendship, good will, and active support of the United States government.

While playing hand in hand with the dictators in the Spanish affair, the Vatican at the same time looked ahead to the impending crisis and to the possibility of a new European war which would make radical changes in the political map of Europe. If, thereafter, the Pope should still be bound by Article 24 of the Lateran Treaty as interpreted by the Fascist regime, the Vatican would be completely isolated from political affairs and its exclusion from even indirect participation in the rearrangement of Europe would be certain. Of course, it was then too early to foresee what the alignment of the nations would be in case of war and whether or not the United States would be involved in it. One thing was sure, however, that the United States with its power, its resources, and its influence was the friend the Vatican needed, no matter what the result of the war might be. A powerful friend such as the United States would be able to extend valuable protection, especially if, as then appeared probable, America should finally act as an intermediary in the re-establishment of peace.

There was no time to lose and in the fall of 1936 Cardinal Pacelli, Secretary of State to His Holiness, paid a visit to the United States. The President was certainly informed in advance of the Cardinal's trip at election time, and obviously he did not discourage it. His Eminence landed in New York on October 9, 1936, just at the time when the presidential campaign was at its height. After spending a couple of weeks in the East, he visited Washington, without, however, seeing President Roosevelt. Then he went on a whirlwind visit to the Middle and the Far West. This trip lasted a week and took him to Chicago, St. Paul, San Francisco, Los Angeles, and then to St. Louis and Cincinnati. By the first of November he was back in New York, and on November 6, after the election, he paid a visit to triumphant President Roosevelt at Hyde Park, where he was entertained at a family luncheon.

The Papal Secretary of State does not usually visit a foreign country unless he has a very important reason for doing so. More unusual was his choosing the last period of an election campaign for such a visit. All kinds of rumors were circulated by the newspapers as to the purpose of this visit. The Nazi and Fascist newspapers were especially convinced that he had come to deliver the Catholic vote to President Roosevelt; others suggested that he had come to silence Father Coughlin, who was then campaigning against Roosevelt and suggesting textually that if ballots failed to oust him, the American people should use bullets. It was also said that Pacelli's mission was to establish diplomatic relations with the United States. Pacelli took great pains to show that he was not at all concerned with the election; with extremely correct diplomatic behavior, he refrained from paying a visit to the President before election day. On the other hand, Father Coughlin was left undisturbed to carry on his vitriolic campaign. If the Vatican wished to urge the Catholics to vote for Roosevelt, it could have done so earlier through the usual channels of bishops and parish priests without involving the Secretary of State in such a delicate matter.

What was said and done at Hyde Park is still the secret of Mr. Roosevelt and Cardinal Pacelli, now Pope Pius XII. But from the events which followed we know that at that time two main subjects were under the consideration of both the Vatican and the President. It is, therefore, natural to think that they were discussed at Hyde Park. The two questions were, first, the policy of the United States toward the Spanish rebellion and, second, the plan of establishing diplomatic relations between the Vatican and the United States.

It is distressing to look back and see how inconsistent and irrational our policy was at that time. In the East, we kept our markets open to the Japanese army and navy in the name of neutrality, knowing full well that China with neither cash nor shipping facilities at her disposal could not take advantage of our generosity in keeping the market open. In Europe, likewise in the name of neutrality, we shut the market to Spain, knowing that we were thereby greatly benefiting the rebels, who meanwhile were being assisted actively by the Fascist and Nazi armies.

Cardinal Pacelli won his point with the President. Future historians will wonder how it happened that we played second fiddle in the Axis-Vatican orchestra. Did the President, at the meeting at Hyde Park, commit himself to establishing diplomatic relations with the Vatican? Since the plan was carried out only three years later, it is logical to assume that, if there was a commitment, it was made with the understanding that the time was not yet ripe for such a step. The President knew well that the great majority of the American people would not relish such a close connection between the government and the Vatican. He was also aware that if such a proposal were to be put before Congress, it would have no chance for success.

On June 16, 1939, six months before the embassy of Mr. Taylor, the correspondent of the *New York Times* in Rome informed the American public in a dispatch from Vatican City that "steps to bring relations between the Holy See and the United States on a normal diplomatic footing are expected to be taken soon by Pope Pius XII." The correspondent then gave a retrospective history of the negotiations. He affirmed that "in the last years of the reign of Pius XI, efforts were reported to have been made to obtain the United States' approval of a Nuncio at Washington and an American Ambassador at the Vatican, but no progress was made." But now, according to the same correspondent, Pius XII had proposed a solution which consisted in adopting the English method; that is to say, "to retain the Apostolic Delegate in Washington as a papal representative with diplomatic powers and have the American Ambassador accredited to the Vatican."

On July 29, 1939, Cardinal Enrico Gasparri, whose famous uncle, Cardinal Pietro Gasparri, was Secretary of State to Pius XI and signed the Lateran agreements, arrived in New York for a visit to the United States. A correspondence from Rome, dated July 28, informed the American public that "Cardinal Gasparri has a mission of preparing the juridical status for the possible opening of diplomatic relations between the United States State Department and the Holy See, it was learned from good sources at the Vatican today. That is to say, Cardinal Gasparri bears no personal or specific message from Pope Pius, nor is he authorized to negotiate for the establishment of relations; he is to work out a legal framework within which such a relationship could be placed if established" (New York Times, July 29, 1939).

Events proved that the correspondent had been correctly informed as to the fact that an agreement was imminent, but, for obvious reasons, he had been misinformed as to how these diplomatic relations were to be established.

On July 29, 1939, Cardinal Enrico Gasparri, nephew of the late Secretary of State of Pius XI landed in New York, spent three days with Archbishop Spellman, and then went for a vacation to Canada, where he had been years before as Apostolic Delegate. The American correspondent of the New York Times (July 29) informed us that according to "good sources at the Vatican," Cardinal Gasparri had "a mission of preparing the juridical status for the possible opening of diplomatic relations between the State Department and the Holy See. . . . He is not authorized to negotiate for the establishment of relations; he is to work out a legal framework within which such a relationship could be placed, if established." The difficulty which stood in the way of having a regular Nuncio in Washington and an American ambassador at the Vatican was the fact that the plan had to be submitted to Congress, which alone has the power to make an appropriation for the maintenance of a legation. The same difficulty existed, if, instead of a Nuncio, the Pope should be represented by the Apostolic Delegate, as long as a regular legation of the United States had to be established at the Vatican. If it was to be done at all, it could be done only over the head of Congress; in other words, it could be done only over the heads of the people of the United States. Hence, Mr. Myron Taylor was appointed, not as an ambassador from the United States, but as a personal ambassador from the President to the Pope. Mr. Taylor, being a wealthy man, pays his own expenses, and therefore it has not been necessary to ask Congress for an appropriation.

Of course, the Vatican would have preferred a regular embassy, which could have come through the main entrance rather than the kitchen door, but the happy solution adopted by Washington had its advantages and from a certain point of view fitted in well with several of the premises so dear to Vatican tradition. An eminent canonist, Father Wernz, who was for years Professor of Canon Law at the Pontifical Gregorian University in Rome and then became General of the Jesuits, remarks in one of his formidable books (*Jus Decretalium*, I, 166): "The Apostolic See, to avoid the risk of mockery, usually enters into solemn undertakings only where a civil government is under no obligation to seek the consent of a representative body, or where there can be no reasonable doubt that such consent will be granted." Since President Roosevelt could neither guarantee the consent of Congress, nor prevent a congressman or senator from saying something unpleasant about the Vatican during the debate, the Holy See was satisfied to deal with the United States as if it were a country in which the government is under no obligation to seek the consent of a representative body.

This solution was so simple that it must have occurred from the very beginning to both the President and Cardinal Pacelli. The reason for the three-year delay is then to be attributed to the fact that the opportunity to put their plan into practice did not occur earlier. The opportunity came with the war. During the months which preceded the German invasion of Poland and the consequent Franco-English declaration of war, President Roosevelt with sincere zeal and the best of intentions used all his influence for the sake of peace and offered his services and the support of the United States for a peaceful solution of the conflict. But since Hitler was disposed to accept nothing by way of solution but another Munich of colossal proportions, war was inevitable. The President, hoping that the Fascist regime might refuse to fulfill the obligations assumed in the Axis pact and stay out of the war, then centered his attention upon Italy. On August 24, 1939, the President wrote a letter to the King of Italy "in behalf of the maintenance of peace." Of course, to write to Hitler again was out of the question after the insulting remarks the Führer had made about the President in his public reply to previous appeals. Neither did the President think it advisable to appeal to Mussolini; hence the letter was addressed to the King.

Even so, the President was wise enough to pay his compliments to Mussolini by mentioning "the great achievements which the Italian nation in particular had attained during the past generation." The President, in his effort to touch the Duce's heart, went so far as to say that "the government of Italy and the United States today advance those ideals of Christianity which of late seem so often to have been obscured." Evidently the President had not had time to read the encyclical of Pius XI which indicted Fascism and the Fascist regime as being at the antipodes of Christianity.

On the same date, August 24, Pope Pius XII addressed to all governments and peoples a warm and at times moving appeal, imploring them "to return to the way of justice and peace," and warning them that "it is with force of reason and not with that of arms that justice advances. Empires which are not founded on justice are not blessed by God. . . . Humanity awaits justice, bread, and liberty, not iron that kills and destroys." This was a noble appeal in the best tradition of the Christian spirit and of the mission of peace and justice that belongs to the Church.

The concerted appeals of the Pope and the President, and Mr. Roosevelt's effort to bring out of obscurity the name of the King of Italy as a possible hope, which was followed by Italy's declaration of non-belligerence, gave the American people the illusion that they had some influence at least in keeping Italy from actual participation in the war. It was, however, clear even then to all unbiased observers, that "if the Duce delayed his participation in the struggle, he did so, not because of any anxiety, but for a twofold purpose, which was to be useful to Germany as a non-belligerent in the period of the Blitzkrieg and in the meantime to set in order the war production and the army" (L. Sturzo, "Italian Problems in War and Peace," in *The Review of Politics,* January, 1943, p. 55). The governments of England, France, and the United States were fooled once more into believing that appeasement would work; therefore, they rushed to put at Mussolini's disposal both raw materials, especially oil, and large sums of money in the form of commercial transactions for war supplies, which Italy was expected to deliver to the Allies beginning in June, 1940. Instead, in June, 1940, Mussolini delivered to the Allies a declaration of war!

But in the fall of 1939 the hope to keep Italy out of the war was high in British and American official circles, and since the co-ordinated effort of the President and the Pope seemed to have been successful, it appeared obvious that this happy co-ordination of the two forces had to be kept at work.

The opportunity to establish diplomatic relations with the Vatican had finally come. The psychological ground had been broken, so that such a step would appear most useful in the eyes of the American public. President Roosevelt could now act without fear of causing serious religious frictions in the country. Hence, on December 23, 1939, he wrote his letter to Pope Pius XII, asking his consent to send a personal ambassador to the Vatican.

In this letter the President, after a few homiletic considerations suggested by the Christmas date, expressed his hope that a new order was at hand and was being built up even now in the hearts of the masses amid the grief and terror of war. In view of this new order, added the President, "it is well that we encourage a closer association between those in every part of the world— those in religion and those in government—who have a common purpose." Then the President spoke of sending his personal representative, in order that "our parallel endeavors for peace and the alleviation of suffering may be assisted," because in establishing a firm peace, "it is of the utmost importance that common ideals shall have a united expression." Finally the President mentioned also that "when that happy day shall dawn, great problems of practical import will face us all. Millions of people of all races, all nationalities, and all religions may seek new lives by migration to other lands or by re-establishment of old homes. Here, too, common ideals call for parallel action."

No one can blame the President and the Pope for having used all their influence to the utmost in an effort to preserve peace, and no one can doubt that Pope Pius XII was very eager to keep Italy out of the war.

On December 21, 1939, the King and Queen, accompanied by Foreign Minister Ciano, paid an official visit to the Vatican. The Pope bestowed high praises on the "King-Emperor" (of Ethiopia) and expressed his satisfaction at the fact that while "other peoples are convulsed or menaced by war. . . . Italy instead, always vigilant and strong under the august and wise hand of the King-Emperor of Ethiopia and the far-seeing guidance of her rulers, remains peaceful in civil life in concord of spirit . . . and in the solemn rites of the Catholic religion."

On December 28, the Pope returned the visit at the Quirinal Palace and expressed his great admiration for "the glorious dynasty of Savoy, crowned by its saints and its blessed." He then spoke of the bliss of peace, thanks to which "on the Tiber shores olive branches are now blossoming out." The Pope did not forget to invoke God's protection in behalf of "the illustrious chief of the Italian government and his ministers."

According to Don Sturzo "All believed that this gesture intimated a mutual understanding between Monarchy and Papacy to prevent Fascism from drawing Italy into the war" (*ibid.*, p. 68).

These gestures made in behalf of peace by the Pope and the President were at the same time calculated moves having another purpose. Behind the action of the President, behind the noble words he addressed to the Pope, there was an element of subtle political maneuvering. To make this innovation of sending a representative to the Vatican more palatable to the American people, and to take the edge off any possible opposition, President Roosevelt sent at the same time letters to the Presidents of the Federal Council of Protestant Churches and of the Jewish Council.

In these letters he repeated the homiletical part of his epistle to Pope Pius XII, but ended merely with a courteous invitation to those modest religious leaders to drop in occasionally at the White House for consultation with the President. Thus, the appeal of the President assumed the aspect of being directed, not to the Pope alone, but to other leaders holding positions of responsibility in other religious bodies. These invitations were merely a screen and had little or no significance. The letter to the Pope and the establishment of a personal embassy at the Vatican were, on the contrary, a significant and far-reaching step in the direction that American diplomatic action was to follow from that time on.

The President's letter, when all its edifying considerations and verbal ornaments are set aside, may be paraphrased as saying to the Pope: "We, the United States and the Vatican, have common ideals and purposes which call for common expression and action in reestablishing peace and in reorganizing the world when the time comes. These common ideals and activities extend to various problems which will arise at the end of the war. My ambassador comes to establish a regular channel for the exchange of views and plans necessary to make effective our common action." This was a direct and explicit invitation to the Pope to take part in international politics and to have a voice in international councils, either directly or through the United States.

On the other hand, the identity of ideals, purposes, and action which the President assumed to exist between the United States and the Vatican might have been interpreted as an invitation to the Holy See to throw the whole weight of its religious and moral authority on the side of the democracies, whose cause the United States had espoused by becoming their arsenal. Italy, which was not neutral but only non-belligerent, was, on the contrary, bound to Germany by the Iron Pact. The Pope had to be very careful in replying to the President's letter. As a matter of fact, Pius XII, after praising the President highly for his Christian views and his zeal, stated in generic terms that "only men of such moral stature will be able to create the peace that will compensate for the incalculable sacrifices of this war and clear the way for a community of nations, fair to all, efficacious and sustained by mutual confidence." Accepting with thanks the offer to send an ambassador to the Vatican, the Pope said that the representative of the President would be received with all due honors, but added significantly that his mission was to be "the faithful inter- preter of your mind regarding the procuring of peace and the alleviation of sufferings consequent upon the war." He made no mention at all of any post-war problems, or of any common action of a political character.

Mr. Taylor was wont to spend part of each year in his beautiful villa, Schifanoia, near Florence. According to the biographical sketch published by the *New York Times* at the time of his appointment, Mr. Taylor was born with a golden spoon in his mouth and was "reared in a conservative atmosphere." He had had a brilliant business career ending in the chairmanship of the finance committee of the United States Steel Company. Born of Quaker stock, Mr. Taylor is a "high" Episcopalian. Though usually shunning publicity, Mr. Taylor had once come forward to express his admiration of Fascism. On November 5, 1936, he presided at a great banquet at the Waldorf Astoria in honor of the Fascist ambassador, Fulvio Suvich. Mr. Taylor acted as chairman of the committee for the banquet and represented also the Italy-America Society and the American Society of the Royal Italian Orders. In his speech Mr. Taylor said that "the whole world has been forced to admire the successes of Premier Mussolini in disciplining the nation." He added also: "Those who have had the pleasure of paying frequent visits to Italy know what great progress has been made." Finally, expressing his approval of the recent conquest of Ethiopia, Mr. Taylor concluded: "Today a new Italian Empire faces the future and assumes its responsibilities as guardian and administrator of a backward people of ten million souls" (*New York Times,* November 6, 1936). Mr. Taylor was thus *persona grata* in Fascist circles, and furthermore, as it is said in his biography, "he was personally acquainted with many important personages in the Roman Catholic hierarchy and with persons prominent in the Italian government."

One cannot fail to admire the wisdom of President Roosevelt, who by Mr. Taylor's appointment was able to kill so many birds with one stone. He had chosen the right time and the right way to execute this plan, pleasing both the Vatican and Mussolini, and had caused only a little ripple in American public opinion. As a matter of fact, the mild protest voiced by representatives of several Protestant denominations and by a few individuals was counterbalanced by the high praises with which the appointment of Mr. Taylor was welcomed by representatives of the Catholic Church, of some Episcopalian groups, and by several Jewish rabbis and various preachers of other denominations. The whole affair caused no great stir and was soon forgotten by the public whose attention in the following months was fully absorbed by the more important news of the battle of France.

The following February Mr. Taylor went to Rome, traveling

on the same boat with Mr. Sumner Welles, the Under Secretary of State, who was then going on his diplomatic tour of Europe in order to test the possibilities of a restoration of peace. Mr. Taylor was also on a mission of peace, because, as Arthur Krock said in his column in the *New York Times* for March 7, "The Pope is an indispensable factor in bringing about a conference." Presented in this light, the mission of Mr. Taylor appeared wholly justified and even the Executive Committee of the Federal Council of Protestant Churches could state: "Surely it would not be to the credit of Protestantism if it should find itself in the situation at some future time, of having blocked a movement that was able to contribute to the ending of the war and to saving the lives of countless men" (quoted by *Time*, March 11, 1940).

How flimsy these plans and hopes were, and how paltry was the supposed influence of the Papacy in European political circles, though it had been so extravagantly magnified by the American press, soon became evident when the "phony war" turned into the sweeping blitzkrieg of 1940, and more than evident when Mussolini and the King of Italy, neighbors of the Vatican, entered the war on the side of Germany.

On April 20, 1943, several newspaper correspondents sent from Washington the news that

An outstanding development is expected soon in the diplomatic world. The Administration will request Congress to appropriate the necessary funds to establish an American Embassy at the Vatican. . . . There is a growing demand from the State Department and from the Office of Strategic Services for a permanent representation at the Vatican and the belief in Washington is that, because of changed conditions, there will be no opposition to such a move.

We spare our readers the fanciful and often childish comments made about this item by the correspondents. This move of the Administration was to be expected as soon as circumstances were such as to promise a favorable reception of the proposal by Congress. But are the American people ready to start a new permanent system of official relations with the supreme head of one of its religious bodies, which forms only a fraction of the population of the United States?

3. The Vatican and the War

The pontificate of Pius XI marked a turning point in the history of the Papacy. His policies reflected a rather unbalanced combination of the ambition and the great, sometimes even bold, vision of Leo XIII, and the narrow-mindedness and hysterical fear of Pius X. Like Leo XIII, he wished to make the Papacy a primary political and social force in the modern world. By taking full advantage of the favorable conditions at the end of the first World War, he successfully established diplomatic relations and made concordats and agreements with many nations; in activity of this kind he proved more adept than any of his predecessors had been. On the other hand, like Pius X, he wished to appear as a religious and not as a political pope. His predecessor, Benedict XV, who after World War I believed for a while, as all of us did, that democracy was victorious and had come to stay, had tried to adapt the policies of the Vatican to the new conditions. He had allowed, if not favored, in all countries, even Italy, the formation of political parties having a Catholic membership and a Christian program. Pius XI hastened to undo what Benedict had done, and steered the Vatican in the opposite direction.

Essentially, Pius XI was a reactionary dominated by fear. His successes were short-lived; most of his concordats had ceased to be effective when he died. What he considered the most important achievement of his pontificate, the solution of the Roman question, by which he had hoped to tame and Christianize Fascism, turned out to be a source of new disappointments and new fears.

Pius XII, who shares the responsibility for many of the policies of his predecessor, is a man of different temper. He is confronted with the unfortunate situation of ruling the Church during another World War, far greater than the first. He does not possess the calculated boldness of Leo XIII, nor is he inclined by temperament to the passionate outbursts of Pius XI. The latter, in moments of anger and indignation, spoke his mind bluntly and courageously, although when his wrath had cooled, he could be induced to compromise with reality, often at the cost of logic and consistency. Pius XII never loses his calm. A master in the language of diplomatic ambiguity, Pius XII assumed from the beginning of his reign a strictly religious, even mystical, attitude in deploring the evils of the world. He has at various times, and always in the most general terms, assigned the causes of evil to the totalitarian states, to the democracies, to everybody, and to nobody.

In the last month of his life Pius XI had convoked a large gathering of bishops in Rome before whom he planned to give an address already written for the occasion. It was known that the old Pope had long been brooding over the wisdom of his policy of compromise towards the Fascist and Nazi dictators. There was, therefore, a tense expectation that this address would be a firm, outspoken declaration of the pessimistic conclusion to which his experience with totalitarian regimes had led him. The address was never delivered. On the day set for the convocation, Pius XI was on his death bed; the next day, his lips were sealed forever. His successor never published his document.

During his long career in the Vatican diplomatic service, Pius XII had learned that prudence is a great virtue. At the time of his election in February, 1939, the crisis was approaching; Hitler's power had already assumed menacing proportions and the terrified democracies were groping in the darkness of disastrous appeasement. Since the war began, Pius XII has performed, and is still performing, the miracle of keeping the Vatican on good, or at least officially correct, terms with the Axis powers, on the one hand, and with the United Nations, on the other. The Pope must maintain good relations with both sides in order to carry on such work for the relief of material and moral suffering as may be possible under the circumstances. Moreover, he must look forward to a post-war program which, according to his view from the papal throne, will best serve the cause of Catholicism. In this connection the aims of the Vatican can be summarized in a few words: to save all that can be saved of the interests, power, and influence of the Church while the world is at war; and when peace comes again, to obtain restitution from the victors for any losses the Church may have suffered; and, finally, to make certain that all privileges and advantages secured through concordats or other agreements will be honored, and that new concordats guaranteeing the rights, liberties, and prerogatives of the Church may be made in the future.

These aims are not, from the Catholic point of view, an end in themselves; they are only necessary means to aid the Church in performing its spiritual and social functions. The Church is an indispensable agency of God's grace, established on earth to secure peace among all nations and peoples, to maintain justice and order in the political, social, and economic relations of mankind, and to make possible to man the salvation of his soul in the world beyond. To expect the Vatican to favor a policy which opposes or fails to consider the claims of the Church is as absurd as to expect that Mr. Churchill would be willing "to assist at the liquidation of the British Empire." It is only by considering the above aims that we can see in the proper perspective why the Vatican professes to keep a neutral attitude in this war, and what its plans and expectations are for post-war settlement.

The idea of neutrality as it applies to the Papacy is quite different from the neutrality of an ordinary state according to the theory of international law. The neutrality of the Holy See is not merely the territorial neutrality of Vatican City, which in this case has little or no importance, but it is primarily the neutrality of the Papacy as the supreme central government of the whole Catholic Church. The neutrality of Vatican City as stated in the Lateran Treaty is only a corollary of the neutrality of the Papacy as such. But the neutrality of the Papacy as the supreme organ of Church government does not mean at all the neutrality of the Catholic clergy and laity which in each belligerent country is expected to, and does, in fact, take part in the war, assisting the national government with all the moral and material means at its disposal to secure the victory of its armies. The Pope is like the supreme commander of a large army who declares that he will remain neutral, while his soldiers (the Catholic laymen) and his officers (the Catholic hierarchy and the clergy) range themselves some on one side and some on the other side of the belligerents and take an active part in the war.

In conclusion we may say of the Vatican neutrality that it consists in refraining from the expression of any opinion as to which of the belligerents is right and which is wrong. Thus it denies to both sides such moral support as they could derive from a judgment in favor of their cause. At the same time, the Holy See tells all Catholics that they are duty-bound to fight and to fight well for whichever side they are on. Absurd and illogical as this peculiar notion of neutrality may be, it is in fact the only alternative left to the Papacy, when it abandons the difficult and often impossible task of passing moral judgment on a conflict in its capacity of "supreme guardian of morals." The other alternative would be to assume an absolute pacifist attitude and to impose upon the Catholics of both sides the duty of abstaining under penalty of excommunication from fighting for their country, and from assisting their national government in the war effort.

This external and official neutrality of the Papacy does not imply that the Pope and his collaborators cannot or do not sympathize with one party rather than another, or that they should not prefer the victory of one belligerent to that of the other. In a moment of distraction, President Wilson, at the beginning of the first World War, urged the American people to be neutral, not only in their actions, but in their thoughts. He could not do this himself; neither can the Pope. It is natural that the Vatican should be influenced in its preference for one side or the other by the religious and ecclesiastical interests involved. In the present war, as is almost always the case, the Papacy has interests to safeguard and protect. It has something to gain and something to lose from the victory or the defeat of each belligerent party. The problem of the Vatican, therefore, is to determine which side can be trusted to inflict fewer losses and to secure more advantages.

It is obvious that once the Holy See has made up its mind on this point, it will, while remaining officially behind the screen of neutrality, endeavor to favor by indirect and prudent action the cause to which it has given preference. Such policies, however, are inevitably affected by the fortunes of war and by the changes which take place in the general picture as the result of military failures and the consequent shifting of the probabilities of victory.

At the beginning of the war, down to the collapse of France, the pendulum in the Vatican, though officially swinging with regular alternation, nevertheless indicated a slight preference for the cause of the Allies. The accord between the Nazis and Soviet Russia, together with their invasion of Poland, had caused consternation in papal circles. Nazi Germany, towards which the Holy See had been so lenient in the expectation that it would destroy forever the monster of Bolshevism, had, on the contrary, become virtually the ally of the Soviets. This was more than the Vatican could stand. German atrocities in Poland, the destruction of churches, and the persecution of the clergy were loudly deplored by the Pope and widely denounced in various languages by the Vatican radio station. Russian "atrocities" were not omitted in this denunciation, though the worst of them appeared to be that "Soviet agents dressed in priests' robes were going around the schools, hospitals, seminaries, and churches making favorable propaganda for the Soviets and in some cases organizing heretical cells" (*New York Times,* January 24, 1940).

But these attacks on Nazi and Soviet practices did not mean that the Vatican wished the victory of the Allies; it still preferred a peace of compromise such as it had urged before the war. The "phony war" which was going on during the winter of 1939 on the western front, seemed to encourage the probability of such a peace.

The five-point program offered by the Pope in his address of December, 1939, advocated the independence of the small nations, disarmament, an international organization capable of securing peace and justice, respect for ethnical minorities, and a return to the principles of love and social justice set forth in the Sermon on the Mount. December 24 was also the date of President Roosevelt's letter to the Pope, announcing the establishment of his diplomatic mission to the Vatican.

Hitler, who was then preparing his massive attack on the West and did not want at that moment an open conflict with the Vatican, since it might have caused disturbances among German Catholics, sent his Foreign Minister, Ribbentrop, to Rome on a mission of appeasement. According to information coming from Vatican circles and transmitted by American correspondents, Ribbentrop reassured the Pope that Germany's policy towards Russia had not changed. He even "expressed a willingness in behalf of the Reich to join the Pope in a crusade against Bolshevism" (*New York Times*, March 11, 1940). Undoubtedly he also made promises concerning the Polish situation. The Vatican radio stopped its anti-German broadcasts.

Soon Hitler's refusal to let a papal representative visit Poland made it clear that Ribbentrop's only aim had been to gain a little time. On April 3 the Vatican radio expressed its disappointment: "Reports from Vienna and Berlin do little to encourage a forlorn hope" (*New York Times*, April 4, 1940). The stories of atrocities in Poland were resumed.

Then the blitzkrieg began with the invasion of Holland and Belgium. Pius XII did not hesitate to send messages to the rulers of these two countries saying that he was praying for their triumph. At this point, Mussolini stepped forward armed with Article 24 of the Lateran Treaty, as well as with threats of harsh reprisals, and imposed silence upon the Pope. From that date, the Vatican daily, *Osservatore Romano,* ceased to publish political news. Within a few weeks France lay prostrate, England seemed doomed, and Fascist Italy had joined Germany in the war. The picture had changed and the Vatican pendulum began swinging slightly to the other side.

Confronted with the reality of a German victory which appeared decisive, the task of the Pope was now to use whatever influence he could bring to bear on the peace terms which the victor was going to impose upon Europe. Whether or not the Nazis would undertake a "crusade" against the Soviets, as Ribbentrop had promised they would, the fact seemed clear that the colossal military power and the incredible success obtained in so short a time by Germany closed the door on all possible Russian aspirations to dominate Europe. In a Europe controlled by Nazi Germany, democratic institutions could not longer exist. But the Vatican had no reason to shed tears over their disappearance, provided they were superseded by governments willing to accept the collaboration of the Church on such terms as the Pope deemed to be essential or at least acceptable.

Pius was fully aware that in a Europe dominated by the Axis the Church would have to accept a degree of subordination to the state. Both systems, subordination to the state and separation of church and state, are condemned by the Church; but of the two, subordination, when limited to certain aspects of ecclesiastical institutions and temporal administration, is the lesser evil. Under the system of partial subordination there are important advantages for the Church, for instance, the financial support of the clergy by the state, the protection of the law, and possibly a degree of religious monopoly such as the Church had already secured from the Fascist regime. The hope that, after the victory, Hitler, or better Hitler's successor (the Church can wait), might come to terms with its large Catholic population and with the Holy See was indeed an alluring one. Under such conditions the Vatican expected nothing worse than to go back to the situation in which the Church had lived and prospered for several centuries, when absolute monarchies flourished and the blight of liberalism had not undermined the strength of both throne and altar. Thus it is easy to understand the attitude taken by the Vatican towards Italy when Mussolini "stabbed France in the back." Pius XII no doubt would have liked Italy to remain neutral. But since neutrality had vanished, the mourning for Italy's entrance into the war did not last long. Cardinals, bishops, and priests were soon busy arousing enthusiasm for the war among the unwilling and bewildered Italians and pinning medals and bestowing blessings on soldiers. Thirty Italian bishops sent Mussolini a telegram urging him "to crown the unfailing victory of our army by planting the Italian flag over the Holy Sepulchre" (*New York Herald Tribune*, June 28, 1940). The *Civiltà Cattolica*, the organ of the Jesuits, addressed a fervent appeal on July 15 to Italian youth, exhorting them to "carry out their duties with the loyalty proper to citizens and soldiers. Catholic youth mindful of the heroism and the spirit of sacrifice of the last war, will give proof of the same heroism in its task of assuring prosperity to this nation, the centre of Catholic faith and civilization." Somebody who had a good memory remarked that in May, 1915, when Italy entered the war on the side of the Allies, the same *Civiltà Cattolica*, far from urging heroism on the Italian soldiers, had written a vitriolic article against the war and against our modern "Godless civilization" which "had promised freedom and has made the nations slave to oppressive militarism; had promised happiness and has brought slaughter among nations."

The war enthusiasm of the rank and file of the Italian clergy reached such a pitch that the Vatican felt the need of warning the world through an official communication in the *Osservatore Romano* that the Holy See did not assume any responsibility for the patriotic exuberance of the Italian Church. The Vatican had felt no need to make such a statement in connection with similar patriotic activities carried on by the clergy in other countries.

It will not be amiss to remark at this point that the Italian clergy is not on the same level with that of other nations as far as its relations to the Holy See are concerned. The connection between the two is much closer and gives the Italian clergy a unique position in the Church. This is due to the fact that the Pope and the papal Curia are in Rome, that the largest part of papal officials are Italians, that a majority of the Cardinals are Italian, and that the Pope himself has, for several centuries, been chosen from the ranks of the Italian Cardinals. Likewise, with very few exceptions the members of the papal diplomatic corps, and the majority of the personnel of the Roman congregations or departments of the central government of the Church, are Italians. It is only natural that a clergy which supplies the Church with its most important dignitaries, not to mention the Pope himself, should be bound by closer ties to the Holy See than are the clerics of other countries.

There is, moreover, a long tradition of close control by the Vatican over the political conduct of the Italian clergy. For seventy years Italian bishops were forbidden by papal order to manifest any public approval whatsoever of the national government and were expected to shun any public political manifestation of loyalty to the constitutional regime. This tradition could not easily be forgotten by the people, nor by the bishops themselves. Furthermore, the Italian clergy is also bound by the Concordat, to abstain from all political demonstrations. Of course, the Fascist government not only was delighted but expected as an obligation that the clergy disregard the Concordat on the occasion of Italy's declaring war, but it was certainly the right and the duty of the Vatican to see to it that such violation of the Concordat did not occur. It was inevitable that the conduct of the Italian clergy should be considered the result of a positive order issued by the Holy See.

Meanwhile, the Pope, according to the *Osservatore Romano* (*New York Times*, September 2, 1940), was exerting himself to bring about peace, which would have meant at that moment a peace dictated by Hitler. In a sermon preached at St. Peter's on November 23, the Pope offered prayers to God for a "more just and more harmonious order." The Nazi and Fascist presses took these words as an expression of approval of the new Nazi and Fascist order, but the *Osservatore Romano* assured them that the Pope was speaking of a Christian, not of a political, order. Pius XII tried to express his thought more clearly in his customary Christmas address of December 24, 1940:

Europe and its system of states, it is said, will not be as they were before. Something new and better, more organically evolved, sounder, freer and stronger, must replace the past in order to eliminate its defects, its weaknesses and its deficiencies, which are said to have been disclosed convincingly by recent events. In the midst of contrasting systems which are part of our times and dependent upon them, the Church cannot be called upon to favor one more than another.

This was a new declaration of neutrality covering, not only the war in general, but specifically the aims of the war, as stated by each of the belligerents. By his wording the Pope seemed to suggest that the Vatican would accept any of the contrasting new orders planned by the belligerents, but not one more than another. In fact, at that moment, this declaration meant that the Holy See did not shrink from the Nazi and Fascist new order as such. Passing from a negative to a positive stand, the Pope declared first that the only interest of the Church is to perform its educational and religious mission in a society based on Christian moral principles. The indispensable prerequisites of a new order in such a society are triumph over hate and mistrust, over the principle that might makes right, over economic and political imperialism. The Pope did not elaborate on this. It is only by implication that the reader can conclude that the Church would favor among the contrasting systems any new order which would fulfill these prerequisites, or which would at least more nearly approach the ideal represented by them. It was also left to the reader to submit the various new orders to a searching analysis and to find out which among them, if any, realized or approached the standard set by the Pope.

One may admire the diplomatic skill with which generalizations in matters of principle, and reticence in regard to concrete situations, are used to avoid stating frankly and without hesitation the papal mind. On the other hand, one cannot help thinking that it is not by generalizations and reticence that the moral leadership of the world, which is, after all, the function of the Papacy, can be rendered effective. The ghost of Article 24, the fiction of neutrality, and the fear of unpleasant reactions were all stronger than the impulse to state frankly and concretely the moral issue at stake. The Vatican does not share Don Sturzo's view that it is time for the Church to feel the compelling duty of taking a stand, even if by doing so it has to go back to the catacombs. As a consequence, the Fascist newspapers continued to affirm that the ideals of the Pope and the ideals of Mussolini were in perfect harmony, and that the Pope was denouncing the British and American imperialisms; while the American newspapers were sure that the Pope had come forward to favor the cause of the Allies.

To be sure, the five points of Pius XII, given in December, 1939, as well as the prerequisites of December, 1940, were nearer to the new order envisaged (also in general terms) by the Atlantic Charter, than to any description of the new order contemplated by the Nazis and the Fascists. However, by tossing weights on each side of the scale Pius XII was endeavoring to restore equilibrium. The theoretical declaration of principles made in those addresses was counterbalanced and robbed somewhat of its character by other utterances and manifestations of sympathy with the Axis side. Pius XII joined the Italian clergy in urging Italians to "defend the fatherland," admonishing them, however, "to abstain from hate." On September 4, 1940, he received

five thousand members of the Italian Catholic Action and told
them that they "must be ready to give up their lives for their fatherland," and "must give due respect and loyal, conscientious
obedience to the civil authorities." These are general principles,
which the Church has always taught to the faithful, but uttered
at that moment to an audience of Italians, it was impossible not
to understand the papal exhortation as having the actual purpose of favoring Italy's war.

Still more significant was the fact that during the following
months Pius XII received again and again large groups of Italian
soldiers and officers, and several times German soldiers and
officers in uniform were granted an audience. He told them all
that they "were particularly dear" to him, and that he was happy
to receive them and to give his benediction to "those who serve
the beloved fatherland with loyalty and love." When the news
of the reception of German soldiers at the Vatican appeared in
the American press, there was a flood of protest, the Catholics
maintaining that the story was a trick of Nazi propaganda which
ought to be stopped. Unfortunately, the source of information
was the *Osservatore Romano,* which had published the story
in the "official section" of communications and lists of recep-
tions passed to the editor by the Vatican bureau.

It is reasonable to think that no one urges soldiers to make
the supreme sacrifice, unless he believes in the cause for which
they are fighting and earnestly desires their victory. It is inconceivable, for instance, that an American bishop would encourage German soldiers to fight heroically; given the opportunity, he would undoubtedly tell them to give up the fight and
surrender. Had the Pope, when addressing the Italian and
German soldiers, forgotten that as Pope he was above all national
quarrels and a neutral in the conflict? Did he speak merely as
an Italian carried away by sentiment and patriotism? At any
rate, it was difficult not to receive the impression that the "cause"
of Fascist Italy was much nearer to his heart than the fiction
of his neutrality. Neither Benedict XV during the first World

War, nor Pius XI during the Ethiopian War ever admitted uniformed soldiers from belligerent countries to public or private audiences at the Vatican. This was a novelty introduced by Pius XII for the exclusive benefit of the Fascist and Nazi soldiers, who alone had access to Rome.

Of even greater importance was the attitude of the Vatican towards the newly created kingdom of Croatia. Its crown was offered to King Victor Emmanuel who, having enough flimsy crowns of his own, passed it on to his cousin, the Duke of Spoleto. A delegation led by that very Ante Pavelich, who five years before had been sentenced, in absentia, to death, by a French court as the instigator of the murder of King Alexander of Serbia, and who had now become the Quisling of Croatia, went to Rome. Here, on May 18, 1941, the ceremony of the acceptance of the crown by the new sovereign took place. The plan of detaching Catholic Croatia from orthodox Serbia could not displease the Vatican, and in view of the affection which the Pope had shown for the House of Savoy, the choice of the Duke of Spoleto for Croatia's king could not but meet with his approval. On the other hand, to extend a full official recognition to the new puppet Axis state would have been rightly considered by the enemies of Germany and Italy as a breach of papal neutrality. By one of those compromises in which diplomatic cant, hair-splitting casuistry, and subtle mental reservations work hand in hand, the Vatican solved the problem. The Duke of Spoleto was received by the Pope the day before the ceremony (and therefore before he had become officially the King of Croatia), and Ante Pavelich, his Prime Minister, and the entire Croatian delegation were received "as Catholic individuals" the same day the ceremony proclaiming Croatia a kingdom took place. Unhappily, the *Osservatore Romano* had stated a few lines before, that Pavelich as a mere "Catholic individual" had not visited the Pope alone; he had been accompanied by a stenographer, who evidently recorded the interview, and after the private conversation with the Pope in the stenographer's presence, had introduced to the Pope, according to the ceremonial of official visits, the whole Croatian delegation.

Meanwhile, at the beginning of 1941, there had been some slight changes in the picture of the war. England had not fallen, and the assistance of the United States, which had adopted an impressive program of military preparation, was becoming more effective. The expectation of an early peace imposed by Germany was no longer so strong as it had been a few months before, and the prospect of a long war of exhaustion appeared more probable. Then the sweeping German successes in the Balkans during the following spring revived the hopes of a victorious German peace, and in June the German armies invaded Russia and thus the war picture again took a new shape and created a new problem for the Vatican.

There can be little doubt that Hitler and Mussolini would have liked to receive straightway from the Pope a blessing, and perhaps a papal bull preaching a new crusade against the "atheists" of Moscow. Pius XI might have committed such an act, for he was ever prone to act on impulse and suffered nightmares on account of Bolshevism. A man trained in the game of diplomatic calculation, as Pius XII had been, could not suddenly throw overboard the frail neutrality which he had taken such pains to nurture. No matter how great the pressure exerted by the two Axis partners, and no matter how great the temptation to sanction this attack on the hated Communist regime, the Pope heard the voice of prudence and kept silent.

In England, Mr. Churchill, overcoming all the scruples of his Tory friends and colleagues in the government, rushed to make accords with Russia in the fight against the common enemy. President Roosevelt acted likewise in extending to Russia the benefits of Lend-Lease and in promising further assistance. Common sense suggested that the safest thing for the Vatican to do was to wait for the results of the Russian campaign, in which a swift and crushing German victory over the Red Army was generally expected.

What the Vatican did not do was done by the Catholic hierarchy wherever possible. With few exceptions it raised its voice in protest against the unholy English and American cooperation with atheistic and Communistic Russia, and used all the political influence at its disposal to raise opposition to it. In Franco's Spain, legions of "volunteer crusaders" were organized and sent with the blessings of bishops and priests to the Russian front. Franco's example was soon followed by Marshal Pétain of Vichy, who added his blessing to that of the French cardinals when a legion of French crusaders was dispatched. In England, for obvious reasons, the Catholic hierarchy could not protest and had to admit that cooperation with Russia was to England's advantage. Nevertheless, the more conservative Catholic organs joined the impenitent Tories in spreading suspicion and doubt concerning Russia's aims towards England, thereby increasing that heavy cloud of mutual distrust which affected to no little extent the relations between the Soviets and the Allies. It was in this country that the Catholic clergy made its greatest effort to prejudice public opinion against cooperation with Russia.

The great majority of the Catholic clergy had supported the isolationists and had used the powerful weapon of a well-organized propaganda against American rearmament, the Lend-Lease Act, and assistance to England. The isolationist campaign was carried on vigorously, not only by such known pro-Fascists as Father Coughlin and the editor of the *Brooklyn Tablet,* but by the majority of the diocesan weeklies and Catholic periodicals. It was also constantly commended from the pulpit and in other episcopal utterances. The slogan of this campaign might well have been, "It is not our affair." At any rate the isolationists maintained that we had no interest in Europe's imperialistic war, and that our great enemy was right in this country; its name was Communism. Months before Germany attacked Russia, Monsignor Sheen, Catholic America's most popular preacher, thundered from the pulpit, "Nations which call Russia a friend

cannot say that they are fighting for the Kingdom of God."
Cardinal O'Connell in his denunciation of Washington's policy
towards Russia deplored "this wicked propaganda that is going
about through press, through letters, orations and addresses;
one wonders if some Americans really love their own country.
Let those who have started the war finish it. It is not our affair."
Bishop Cassidy of Fall River denounced the English because
they had betrayed the Arabs of Palestine and had derided Franco
of Spain. Father Low of Boston College said that "the best way
to protect and preserve democracy is not by putting Hitler out
of business, but by eradicating materialism and socialism here
in this country." At that time, American Communists formed
one of the noisiest groups in the isolationist campaign. It was
very edifying indeed to see marching together under the banners
of American isolationism such strange companions as Father
Coughlin and Cardinal O'Connell, Irish Catholics and Italian
Fascists, German Bundists and Protestant ministers, Jesuits and
Communists, disgruntled Democrats and standpat Republicans,
all under different and contradictory slogans, but all united on
the issue of keeping America out of the European imperialistic
war.

The best description of this campaign was perhaps given by
Bishop Joseph Hurley of St. Augustine, Florida, one of the
small minority in the Catholic hierarchy who opposed the views
of their colleagues. Denouncing in outspoken words as un-
American "the flow of invective against everything American,"
which filled the Catholic Press in this country, Bishop Hurley
challenged the assumption that "the enemy number one of
America is Communism," while, in fact, "today the first enemy
of mankind is the Nazi." Then he said:

May I add by way of candid criticism directed against a few of our
National Catholic weeklies and reviews that we Catholics would be
unwise to entrust any of our part in the work of national healing to
practitioners whose only merit is their mastery in the acids of vituperation. Curiously enough, these men who would have us spend all our

energies combatting Communism, are now in reality following th
Moscow party line. That line dictated by Berlin is this: Confus
Americans, sabotage American morale and we need not worry abou
her powder factories and her assembly lines. I deeply regret to sa
that some good Americans, among them a few Catholic publicist
are now following this Berlin party line. (Address at the Florida Stat
Convention of the National Council of Catholic Women, April 3c
1941).

The isolationist ranks were scattered by the bombshell c
Germany's invasion of Russia. Overnight the Communists be
came ardent "war-mongers." The Catholics remained in th
field, more determined than ever to fight against any America
cooperation with, and any assistance to, Soviet Russia. Presiden
Roosevelt, who had successfully resisted other isolationist pres
sure, and who was already in agreement with the British polic
of helping Russia, could not remain indifferent to the devastat
ing Catholic propaganda, in which bishops, Jesuits, and poli
ticians were playing a prominent part and giving the impressio
that their movement was authorized by higher ecclesiastica
powers.

Mr. Myron Taylor was again sent to Rome, where he arrive
September 9 after a brief stop at Barcelona for a conferenc
with Admiral Leahy, who had come down from Vichy. As usual
the newspapers spread rumors about the purpose of Mr. Taylor'
mission. The New York Times correspondent in Rome, Mr
Herbert Matthews, reported that, according to "Vatican sources,
President Roosevelt had requested the Pope to declare that th
war against Nazism was a just war, and that the Pope's repl
"appears to have been a polite, 'No'" (New York Times, Sep
tember 16, 1940). Mr. Matthews knew also that the Pope'
negative answer was accompanied by a threefold explanation
1. theoretically, there is no such thing as a just war, and hence
the Vatican could not take such a stand; 2. England and th
United States had doctrines, interests, and political aims of thei
own and so had the Vatican; 3. though these doctrines, interest

and political aims ran parallel, they were not altogether identical, and "the fact that they are parallel means that they cannot meet." Mr. Matthews discounted altogether the rumor that Mr. Taylor's mission had the purpose of trying "to separate Italy from Germany." The most popular rumor was that Mr. Taylor's mission was to solicit the intervention of the Vatican in a new attempt to restore peace. The *Chicago Times* summarized this view under the caption, "Is Myron C. Taylor Our Angel of Peace?"

It is hardly possible that President Roosevelt asked the Pope to declare that the war against the Nazis was a just war, as Mr. Matthews reported from Rome. The President, unless his ecclesiastical counselors had misled him, must have been well aware that the Pope, having refused to bless the "crusade" against Russia, could not bless the counter-crusade against the Nazis and thus destroy the screen of neutrality behind which he felt more or less secure. The "Vatican sources" which gave Mr. Matthews his information in such detail, were probably pleasing Hitler and Mussolini by bringing into relief the absolute and uncompromising neutrality of the Holy See.

Whatever other purposes Mr. Taylor's mission may have had, we are allowed to guess, in view of what preceded and followed his visit to the Vatican, that one of his tasks was to inform the Pope of the reason why the United States felt obliged to extend its help to Russia, to reassure His Holiness that the United States was exerting all possible pressure on the Soviet government for the adoption of a liberal religious policy, and, very likely, to ask the Pope whether he could discreetly persuade the Catholic hierarchy of America to stop waving the red rag of the Soviet religious question and so stop causing new conflicts and divisions among the American people.

We may reasonably suppose that the Pope's answer was prudently non-committal while he awaited the results of President Roosevelt's action in Moscow. Meanwhile, it was announced by the press, though with some delay, that the American mission to Moscow, headed by Mr. Averell Harriman, "had been instructed to take up the question of religious freedom in Russia with the Soviet Government, and President Roosevelt indicated that the American Ambassador to Moscow, Mr. Steinhardt, already had discussed that question with Soviet officials" (*New York Times,* October 7, 1941). As a result of these steps, the official spokesman for the Soviets, S. A. Lozovski, made a statement on October 4 declaring that Article 124 of the Soviet Constitution guaranteed religious freedom to all and covered sufficiently the demand made by the United States. President Roosevelt echoed Lozavski's statement, hoping that it would satisfy the American Catholics.

The reaction of Catholic circles in America was divided. The Jesuits of Georgetown University through their spokesman, Father Walsh, who in the early twenties had been in Russia to distribute papal relief, denounced the Russian answer as "a hollow mockery" and "cynical pretenses." He added that "the issue was now drawn for the American people who were already involved in assisting the Soviet government in war." Moscow's answer, said Father Walsh, amounts to this: "We want your money, we want your ships, we want your tanks and ammunitions and we expect your blood if that be necessary. But we will not permit you to have a word to say respecting the freedom for which you shall make these sacrifices." In conclusion, the Jesuits proposed that help to Russia be conditioned by the Soviet surrender to the American demand for religious freedom.

This demand was supported by a majority of those connected with the Catholic Press; it was endorsed officially by the Knights of Columbus and was favored by representatives of some of the Protestant bodies. It is difficult to imagine that all these people did not realize that the main beneficiaries of the stubborn Russian resistance to Nazi armies were the democratic countries, and that to deny assistance to the Soviets under the pretext of religious differences would have the twofold and fatal result of helping the Nazis to win and of confirming the Soviets' belief that religion is their enemy Number One. Men like Father Walsh also knew that in a world dominated by Nazi Germany religion would have a slimmer chance than in Soviet Russia, which at least recognizes freedom of religion as a human right, even if, for reasons with which we cannot deal here but for which the churches are partly responsible, the principle of religious freedom has not been fully carried out. Fanaticism is always blind, no matter how advanced a religion or a system of government may be.

The Vatican does not seem to have made any move to put an end to the disagreements and controversies which raged among American Catholics over the Russian question. The campaign against aid to Russia continued unabated despite the denunciations of men like Bishop Hurley. If anything, it became more vituperative; Father Gillis, the editor of *The Catholic World*, speaking on the same platform with Senator Wheeler at a rally in Springfield, Massachusetts, on October 23, 1941, described Stalin as a "murderer, atheist, mongrel and sadist."

There were some who yielded to the evidence that aid to Russia was in our interest, but they did so with ill grace and insulting remarks against Russia, as did Monsignor Sheen who, in an address of October 18 said: "We must aid Russia materially. I do not think it is wrong to accept help from a second gangster when you already are attacked by a first." On December 3, 1941, three days before Pearl Harbor, Archbishop Curley of Baltimore and Washington in an interview given to the *Baltimore News Post* remarked, "More than one dog has bitten the hand that fed it" and then stated:

I would not be surprised to see Stalin and Hitler get together again, in spite of what their nations, Germany and Russia, have done to one another during the last twenty-three weeks. We of the United States are fighting side by side with Stalin, the greatest murderer of men the world has ever known, because he is fighting Hitler, but there were days and years when Stalin was not fighting Hitler, but rather fighting in behalf of Hitler. . . . The cry of peace no longer rings in the air from our own peace organizations. Even Mrs. Roosevelt's American Youth Congress is crying out today for war! war! war! . . . We say, we all hate communism . . . but I wonder just now, if communists are not taking advantage of the situation to build up here in this free republic of the United States a system which has for the past twenty-one years had but one object, namely, the destruction of the very government from which help is now going to the head of communism today. I have no more confidence in Stalin than I have in Hitler.

Then on December 7 came the Japanese attack on Pearl Harbor and the subsequent declaration of war on the United States by Hitler and Mussolini. Moreover the collapse of Soviet Russia upon which the reactionary American Catholics had perhaps counted so much, did not take place; on the contrary, the winter counter-offensive of the Soviet armies gave evidence of a Russian strength far from declining. The picture had changed so radically that the best prophets could not have foreseen such a difference.

In his long broadcast on Christmas Eve, 1941, Pope Pius recognized that "there appears today to be no open road to agreement between the belligerent parties whose reciprocal war aims seem to be irreconcilable." He spoke of the foundations upon which a future peace must be built, stating again at length the principles already contained in his five points and in other pontifical addresses. Then he added: "We love with equal affection all peoples, without any exception whatsoever, and in order to avoid even the appearances of being moved by partisanship we have maintained hitherto the greatest reserve."

A practical demonstration of his impartiality can be found in the same address. Deploring the "dechristianization" of modern society, an evil which is the root of all others, the Pope remarks, not, however, without a certain reluctance: "Here we do not wish to withdraw the praise due to the wisdom of those rulers who . . . were capable of restoring to their place of honor . . . the value of Christian civilization in the amicable relations between Church and State, in the safeguard of the sanctity of marriage, in the religious education of youth." In this statement, the Pope clearly referred to the three main points of the Lateran Concordat, and hence the praise "which was not withdrawn" was addressed to Mussolini. But near the end of his sermon, Pope Pius bestowed a special benediction "upon those who though not members of the visible body of the Catholic Church, are near to us in their faith in God and in Jesus Christ, and share with us our views with regard to the provisions for the peace and its fundamental aims." There can be no doubt that the primary beneficiary of this benediction was President Roosevelt.

During the following period, down to September, 1942, the Vatican remained silent; it was almost as if the Pope had had his say for the duration. But on September 17, the Secretary of State, Mr. Hull, announced that Mr. Myron Taylor had resumed his mission at the Vatican and was on his way to Rome with a safe-conduct from the Fascist government. According to information coming from Vatican circles and relayed to American correspondents in Berne, Mr. Taylor's objective was "that of presenting personally what the United States had set out to accomplish, how the United States proposes to do so, and what the country hopes to accomplish in guaranteeing world peace when and only when the victory is decided."

Periodical consultations between the White House and the Vatican will undoubtedly continue throughout the war, especially through members of the Catholic hierarchy, who, like Archbishop Spellman, cannot be denied by the Fascist government a safe-conduct to perform their duty of periodical visits to the Pope. The harmonious relations between the United States and the Vatican as regards the post-war reorganization of Europe will be kept up to date. It is natural that this harmony be especially sought where the settlement of the Italian problem is concerned, for the Holy See regards that as the paramount problem, since it affects more directly its ecclesiastical and political interests.

While the Vatican was following its see-saw technique,

the American Press in general has done its best to persuade the American people that the Vatican is against the dictators and for the democracies. The idea that "the Pope is with us" has been hammered in our heads day in and day out. Hence, we have been steeped in the opinion that we must follow papal suggestions and papal directions, when the time comes for a just and lasting peace. The Pope, on the other hand, has done his best to tell us frankly that he is neither with us nor against us, that he has no preference regarding the new order to be established in Europe or its founders, be they Italian, German, British, or American. His only concern is that the new order recognize the claims of the Church. In the same breath Pius had bestowed praises and blessings on Franco's dictatorship because it represents "a triumph of religion and of the Spirit"; on Mussolini's Fascist regime because it "restored amicable relations between Church and State"; and on Mr. Roosevelt, the President of a democratic republic, because "he shares with us our views with regard to the provisions of peace."

Though this is not a matter in which the Pope claims to be infallible, no one would think of challenging the papal statement that President Roosevelt shares the Vatican's views as to the "provisions for peace." The historian, however, cannot accept this a priori inference, unless it is confirmed by the facts.

4. Post-War Plans

> In establishing a firm peace it is of the utmost importance that common ideals shall have united expression. . . . When that happy day shall dawn, great problems of practical import will face us all. . . . Here too common ideals call for parallel action.
> —President Roosevelt to Pius XII. Letter of December 24, 1939.

This official invitation extended by the President of the United States to the Pope for "parallel action" in dealing with post-war problems was taken at its face value by the Vatican.

Mr. Taylor's mission was to convey the Pope's plans to the President. Whether our State Department suggested modifications to those plans we do not know. But the "parallel action" promised by President Roosevelt to the Pope will be in fact a wholly unilateral affair. The Vatican has remained and will remain, neutral to the end, while we do the fighting. When the war is over, we will do all the work of putting the plans into effect.

Unlike our State Department where everything is shrouded in deep mystery, the Vatican has never concealed its views. These are fully consistent with its well-known religious and political principles, with the policies followed during the war, and with its primary purpose of safeguarding and fostering the interests of the Catholic Church.

The Swiss Catholic newspaper, *Die Tat*, published on October 12, 1942, an article on "Vatican Policy in the Second World War" which was circularized in English translation among the three hundred Catholic diocesan periodicals in this country by the news service of the National Catholic Welfare Conference. Among others it was reprinted in full by *The Tablet* of Brooklyn, New York (October 24) from which we quote below. The paper enumerated the many difficulties which beset the Holy See in maintaining its neutrality. Then it remarked that this neutrality of the Vatican does not mean that "they renounce the liberty of taking a moral stand in the face of events." Then the writer described the "religious" policies of the Holy See and concluded:

If one keeps in view the religious aims of the Curia, he may well be satisfied with the success attained thus far in this war. It is different if one looks at the Vatican's possibilities of action in the purely political field, and if we consider the political aims, which the Curia must have, even though the motives be religious, in its farsighted policy.

According to the opinion of Vatican circles, "there is no chance at present or at any future date for Papal mediation between the fighting nations." However, the Vatican, even from the political point of view, has made some gains:

Among positive changes, the Curia hails with satisfaction: the change in France; a greater stability in the present governments in Spain and Portugal; Catholic domination in Slovakia and Croatia. Relations with Fascist Italy and with Hungary continue splendid. That holds, too, for relations with the United States which have never been disturbed and thoroughly satisfactory relations, for the present, with the South American States, with Japan and China and with Turkey. A passing cloud of discord in England, after the naming of the Japanese ambassador [to the Vatican], has been quickly cleared away.

The Swiss newspaper is neither an official nor an unofficial organ of the Vatican and its words would have no weight, if it were not for the fact that the American bishops who head the National Catholic Welfare Conference have adopted the article and have taken pains to bring it to the notice of all American Catholics. More recently, Count Michael de la Bedoyère, editor of the London *Catholic Herald,* published an article on the same subject of papal neutrality. In the periodical, *The Fortnightly,* April 18, 1943, he states frankly:

The Church sees things hidden from the average Englishman or American, who is concentrating on destruction of the evils of Hitlerism. The Church sees that a new order in Europe, under the leadership of Great Britain, America and Russia might turn out to be a Europe dominated by Russia. Just as the creation of a moderately authoritarian bloc in good time might have prevented war from breaking out, so the nursing, so to say, of the same element at the present time may help to stabilize a very dangerous and difficult situation after the war (*New York Herald Tribune,* April 19, 1943).

These remarks about the Holy See's satisfaction over the change that took place in France, over the regimes of Spain, Portugal, Slovakia, and Croatia, and above all, over the "nursing [of] moderately authoritarian" regimes to be established after the war, represent faithfully the views of the Vatican and coincide point by point with its policy and its program of political action.

To understand why the Holy See would greatly prefer to see authoritarian rather than modern democratic regimes established in Europe, especially in countries with Catholic populations, we must keep in mind the general principles which dictate Vatican policy. That the Church objects to modern democracy may seem absurd to the ordinary American citizen, who is so used to hearing Catholic bishops and priests in this country publicly profess their faith in democracy and seeing them demonstrate by actions their devotion to the American system of government. Indeed, it has become fashionable now among Catholics to claim that the American Declaration of Independence and even the American Constitution are derived directly from the teachings of St. Thomas Aquinas or, at least, from Cardinal Bellarmine.

A great deal of mental confusion has been artfully created in the American mind by the fact that Catholic writers and preachers use indiscriminately the terms "democracy," "modern democracy," and "Christian democracy," as if these terms were synonymous and the writers had the same type of democracy in mind. This is not the place to discuss this problem, but a simple explanation is necessary in order to clarify the main issue with which we are concerned, i. e., the post-war settlement of the Italian question.

In ancient times "democracy" meant simply a government of the people as against the government of one. But by "people" was meant merely the dominant class or an oligarchy, to the exclusion of the rank and file of the population. Aquinas, who derived his notion of democracy from Aristotle, had no historical knowledge of other types of democracy.

"Modern democracy," on the contrary defines "people" as including all classes and all individuals, all with equal rights and equal duties towards the community. It implies, above all, individual freedom within the law, and freedom of speech, of the press, of association, of conscience, and of religion, and the right to be represented in central and local government. We are now striving to add to these freedoms one other: freedom from want, to be achieved through social-security measures, so that social justice and not mere charity will take care of human need.

Freedom of religion implies the equality of all religions before the law and this leads logically to the separation of church and state, since religion is a matter of individual choice and the state has no power to make laws regulating religion. This in turn precludes the state's making concordats or agreements with the Holy See or with any other spiritual sovereignty. Each religion is free in its internal organization to establish hierarchical powers of its own, at home or abroad, but such powers have no juridical existence as far as the state is concerned. It is obvious that the Catholic Church must dislike and disapprove of this kind of democracy, which puts Catholicism on the same level with other religions, and that the Holy See must consider it as a great heresy. From the Vatican's point of view, concordats with states are needed, not only because they regulate the relations between church and state, but primarily because they necessarily imply state recognition of the sovereignty of the Pope over the Catholic Church within the State.

"Christian" democracy is something different. Pope Leo XIII, whose encyclicals are the primary source of the teachings of Christian democracy, tells us in his *Graves de communi* that the word democracy may be interpreted in two different ways. If it is understood in the political sense and holds that popular government is preferable to any other form of government, then it is illicit:

The intentions and activities of those Catholics who work for the betterment of the proletariat, can never bend to preferring one civil regime to another.

The only lawful Christian democracy is that which has been freed from all political significance, and to which is annexed no other meaning than that of beneficent Christian action among the people.

To carry on this beneficent action, Pope Leo XIII invoked the cooperation *above all* of those who, because of their wealth, their social position, their intellectual and moral culture, exercise the greatest influence over society.

In accordance with these principles, the *Catholic Encyclopaedia of America* in its article "Democracy (Christian) teaches us that Christian democracy has been in existence at least since the times of Constantine and gives evidence of this fact in the following words:

Constantine in a period of famine chose the Bishops rather than the civil officials to distribute corn among a starving people, and thus showed his appreciation of Christian democracy (IV, p. 709).

The notion of Christian democracy of Leo XIII, who had in mind its social, to the exclusion of its political, aspects, has been superseded, according to the directions of Pius XI, by the more general notion of "Catholic Action," which affects the whole range of religious, social, and economic institutions but always held fast to the principle of the "indifference" of the Church to any form of government. This indifference, however, is only relative; that is to say, it exists only in relation to the hypothesis or actual conditions of the political society. It is not absolute indifference in relation to the thesis or doctrinal principles of the Church, adherence to which is required for the positive approval by the Church of any system of government.

Modern democracy does not meet these requirements. On the contrary, it violates the fundamental claims of the Catholic Church of possessing alone the true divine revelation and the true way of salvation. Hence, modern democracy is condemned as unchristian, agnostic, and as leading to paganism. As a matter of fact, recent Catholic writers in this country do not call it democracy but prefer to classify it under the old name of "agnostic liberalism" and have engaged in a relentless campaign in the press and in the pulpit against it. It seems that, though they themselves enjoy all the advantages of the American system of religious freedom, Catholic bishops and priests who are bound by the essentially intolerant spirit of Catholic theology, cannot admit that similar freedom ought to be granted to all other religious bodies. Thus, while praising American democracy because the Church has prospered under a regime of liberty, they at the same time look upon this system as wrong and as leading inevitably to disaster.

The Reverend Joseph Cody of the Catholic University of America, editor of the *Catholic Historical Review,* makes the following statements in an essay published in Italy (1939) as part of a large volume on church and state edited by the Catholic University of Milan:

The American form of government as it relates to religion *is not the desired model* for the Christian State (p. 531). . . . Separation of Church and State in America has resulted in the separation of a great number of people from the practice of any religious belief. . . . Thus a race of neo-pagans is being raised up who will someday be entrusted with the destinies of the nation. . . . The Church looks upon the clinging of Protestantism to the *shibboleth of separation of Church and State* as nothing more or less than the paganization of America (p. 533) [*italics ours*].

The phrase "shibboleth of separation of Church and State" is now current among American Catholics and was used even by patriotic Archbishop Spellman in a public answer to criticisms made of Mr. Taylor's appointment as presidential ambassador to the Vatican. It must be said that the Holy See, more indulgent than its theologians, does not look with disfavor upon the United States, in spite of its being a modern democracy. As the present Pope once remarked, in this country there is no real separation of church and state, but only a "benevolent neutrality" of the state towards the church.

In our times, according to Catholic opinion, the "model Christian State" which Father Cody considers the goal of all Christian nations, is realized almost fully in the dictatorial regime of Salazar in Portugal, which has been described several times by the Vatican organ, the *Osservatore Romano,* as fulfilling all Catholic requirements. To a lesser degree, the Franco regime in Spain represents a model government. It is only logical to assume that the Vatican will fight to the last ditch not only to preserve those two regimes unaltered, especially Franco's dictatorship, which was established at such great cost, but to have similar regimes established in all other so-called Catholic countries.

The true history of the Spanish rebellion is still to be written, and only then will it become clear upon whom the responsibility must primarily rest for three years of civil war. From the very beginning, Pope Pius XI blessed the rebels who were "defending the rights of God and of religion." But the Pope seems to have had some doubts about the good faith of these "crusaders" whom God had chosen to defend his rights, because he warned them that "intentions less pure, selfish interests, and mere party feeling may easily enter into, cloud and change the morality of what is being done" (September, 1936). Speaking in the same address of the Republican Loyalists who were held responsible for the burning of churches and the murder of priests, Pope Pius said that he could do only one thing, "love them with a special love born out of pity and compassion," and since he could not do more, "pray for them."

Pius XII has had plenty of time and ample opportunity to see for himself whether the doubts of his predecessor about the intentions of the crusaders were justified, and whether the morality of what was done lived up to his specifications. Evidently the present Pope finds that all is well with Franco, that Spain is a model of order and discipline, that the people are happy, well fed, and prosperous, and that all the Christian virtues are practiced there under the paternal guidance of the Church. As a matter of fact, Franco has restored to the Jesuits and to other religious orders all their former possessions, rights, and privileges, and has put the schools under their control again. Furthermore, he has returned to the Spanish grandees the land which they formerly held, has outlawed Freemasonry, has expelled Protestant missionaries, and has forbidden the public practice of any save the Catholic religion.

It was fitting, therefore, that Pius XII should, from the beginning of his pontificate, show his absolute confidence in, and boundless affection for, the Spanish dictator and all those who helped to secure his victory. Shortly after his election, Pius XII in a broadcast to Spain (April 16, 1939) expressed his feelings in an almost lyrical vein:

Peace and victory have been willed by God to Spain . . . which has now given to proselytes of the materialistic atheism of our age the highest proof that above all things stands the eternal value of religion and of the Spirit.

How "the eternal value of religion and of the Spirit" found its "highest proof" in a civil war, or in the following four years of shooting prisoners by the hundreds, His Holiness did not explain.

As for the Loyalists, Pius XII, being of a sterner fiber than his predecessor, urged Franco to "use justice towards crime and benevolent kindness towards those who had been led astray." But since in Franco's eyes all Loyalists, without distinction, were criminals, there was little room for displaying the "benevolent kindness" recommended by the Holy Father.

On June 11, 1939, Pius XII greeted at the Vatican 3,000 of Franco's soldiers, who had been brought to Italy to celebrate with their Fascist colleagues. They were accompanied by that great friend of Hitler and Mussolini, Serrano Suñer. The Pope told them that they had fought "for the triumph of Christian ideals," and that they had brought him "immense consolation" as "defenders of the faith." As recently as June 20, 1942, the same Serrano Suñer again visited the Pope, "from whom he received the Grand Cross of the Order of Pius IX, together with a blessing for Spain and for General Franco, *benemerito de la causa de Dios y de la Iglesia*" (*Bulletin of Spanish Studies,* Institute of Spanish Studies, Liverpool, January, 1943).

We may suppose that Franco's dictatorship in Spain represents only a period of transition which will be terminated some time after the war is over with the restoration of the Catholic monarchy. It would seem that our State Department shares in full the Pope's views on Spain and that our government is determined to prevent any molestation of Franco, both now and when the war is over. We are told that, at present, strategic reasons justify this policy.

As the ruler of a "model Christian State," Franco occasionally derives great pleasure from slapping these "pagan" United States in the face. He constantly throws in our teeth the fact that he is a totalitarian dictator and that his cause is the cause of his friends, Hitler and Mussolini, to whom he owes so much. Two weeks after Mr. Carlton J. H. Hayes, our ambassador to Franco, had informed the world in a public address from Barcelona that the United States was sending large amounts of valuable material to Spain, the Caudillo boasted in a speech to the Cortes: "When the echoes of the great struggle die down . . . the world will be surprised to see that, in spite of the great catastrophe unleashed by the Reds, Spain could re-establish her situation, *without any outside help*" (*Time*, March 29, 1943, p. 25).

At the same time the Spanish ambassador in Washington, De Cardenas, presented a protest to the State Department over the publication in America of T. J. Hamilton's book, *Appeasement's Child: The Franco Regime in Spain*, in which the author, who spent three years in Spain as correspondent for the *New York Times*, gives a graphic, documented picture of the horrors, confusion, and misery of that country under the rule of the Caudillo. To placate Franco we recently sent the good Archbishop of New York, who, as he told American soldiers in North Africa (*New York Times*, March 15, 1943), has reassured the two model Christian dictators of Portugal and Spain that "we have engaged to respect the territorial integrity of Spain and Portugal." Since we have not menaced the "territorial integrity" of these countries, this reassurance can mean little unless we are to undertand thereby that the "integrity" of their dictatorial regime is not to be molested.

Marshal Pétain's coming to power after the downfall of France was regarded with no small approval by the Vatican. Painful as the French catastrophe may have been from other points of view, it was believed to have had the happy effect of putting an end to the Republic and replacing it with an authoritarian regime. Around Pétain, onetime pupil of the Jesuits, gathered the French Catholic hierarchy, placing all their influence and power over the faithful at his disposal. On July 3, 1940, the *Osservatore Romano* published "an editorial full of praise for Pétain and his effort to reorganize France" (*New York Times,* July 4, 1940). On July 16, the *Osservatore Romano* published another, almost extravagant panegyric of Pétain, stating that under his guidance France "would experience a spiritual regeneration which would mark the dawn of a new, radiant day, not only for France but for all Europe and the world." As if this were not enough, the Vatican writer added some considerations on the advantages of an "authoritarian regime," pointing out as a model the regime of Salazar in Portugal. An authoritarian regime is best for creating "a civic conscience that opens and prepares the way for spreading and strengthening the moral conscience." And, added the writer, "this is also the desire, aspiration, and program of the Church." An American correpondent informed the public of America that "German foreign circles expressed marked satisfaction over what they consider as a complete about-face by the Vatican in its position towards totalitarian states" (*New York Times,* July 18, 1940).

These eulogies of Pétain indicate the extent of the Holy See's appreciation of the marshal's services to the Church in France. The Republic had given the Vatican so many headaches, had been so unsympathetic towards the Church, so ruthless in its anti-clerical laws, and finally, France, the oldest daughter of the Church, had been such a hotbed of revolutionary and radical ideas, that its end could not be much regretted. Pétain hastened to revoke all laws which were objectionable to the Church. He restored to the Jesuits and other religious orders their former

privileges, especially in the matter of schools; he proscribed Freemasonry and restricted such liberties as were still to be had under
the German control of the Vichy government.

In view of these facts, the ardent support that Pius XII has
given the Pétain regime was to be expected. An authoritarian
regime of the Pétain type, or perhaps better, a restored monarchy, would meet with his full approval.

In connection with France also the policy of the State Department seems to have moved along lines parallel to those of the
Vatican. It is perhaps significant that the *Osservatore Romano*,
after its editorial of July 8, 1940, praising Pétain, published
another editorial two days later, filled with commendation of
President Roosevelt, "who has known how to defend the democratic institutions of his country," and who "has always acted
with great ability both in internal and foreign politics." These
remarks were undoubtedly intended to dispel the danger that
the American public might have interpreted the policy of the
Holy See towards Pétain as meaning that the Vatican had ranged
itself openly against the democracies and disapproved of the
democratic institutions of the United States. Did those flattering
remarks mean also that the Vatican was hoping that President
Roosevelt would lend his support to the "good Marshal"? How
large a part the Vatican played in determining the policy of our
State Department towards Vichy is, of course, a diplomatic mystery. But in view of the harmony between the American attitude
and that of the Vatican, it is reasonable to assume that the voice
of the Pope was not without weight in this important episode.

Anyhow, the fact is that our government put all its faith in
Pétain and gave the cold shoulder to De Gaulle, the leader of
those whom Mr. Hull called "the so-called Free French." This
policy reached its height when the American forces landed in
North Africa. Our dealings with General Giraud may be plausi-
bly explained from the point of view of military strategy, for the
general, though known to be unfriendly towards democracy,
was not responsible for the policies of Vichy. But Darlan's mys-

terious appearance on the spot at just the right time to assume
government of French North Africa, with the consent of the
American authorities, overshadowed all other features of that
painful episode. There are many things in this affair which are
unexplained. While American and British soldiers were fighting
in North Africa, General Nogues, an outstanding Vichyite, was
allowed to fly from North Africa to France and back, after con-
ferring with Pétain. Darlan's proclamation to the effect that he
was assuming the governorship "on behalf of Pétain" was broadcast from Algiers to Vichy and came to America via Vichy. On
November 17, the Associated Press sent to America from London the news that a Swiss agency at Berne had had a report from
Vichy saying that Rear-Admiral René Platon, State Secretary
under Laval, had returned to Vichy the day before, after several
days in North Africa. On his return, he had a long conference
with Pétain and Laval. On November 19, Darlan, speaking on
the Algiers radio, said that though he was working with the Allies, he was "fulfilling Marshal Pétain's mandate." Last but not
least Mr. Edwin James (*New York Times,* November 15, 1942),
who seems to be unusually well informed of what goes on in the
State Department, gave us this sybilline information:

It is anybody's guess whether, in offering to work with the Americans, he [Darlan] is or is not following the real wishes of Pétain. It
will take some time to know. It is quite evident that the position,
present and former, of Darlan has something to recommend him to
the Americans.

It seems thus that there was a pre-arranged plan and a deal
not only with Giraud, but with a Darlan-Pétain combine. One
cannot fail to notice the fact that the presidential ambassador
to the Vatican, Mr. Taylor, journeyed to Rome in early September, the very time when the African affair was taking shape.
Had Mr. Taylor's mission anything to do with the plot? Did
he ask or receive any assistance from ecclesiastical circles in
Rome? These are unanswered questions.

But why did the United States show its unfriendliness to De Gaulle and his followers so ostentatiously, and why did our State Department bring pressure upon England to keep De Gaulle in the background? Then again, why did the United States assume all the responsibility for all the dealings with Darlan and his crowd? Why should the United States favor an authoritarian regime in France, what interests had she in strengthening the reactionary forces there, especially after it became evident that Vichy could not break the German stranglehold and that Pétain's game was Laval's game?

Our change of policy in North Africa—at least, we hope it was a change—accompanied by Giraud's public statement as to the future of France, coincided with Archbishop Spellman's visit to the Vatican. It is natural to suppose that the archbishop had, among his other missions, that of explaining to the Pope our reasons for deviating from our pro-Vichy policy, and of informing him as to our plans for the future. According to the newspapers, one of the archbishop's reasons for visiting London after his North African tour, was to act as an intermediary for the final fusion of the De Gaulle and Giraud forces, a difficult task, which up to then we had failed to accomplish, and which, if accomplished with the Vatican's aid, would appear as another obligation towards the Holy See. A coalition of ex-Vichy men, of *cagoulards* and army generals, who can count on their Senegalese and Algerian troops, with the active support of the Catholic hierarchy, the leadership of Giraud, and the blessings of the Pope and of the State Department might well strangle in the cradle any effort to reestablish a French democracy.

Let us now turn to Mr. Otto Hapsburg. It is not a secret that the Vatican has always mourned the disappearance of the Hapsburg monarchy in Austria-Hungary. The Austrian Empire was the bulwark of Catholicism in Central Europe, the only empire in which the Church was still in possession of substantial rights, and in which, despite the often high-handed policy of the emperors in church matters, Catholic religion was actively protected and fostered by the state. The reconstruction of the Hapsburg Empire has been regarded by the Holy See as an essential barrier against the spreading of Protestantism from the north, of Communism from the east, and of Greek orthodoxy from the south. This is a vital issue from the point of view of Catholic interests.

But why the United States should encourage the hopes of the Hapsburg pretender and help him get back into the limelight is another diplomatic mystery. It was soon after the landing of our troops in North Africa, that the official acceptance by Mr. Stimson, the Secretary of War, of the offer made by Mr. Otto Hapsburg to raise an Austrian legion in America was announced. When confronted with the uproar caused by this move, Mr. Stimson offered explanations in which it was clear that he himself did not believe. The fact was that Otto had thrown his hat into the ring under the auspices of the United States; no palliative could camouflage the real meaning of the gesture. The State Department disclaimed any responsibility in the affair; the decision evidently came from President Roosevelt, who acted through the War Department as the commander-in-chief of the United States Army.

This action of the War Department came, as we have already noted, close upon the heels of our landing in North Africa, and this latter event came shortly after the mission of Mr. Taylor to the Vatican. Were these events interrelated? Was Otto's new emergence into the limelight the price paid by the United States for some favor received from the Vatican? Or was it a gracious gesture of appeasement to calm Pius XII's irritation over, and fears concerning, our close connection and cooperation with Soviet Russia? Most likely this was the real motive prompting the wise men in Washington to take this step. Its meaning is clear. Mr. Taylor will perhaps some day tell us to what extent he engaged the United States to support the restoration of the Hapsburg Empire, a matter so fraught with momentous consequences for all Europe.

Of all the problems of European post-war reconstruction, the one of most concern to the Holy See is that of Italy. Having failed to keep the Fascist regime out of the war, and having failed to bring about a peace of compromise, the Vatican, after the Italian disasters in Greece, Cyrenaica, and Ethiopia, when it became clear that an exhausting war was inevitable, began to share with the Foreign Office in London and with our State Department, and perhaps fostered, the hope that Italy could be detached from the Nazi alliance and led to conclude a separate peace. In spite of the fact that Hitler took the precaution of putting Italy virtually under Nazi control, the hope for a separate peace continued to be cherished by the British and American governments.

If such a hope had materialized, the solution of the Italian problem would have offered no difficulties at all; the peace agreement would have been made with the existing government, which certainly could not have been expected to commit suicide. Fascism with or without Mussolini would remain in power. This solution would have suited the program of the Vatican to perfection. This program has two aims: first, to prevent at all costs the establishment in Italy of a government controlled by anti-Fascists, be they Communists, Socialists, or democrats; second, to secure the preservation of the Lateran agreements, both the Treaty and the Concordat, made under the Fascist regime. These two aims are interdependent and they can be realized by preserving not only the Savoy Monarchy but the authoritarian government as well, no matter under what name.

On February 12, 1943, President Roosevelt stated that no nation in the world "is going to set itself under the Fascist form of government," and that this war is not being fought with even the "remotest idea" of putting Quislings in power. These words, together with the proclamation made at Casablanca in which the President and Prime Minister Churchill jointly declared that only the "unconditional surrender" of the Axis powers would put an end to the war, must have caused considerable apprehension in high Vatican circles. These declarations not only sounded as if all prospects for a separate peace of compromise with Fascist Italy were to be ruled out, but they also boded ill as to what kind of government would be established in Italy when victory comes to the United Nations. Did they mean that Italy was going to be free to choose her own government? Did they mean that Soviet Russia would be allowed to impose its terms upon the whole of Central Europe? Of course, the absence of Stalin from the Casablanca meeting and the comments made by both Allied and Axis presses on it confirmed the general impression that there were divergencies and a degree of mutual diffidence among the big European three. This was somewhat reassuring to the Vatican. Nonetheless, it had reason to be apprehensive. Of prime importance was the fact that the plans which had been made in the expectation of a separate peace with Italy's present government had to be revised in the light of "unconditional surrender."

Archbishop Spellman was then sent to Rome on a new mission. It is significant that the visit of the Archbishop to the Vatican in March, 1943, coincided with the sweeping changes in Mussolini's cabinet, by which his son-in-law Ciano was removed as head of the Foreign Office and appointed ambassador to the Vatican.

Did Mussolini see the handwriting on the wall? Being hopelessly under the Nazi thumb, he continued to send Italian youth to be killed for Germany. After all, the war was not over yet, and there was still a possibility, although it was slim, that if German resistance could be prolonged several years, there would be a compromise peace in spite of all declarations to the contrary. On the other hand, Mussolini knew only too well that the downfall of Germany would be his own end. It was natural that he should start making plans for saving the lives and fortunes of his family. In view of the connections between the Vatican and Washington, the ambassadorship to the Holy

See had become the key position for any plan of salvage. The Vatican might even be a convenient, though temporary, place of refuge for Mussolini and his family if the time came when all other avenues of escape were cut off. The embassy to the Vatican had thus to be entrusted to a member of the family. Who better than Ciano could have been selected to tell Archbishop Spellman the Duce's troubles and to convey to Mussolini and the King the plans of the Vatican? It is reasonable to surmise that such plans as may have been under advisement for a long time by the Vatican and our State Department have taken a more concrete form during this last period, in which the English and American armies are getting nearer to Italy as a result of the African campaign.

One of the most important problems is the choice of a man to head the new regime. After the search for an Italian Darlan proved fruitless, and after all prominent Fascists—politicians, diplomats, generals, and even mummified premiers—had been appraised, it seems that the choice finally fell on Dino Grandi, the former Fascist ambassador to England. At the same time that Ciano was sent to the Vatican, Grandi was relieved of his cabinet post as Minister of Justice and thus ceased to have any responsibility in the Fascist administration. American newspapers, which have always described Grandi as "a pronounced anglophile," though there is no evidence for this and plenty of evidence to the contrary, interpreted Grandi's dismissal from the cabinet as a clear sign of a final breaking down of the Fascist high ranks, and of an open opposition to Mussolini led by Grandi.

But a few days after Archbishop Spellman's arrival at the Vatican, where, as the newspapers informed us, he had long colloquies with several members of the diplomatic corps accredited to the Holy See, an official communiqué was issued in Rome on March 25, 1943, announcing that the King had bestowed on Grandi the Supreme Order of the Annunziata. This is Italy's highest decoration, reserved to persons of royal blood and to statesmen who have rendered extraordinary services to the kingdom, such as the acquisition of new territories. The wearer of the insignia of the Order of the Annunziata becomes a "cousin to the King" and takes precedence over all other dignitaries at the Court. Of course American newspapers discovered in this action of the King another evidence of "a renewed friction existing between Victor Emmanuel and Premier Mussolini" (*New York Times*, March 26, 1943). Newspaper correspondents certainly know that Mussolini himself is a "cousin to the King" and that, as Premier and Duce of Italy, he must not only have known of the award to Grandi, but have given his consent to it. Likewise, they could not have failed to notice that, while Grandi is no longer a member of the cabinet, he has retained nonetheless the strategic position of President of the Chamber of Fasces and Corporations, a supposedly representative body, which may be called to play a part in the crisis when it comes.

The inference from all these facts is clear: Grandi is the choice of the Vatican to head the Italian government after Mussolini; our State Department through Archbishop Spellman has given its consent to this choice. It has also been accepted by Mussolini and the King as the only alternative left after the debacle. Indeed, this is the only way left open to them to save what can be saved of Fascism.

The question of possible Russian predominance in after-war Europe, which is of so much concern to the Holy See, was also connected with Mgr. Spellman's mission to Rome. A Catholic journalist, Mr. Michael Williams of the *Commonweal*, at first informed the American readers that the mission of the Archbishop of New York was that of making arrangements for the escape of the Pope to the Canary Islands or perhaps to New York. But later on Mr. Williams announced that Mgr. Spellman intended to go to Moscow where he was sure to obtain, if not the outright conversion to Catholicism of Mr. Stalin, at least

a Soviet concordat with the Holy See. It is natural that the Holy
See should be apprehensive of the Soviet danger in post-war
Europe; there are many others who share the same fear for non-
religious reasons. It is natural also that the Holy See, in view of
the close connections now existing with our government, should
be anxious to see some agreement reached with both England
and America as to the ways and means to offset that danger.

It is very doubtful whether any further pressure on the Soviet
government to make more definite promises than its previous
statement of October, 1942, would be successful. The precaution
which the Holy See would like to see adopted is undoubtedly
that suggested by the London *Fortnightly,* of "nursing a series
of authoritarian states in central and southern Europe, beginning with Italy."

It seems that there is one more point in the plans of the
Vatican which has been little advertised, for it could not be
made public so long as Mussolini rules Italy. Pius XI, while
the Lateran agreements were in the making, gave up his predecessor's idea of requesting an international guarantee of the Treaty
which was then being negotiated between the Holy See and the
Italian government. To be sure, Mussolini, as the head of a
totalitarian state, could never have accepted an international
guarantee of his accord with the Papacy, because it would have
meant in practice that the guarantor powers had the right to
interfere with Italy's policies at any time, whether the Vatican
asked for their intervention or not.

It would seem that the experience of these last years and the
strict interpretation given by Mussolini to the article of the
Treaty concerning papal aloofness from all political quarrels and
conflicts among states, not to mention the Vatican's fear that a
democratic regime might be established in Italy, have resulted
in a change of heart in the inner circles of the Holy See as regards
the question of a guarantee of Vatican City and of the sovereignty of the Pope by an international organization.

In February, 1940, at the time of Mr. Taylor's first appearance in Rome as ambassador and of Mr. Welles' visit to the Pope, the Rome correspondent of the *New York Times,* Mr. Matthews, stated that, "according to the best Vatican sources, the Pope would favor the participation of the State of Vatican City in such an international organization." This information was more than premature. The Vatican goes slowly in such matters and would not make any decision before seeing what kind of international organization was being formed. But if the rumor came from Vatican sources, it was certainly indicative of the trend of thought prevailing there on this point. We will deal with this question later on: but it is safe to say that only an Italian government such as the one desired and hoped for by the Vatican could accept an international guarantee of the Lateran agreement. This could be imposed and maintained only by coercion. Moreover, this coercion could only be effectively applied by the United States. Thus, the American government, though not possesssing the power to legislate in religious matters for its own people, would become the bodyguard of the Vatican abroad.

All these plans and policies of the Vatican are consistent with its principles, its interests, and its traditions. But why have President Roosevelt and the State Department embraced these plans, which do not seem to coincide with the interests and the traditions of the United States? As long as the cooperation of Washington with the Vatican had the limited purpose of trying to keep Fascist Italy out of the war, there was a certain justification for it, though it was clearly a hopeless undertaking. These plans, or "provisions for peace," however, concern the future of Europe; in other words, they concern the future of both American and world peace. Why should the government of the United States mortgage this future for the sake of a religious power which—to mention but one vital point—cannot and will not assume any political responsibility for its success or its failure?

We wish we knew a satisfactory answer to this question. We

wish we knew for sure by what process President Roosevelt came
to the conclusion that the interests and views of the Vatican
coincide with those of the United States. Perhaps the first idea
which occurs to anyone familiar with American politics is that
political expediency was behind these dealings with the Vatican
in the beginning. The political power of the Catholic Church
in this country has grown lately by leaps and bounds; it has become aggressive, even boisterous. Politicians of both the Democratic and the Republican parties fear it. President Roosevelt's
New Deal did not meet with the approval of the rank and file
of the Catholic hierarchy, and the refusal of that body to silence
Father Coughlin and stop his personal attacks upon the President
must have caused some uneasiness in the White House. A policy
of appeasement was indicated. The American blockade against
Loyalist Spain was the first step on that slippery ground. As
usual, however, this concession served only to whet the Catholic
appetite for more.

When President Roosevelt, foreseeing that the European crisis
could not fail to engulf the whole world, began to push ahead
his policies of preparedness and aid to Britain, he found himself
confronted with the compact opposition of the American Catholic
hierarchy, of the clergy and of large Catholic groups. The idea
of establishing an open tie of friendship with the Vatican must
have appeared under such circumstances to be a master stroke
of political strategy, a stroke which should not only smother
Catholic isolationism, but range the whole Catholic vote on the
side of the administration. We have seen, however, that Catholic
opposition did not abate; indeed, it assumed a more acute form
in connection with aid to Russia and did not disappear altogether even after Pearl Harbor. Neither does it seem, as far as
we can judge from the elections of 1942, that President Roosevelt succeeded in gaining a strong hold upon the Catholic vote.
Will he get it in his eventual attempt to secure a fourth term?

Political expediency, however, especially not crowned by a
brilliant success, is not sufficient to explain this policy of the

administration. President Roosevelt has gone so far in his dealings with the Vatican as to suggest that in following this policy
he is moved by personal conviction. We have reason to suppose
that he sincerely believes that the path which he is following
is the best, both for the European countries and especially for
Italy and for American interests.

Such a conviction in a statesman as able and intelligent as
Mr. Roosevelt undoubtedly is can be explained only by assuming
that he starts from the premise that in the Latin countries of
Europe—which are supposed to be Catholic by definition—the
Vatican has immense power and unlimited influence over the
people. He believes, perhaps, that in those countries the Catholic hierarchy and the clergy, when mobilized by an order from
the Vatican, will be able, in their turn, to mobilize the masses
and lead them wherever they wish, as they do, for instance, in
French Canada. This is a dangerous illusion, the result of little
familiarity with the entire history, the modern history in particular, of those countries.

To dispel such an illusion one has only to consider that in
Spain the Catholic Church was disestablished by the Republic
and was able to regain its official position only after four years
of bloody civil war, won by a minority of rebels with the assistance of foreign armies. In spite of the official blessings and
lavish praises bestowed by the Pope on the rebels from the very
beginning, the Spanish people fought to the last ditch.

In France, where the separation of Church and State already
existed, the Church could regain a position of privilege only
after the colossal military defeat which put the nation under
German control and put into power a sub-government under
the leadership of a senile general who was nothing more than
a reactionary puppet in the hands of unscrupulous Quislings.
The Vatican blessed Pétain and announced that his regime was
the beginning of a "spiritual rebirth" of France. Events have
shown what to think of Pétain and his regime.

In Italy for over sixty years the Vatican tried to undermine the national independence and the political unity of Italy and to bring about the disintegration of the free regime by forbidding Catholics to vote in parliamentary elections, or to take part in the central government. According to papal pronouncements, deputies and members of the cabinets were supposed to incur the excommunication of the Church. Certainly no one can say that the Italian Catholics, that is to say, almost the whole population, paid much attention to papal protests and papal comments. To wrest a concordat from Catholic Italy the Vatican had to wait for the advent of a dictatorship based on what the Pope considered "pagan" principles, and which was willing to bargain only for the purpose of "fascistizing" the Church. The Italian people had no part in these agreements between the Vatican and the Fascist regime.

American politicians forget that the Latin countries have a long tradition of anti-clericalism, which is a political feature of almost the whole history of Italy. It represents the reaction of the people against the claims of the clergy in general and of the Papacy in particular to control the political life of Italy. The burghers of the Italian mediaeval Communs who built the beautiful cathedrals dotting Italian cities and town, monuments of their faith and their artistic skill, were the same people who often besieged their bishop in his palace, imprisoned or chased away their priests, and challenged the pope and his excommunications. Modern anti-clericalism had its justification in the fact that the Papacy was, to the last, the stumbling block in the way of Italy's national unity and could maintain its temporal power only with the support of foreign armies. After national unity was achieved, anti-clericalism was kept alive by the hostility of the Vatican and the Church, as well as of the reactionary "clericals," to the national regime.

One might think that this anti-clericalism would have disappeared in Fascist Italy after the Lateran agreements. It has not, and not only has it not disappeared, but there is evidence that it has become even more sharp and anti-religious. Could it have been otherwise in a regime based on "pagan" principles? The deterioration of religious life was denounced by no less an authority than Cardinal Lavitrano, chairman of the Committee of Bishops in charge of the Catholic Action in Italy. In February, 1940, he sorrowfully announced that, according to statistics gathered by his office, "sixty per cent of the Italians do not hear Mass on religious holy days and only twelve per cent of Italian men receive the Holy Communion on Easter" (*Time,* February 16, 1940). All these Italians who do not observe such fundamental obligations of the Catholic faith certainly cannot be considered practicing Catholics.

More recently, at the end of March, 1943, the Fascist Archbishop of Milan, Cardinal Schuster, in an article in the Catholic Fascist newspaper *L'Italia* published in Milan made the startling admission that anti-clericalism has gained ground under the Concordat, that some people were "indulging in profanation of the Eucharist" and that others had made "an organization to promote blasphemy" (*New Republic,* May 17, 1943). We shall see later on the results of the so-called religious education imparted in Fascist schools.

It is in the light of these facts that those who have now in their hands the destiny of post-war Italy must judge of the strength of the religious, social, and political forces at play in the Italy of tomorrow. To accept blindly, as President Roosevelt, who is not personally familiar with the Italian situation, seems to have done, the misleading reports of diplomats and of ecclesiastical advisors is a serious mistake.

Diplomats, themselves unfamiliar with the peculiar features of Italian Catholicism, rely often on impressions received in aristocratic drawing rooms and at tea parties. The clerical advisors, brought up in the American College in Rome, reflect more often the ideas and the wishful thinking of Roman ecclesiastical circles than they do the feelings and aspirations of the Italian masses.

There may be other, perhaps more subtle psychological elements which might have concurred in determining President Roosevelt's choice of a policy based on the premise that the interests and purposes of the Vatican coincide with those of the United States, and that the welfare of post-war Italy may be best secured by carrying out the plans of the Vatican.

To be sure, the effective religious Catholic forces in Italy are not to be overlooked or underestimated in the Italy of tomorrow. The Vatican itself, if it could be persuaded to give up its hostility to modern democracy, could be a strong force in rebuilding the Italy of the future. We have confidence in the progressive Catholic forces and in their readiness to collaborate under a regime of liberty. But the history of the past has taught us that such a regime will find the Vatican filled with distrust and hostility.

V. The Old and the New Generations

1. The Pre-Fascist Political Parties

WHEN the mistakes which have been made and may still be made in dealing with the Italian problems have been described, one question remains to be answered: *what to do with Italy?* Which are the solutions we would recommend for those problems?

Whoever tries to visualize the psychological reaction of the Italian people to their present tragic situation should think of a person caught in the spirals of a terrific sandstorm on the Sahara Desert and tossed around in a hot, thick atmosphere of yellow dust with no possibility of orientation or escape. Nobody knows what the configuration of the landscape will be, or what the shape of things will be when the storm is over. Neither can we foresee the direction in which the political forces will lead Italy after the debacle of Fascism. Perhaps it is not very wise to indulge in over-optimistic or over-pessimistic guesswork.

Of one fact at least we may be certain. Pre-Fascist Italy is dead and cannot be revived, no matter how strong may be the nostalgia of some of the men and groups of men belonging to the old generation.

The various political parties into which the Italian people were divided before Fascism seized the power, no longer exist. During the twenty long years of Mussolini's dictatorship, most of the leaders of those parties have either died or sunk into obscurity. Those few among them who found a refuge in foreign countries, and who are still alive, have been cut off for a long time from any direct contact with the Italian people and hence their activities have had little repercussion in Italy. As for those who made up the memberships of these parties, some joined Fascism at the very beginning and became traitors to their former beliefs. Others gave up reluctantly and, by adapting themselves to the new situation, obeying orders, and asking no questions, made a living.

Many others remained faithful to their political principles and opposed the regime by passive resistance. With the passing of time and the dying of all hopes of a change in government, some of these, too, gradually sank into political apathy. Others not only remained faithful to the political beliefs but carried on, insofar as they were able, such anti-Fascist activities as opportunity afforded. The most daring of these underground fighters were caught in the net of the secret police and taken out of circulation.

By way of a broad generalization we may say that the entire large class of reactionaries and conservatives, big business men, bankers, great landowners, the upper clergy, aristocrats of wealth and title, and a large section of the upper bourgeoisie were from the beginning or became afterwards, with few exceptions, firm supporters of the Fascist regime. It is enough to glance over the list of Fascist officialdom, especially of the *podestà,* or administrators of cities and towns; there, side by side with those of the Fascist parvenus, we find most of the names registered in the heraldry of Italy.

As Don Sturzo remarks, the strictly reactionary policy of Mussolini "was supported by three groups of persons—the industrialists, who feared a renewal of the workers' movement; the big landowners who feared a renewal of agricultural agitations—as an aristocracy with resounding titles they gave a significant political dinner in homage to Mussolini—and finally, the clericals, whose little hour of success was firmly, and is, bound up with the destinies of Fascism" (*Italy and Fascismo*, New York, 1926, p. 200).

In pre-Fascist days, most of the men of this class were scattered throughout the various political parties. They were to be found chiefly in the conservative and clerical groups, as well as among the democrats; later they crept into the Populist Party. Their main function in the liberal parties was to block, when they could, or at least slow up, the progressive programs and activities of the more advanced members.

It is reasonable to suppose that all these reactionary groups which made common cause with Fascism shun the idea of going back to the political organizations of pre-Fascist times. Their hope, if they have any left, must be to unite in a new conservative group strongly backed by the upper clergy and perhaps also by foreign armies; thus, they might well prevent a new democratic regime in which social and economic reforms contrary to their class interests would undoubtedly be fostered. In post-war Italy these reactionary groups will not be able to function as they did in the political life of pre-Fascist Italy; either they will be put in power as a new out-and-out reactionary party, or, if a progressive, democratic regime is established, the foundations of their power as a class will be destroyed and they will become impotent.

The party which for the sake of convenience we may call democratic was in reality a motley aggregation of various groups divided not so much by their programs as by their allegiance to different political leaders. If we may judge from the results of Parliamentary elections, this party had the support of the majority of the population. This support came chiefly from the middle class—professional men, public officials, teachers, small landowners, farmers, tradesmen—people who either had democratic leanings or who, for less idealistic reasons, sent to Parliament prominent local politicians, usually lawyers and property owners. This party, which in some measure represented a continuation of the old Left that had held the power with only brief interruptions since the late seventies of the nineteenth century, was for the most part progressive and enacted much social legislation for the improvement of the lower classes. To be sure, they did so under the pressure of the Socialist Party, but, even so, they often took the initiative in broadening the scope of the regime's free institutions.

As is the case of many, if not all, political parties the world over, the moral level of their methods and manipulations was not high, and corrupt practices during elections were not infrequent. Above all, they proved inept and irresponsible when the Italian nation was faced with the greatest crisis of its history up to that time: the post-war crisis which culminated in the Fascist *coup de main* of October, 1922. The fault lay both in the system and in the men, though more in the latter than in the former. Even so, the methods of democracy as represented by the system fell into complete discredit with the nation, and it is not at all desirable that this system, as it was in those days, be revived. The old generation is perfectly aware of this; only a few impenitent worshippers of the past may delude themselves into thinking it will come back. If the Italian people have learned something, as we think they have, from twenty years of dictatorship, the new Italian democracy will not be a revival of the old pattern with its amorphous liberalism and its mongrel institution known as a constitutional monarchy. It will be a new creation, which will not hesitate to discard the fetishes of the past.

The Italian Socialist Party, was organized in the early nineties of the last century mainly by intellectuals under the influence of Marxian theories. To that movement must be given the credit for having broken the iron ring which held in ignorance and abject submission the working classes.

In spite of stubborn opposition from all other political groups, labor unions were formed, Socialist deputies were elected to Parliament, and in time the strength of the Socialist Party and its pressure on public opinion forced the government to introduce much-needed social legislation.

Born and brought up in the cult of Marxian ideologies, the Italian Socialist Party assumed a puritanical attitude of non-cooperation with the parties of the "bourgeoisie," and refused under any conditions to assume the responsibilities of government in coalition with other parties. The Socialists wanted all or nothing and waited expectantly for the proletarian revolution that was going to deliver everything into their hands. In the light of history this seems to have been a mistake. Another serious weakness of the Socialist Party was that it centered its interest especially in the working classes of industrialized northern and central Italy, neglecting the large rural classes of the South, and often ignoring them for the sake of the former.

The disadvantages which accompanied this "isolationism" became so apparent that gradually a Right-wing Socialist group emerged, Socialist Reformists who had strong support in the General Confederation of Labor. At the other extreme emerged another group, the ultra-revolutionary or Communist wing. It was in this divided condition that the Socialist Party faced the crisis which followed World War I. Rent by internal dissensions, its various tendencies pulling in opposite directions, the Socialist Party wavered between revolution or no revolution. Meanwhile, strikes and riots disturbed the economic life of the country. The fact that there was no revolution is largely to the credit of the leaders of the Reformists and also of many of the would-be revolutionary group which opposed the program of the noisy but impotent Communist minority. Finally, the Reformists and the Communists both broke away from the Socialist Party and formed separate autonomous parties. This secession cleared the air but it came too late. Confronted with the prospect of an imminent coalition of the Reformists, who had a considerable following in the labor unions, with the Populist Party and the democratic liberal groups, the Fascists (indirectly helped by Pius XI, who had forbidden the Populists to join the coalition) marched on Rome. In the crisis created by the Matteotti murder neither the Reformists nor the Revolutionary Socialists dared take the initiative against the tottering Fascist regime. This marked the end of the Socialist Party, which was dissolved and proscribed by the Dictatorship.

A bold program of social and economic reform must be adopted by post-war Italy as an indispensable prerequisite for rebuilding the life of the country. But certainly the old men of the Socialist Party, who have not discarded their narrow mentality, their spirit of non-cooperation and their petty doctrinal slogans cannot be expected to perform the vital task of directing Italy's new destiny. Their past leaders, men who were respected and loved, like Turati, Treves, Prampolini, Morgari, are dead. Others like D'Aragona, Reina, and Canepa sold out to Fascism.

A Socialist Party, freed from the prejudices of narrow sectarianism and inspired by a broader vision of national and international problems, will have a function to perform in the Italy of tomorrow. But it will be, root and branch, a new formation.

The third important political party of the pre-Fascist period was that of the Populists. They were the last in the field, having been organized in 1919 under the leadership of the able, honest, and well-intentioned Sicilian priest, Don Luigi Sturzo. The membership of this party was supposedly recruited from the Catholic ranks, though the Party as such had no religious label.

Its program was in fundamental harmony with the principles of democracy and it claimed to embody those currents of thought which, at the time of Leo XIII, had given rise to the movement of so-called Christian democracy. In Don Sturzo's plan, however, Leo's vague notion of charity and benevolence towards the lower classes took a more definite aspect. What was needed was not so much Christian charity as political democracy and social justice in the truest sense. Pius X had repudiated this interpretation of democracy, but times had changed and after the first World War the Vatican was not averse to giving it a trial.

The constituency of the Populist Party was large from the beginning, for it had gained a compact following among the rural classes, especially in northern Italy. All of them soon organized into "white" labor unions, which, though less numerous than the "red" unions, had considerable power. The party appealed also to many people of the middle and professional classes.

Organized almost in a hurry, the party was not conspicuous for coherence in its policies. There were within it three conflicting tendencies. On the Right stood the old clericals, remnants of the reactionary aristocrats who had dominated the first Catholic organizations. This group had opposed the Christian democracy of Leo XIII and had again acquired ascendancy under Pius X. Its members disliked Don Sturzo and his program and in time allied themselves with Mussolini in bringing about the disintegration of the party. On the extreme Left were the "radical" Populists who advocated measures and methods of action so similar to those of the Socialists that they were nicknamed "White Socialists." Between the two stood Don Sturzo and his close followers, who were liberal enough to avoid being clericals, their religious orthodoxy notwithstanding, but not radical enough to become Socialists. The backbone of the party was made up of numerous social and economic institutions, cooperatives and clubs organized by the local clergy in both rural and urban districts.

This source of strength was at the same time the main cause

of the party's failure to function with the necessary autonomy and with sufficient elasticity to enable it to meet the extraordinary needs of the post-war crisis. The Populists had a unique opportunity for becoming a force of primary importance in Italian politics, for they were in a position to seize and hold the balance of power between the other two leading parties, the Democrats and the Socialists, neither of which could achieve alone a majority large enough to control the government effectively. But in spite of the able leadership of Don Sturzo, many of the party's representatives in Parliament, not a few of whom had discovered they were Catholics only on the eve of the elections, were opportunists with no clear notion of what they wanted except the defense of their class interests or personal advancement. These men constantly weakened the party by compromising where it would have been better to remain steadfast, and by assuming a rigid attitude of non-compromise when it was fatal to do so.

The fundamental weakness, however, of the Populist Party lay in an organic disability which had affected it from birth. The party had been organized with the tacit permission of Benedict XV on condition that it was not to be a Catholic party in name, though it had a Catholic membership, and that it should be an autonomous political group for which neither the Vatican nor the Church were to assume any responsibility. In reality, it could not avoid being bound by invisible ties both to the Vatican and the Catholic hierarchy. Its fortunes depended to a great extent upon the active support of the clergy, which held key positions in the organizations on which the party primarily relied.

Such being the case, it was only natural that Populist leaders, when making decisions in public affairs, had always to consider first the possible reaction of the high ecclesiastical circles and make sure that their disapproval was not incurred. It was also natural that the ecclesiastical hierarchy should often bring pressure to bear on the party's attitude in regard to specific problems. Don Sturzo made an honest effort to maintain the autonomy of the party, but he was forced to yield at times to this ecclesiastical pressure, and he incurred the displeasure of the Vatican and the hierarchy when he refused to do so. As a matter of fact, Benedict XV did not seem much pleased with the party during the last period of his reign, and his successor, Pius XI, deliberately smothered it.

If the experiment of the Populist Party means anything, it is that no party which is forced to remain in such an equivocal position regarding both its formal and its essential autonomy can be a constructive factor in the political life of a nation. A party like the old Populist Party, in which democrats and re-actionaries were mixed together pulling in different directions, is not a fit instrument for the political education of the people. Finally, a party which must look at the Vatican weathervane for the direction of the wind every time it wishes to make a serious decision lacks the qualifications so essential to the functions of parties in a democracy. The existence of the Populist Party depended upon the benevolent attitude of the ecclesiastical hierarchy and the Vatican. At the same time, the hierarchy and the Vatican disclaimed any influence on its policies and activities or any responsibility for its decisions. No party in such a position could survive a serious political crisis. The same thing happened in other countries: in Germany with Monsignor Gaas, in Austria with Mgr. Seipel, in Slovakia with Fr. Tiso, and in Jugoslavia with Fr. Korosech. In each case the party failed and the leader went over to the enemy; Don Sturzo alone did not betray.

The restoration of the old Populist Party in post-war Italy with the same old elements and the same misunderstanding as to its autonomy would be a calamity no less than would the revival of the other old political parties. In post-war Italy a party willing to adopt the progressive program of the defunct Populists will have a chance of success only if organized outside and in-dependent of the clergy. Moreover, it must be ready at all times to oppose any policy contrary to the principles and practical exigencies of a progressive democratic regime, no matter how strongly that policy is advocated by the Catholic hierarchy. There is an alternative, that of forming a strictly clerical party with the open support of the hierarchy and the Vatican, which should assume unequivocally the responsibility for its policies.

Brief mention must be made of another small party, which lived on the margin of the political life of Italy: the Republican Party. Mazzini and Garibaldi were republicans. There was a moment at the end of 1848 and the beginning of 1849 when it seemed that Italy's national unity could be achieved under a republican constitution. Most of the cabinet ministers and prime ministers in Italy from 1876 to 1891 were converts from republicanism who had accepted the House of Savoy as a useful medium for the achievement of national unity and the establishment of free institutions, though not as a representative of traditional and despotic legitimacy. A republican party remained in existence even after most of its members had joined the Monarchists. Its constituency was to be found chiefly in the Romagna, the former provinces of the Pontifical States, where the ideas of Mazzini had taken root and had survived these many years. It sent to Parliament a few deputies. The existence of this small group was a symbol of the vitality of the Mazzinian ideal and tradition among the Italians. We hope that this ideal will become a reality in the form of an Italian republic. If such should be the case, and the Italian majority should become republican, then the mission of this small party and of its pre-Fascist organization will have been completed. It can fold the little flag which it has so faithfully carried through two generations of monarchical rule and take its place under the larger national flag of a republican Italy.

These strictures against former parties do not mean, however, that the older generation, which grew up during the regime of free institutions, has no mission to perform in a free post-war Italy. Far from it! The men of that period, now in their fifties, when mental vigor is at its height, have the most important mission of all. Those among them who have suffered physical and moral tortures in Fascist prisons and places of confinement, those, more numerous, who have lived through the Fascist years in silence without yielding their souls to the masters and without cooperating actively with Fascism—those are the links between what is worth reviving of the past and the Italy of tomorrow. They carry with them in one form or another the ideals of liberalism, of freedom, of democracy, of social justice, which the new generation has had no chance to learn or experience. There will be many others of this old generation, men who were able to escape in time from Fascist violence and persecution and find a refuge in foreign countries, who will return to Italy. They have much to give.

In the history of the Italian Risorgimento, the political exiles of the revolutions which paved the way for Italy's independence, contributed greatly, after their return, to the political, intellectual, and technical regeneration and development of the new Italian nation. They were more fortunate. They had found, from 1848 to 1859, an oasis of freedom in the Kingdom of Piedmont under the constitutional government of men like Cavour. From the various countries of refuge they had flocked to Piedmont, where they had kept close contact with the Italian people, had held political offices, and had acquired valuable experience in free government. The political exiles of Fascist tyranny have not had this chance; in Fascist Italy there has been no oasis of refuge.

Even so, the knowledge they have acquired in foreign countries, their painful personal experience of how costly were the mistakes made by the old political parties, their love for Italy, now purified by suffering, and, most important, their full devotion to the ideals of liberty—all give them the right, and make it their duty, to contribute their share to the reconstruction of Italy. But it would be a great mistake for them to think that the destiny of Italy will be put into their hands, or for them to expect, as did the émigrés of the French Revolution, that they can wipe out twenty years of Fascism and just go back to the old way of life as if nothing had happened. When and if they go back to Italy, they will find a new world, a world which speaks a different language and thinks different thoughts.

The young generation will need guides and teachers of democracy. This task can well be performed by the men of the old generation, both those who remained to endure Fascist tyranny and those who went into exile. But they must try to understand the new generation, to be humble, sympathetic, patient, unselfish, and prepared to face difficulties and disappointments.

2. The New Generation: What of Them?

The Fascist dictatorship is twenty years old. During these twenty years a new generation has grown up under the Fascist system of education. Children have been carefully regimented from the age of six or seven until the time they are old enough to be enrolled in the Fascist militia or in some other Fascist organization. Throughout these formative years their heads were crammed with the principles that might makes right, that Mussolini "is always right," and that their duty was *to believe, to obey, and to fight.*

The Fascist totalitarian state saw to it that not even the memory of the old parties survived among them. They were told, day in and day out, that pre-Fascist democracy was rotten and that the men who ruled Italy under that system were without exception crooks, criminals, idiots, cowards and worse.

Yet the generation which was reared in the Fascist climate— men now in their twenties and thirties—will have to bear most of the burden of rebuilding Italy. How far has Fascist "education" perverted Italian youth? How deeply has Fascism penetrated the minds and souls of these young people? Have the events of these last years shaken their faith in Fascism and in their Duce?

A clear and definite answer to such questions would be of inestimable value in making plans for the reconstruction of post-war Italy. Unfortunately, the nature of the problem on the one hand, and the fact that in dictatorial regimes everyone must hide his true feelings on the other, forces us to rely solely upon whatever reasonable deductions we may draw from facts that are relevant to the problem.

The various books, already too numerous, recently published in America by press correspondents who have returned from Italy, say little or nothing on this question. Apart from some generalizations of doubtful value, these American observers, who describe so accurately cocktail parties with eminent Fascists, seem to have lacked opportunity to evaluate the reactions of students and young people in general to the Fascist way of life and to the current events of Fascist history.

One useful source of information has been provided by the scores of young Italians who, after the enactment of the racial laws, were allowed to leave Italy and find refuge in England and America. Their reports, while differing in details, were almost uniformly optimistic as to the extent of growing unrest and dissatisfaction with the regime among Italian youth. Even though their judgment, as was to be expected, was somewhat affected by their unpleasant personal experiences, their reports contained much material worthy of consideration. Yet the present writers, who had occasion to interview several of these young men, could not help remarking that some of them, though embittered against Fascism, were still molded in the Fascist mentality; they had an inherent, ill-concealed contempt for the *homo democraticus* and looked upon free Americans as extravagant, conceited, but gullible simpletons, whose cultural level was lower than that of the Fascists. The Fascist method of educating children, especially the boys of the primary and secondary schools, has been, at least to a certain extent, effective.

A distorted vision of history and present conditions, of life and its significance, of the rights and duties of individuals, groups, and human society as a whole has given too many youths the firm impression that if they have a mission, it is on a par with that

of young lion cubs in the jungle. The strong emphasis placed
on discipline in Fascist schools would have been an asset, had
it been accompanied by a sense of moral responsibility and
by a recognition of the individual's proper place in the social
structure. Unfortunately, this discipline, based as it is on irrational motives and imparted in a formalistic authoritarian
and intolerant spirit, has become a distinct liability.

Another feature of the Fascist system of education which in
principle might have been a real improvement over the old
methods is the importance assigned to physical training in the
schools. In pre-Fascist schools physical education was insuf-
ficient and generally perfunctory; in Fascist schools it has reached
the other extreme, invading the whole system and overshadow-
ing other activities. Still worse, it has assumed a striking military
character. Mussolini taught the school child that he must always
have two pieces of equipment, "a book and a gun." Of the two,
the gun was more important than the book. It is the symbol
of a warlike education destined to provide spiritual and physical
training for future soldiers, who would be needed by the regime
in the conquest of the "Italian Empire."

In addition, the youngsters of the secondary schools, apart
from military drills, marches, and parades, were often mobilized
to stage political demonstrations on the streets and in the squares
of cities and towns, carrying placards and shrieking slogans
in accordance with their instructions. They were even led to
commit acts of violence and vandalism whenever the Fascist
government deemed it advisable to impress the world with a
show of the "'spontaneous unanimity" by which the Italian
people, inflamed with the irresistible and aggressive spirit of
Fascist Italy, supported the policies of the government.

Without being a master of pedagogy, anyone can see what the
results of such an educational system must be. On the one hand,
the cult of force and violence could not fail to awaken in these
youngsters the worst animal instincts, blurring all notions of
morality and preventing the forming of a moral conscience. On

the other hand, the system of strict compulsion, to which were added such features as the encouragement of espionage and secret denunciations, served to foster in them the evil habits of fear, hypocrisy, and contempt for truth and fair play.

Reared in this atmosphere with such principles for moral guideposts, the youngsters, scarcely able to think for themselves, could not possibly react unfavorably to their Fascist education, unless they happened to live in an anti-Fascist family environment or eventually to come in contact with and be influenced by nonconformist groups.

Yet, when all this has been said, there still remain reasons for hope and optimism. The results of Fascist education cannot be stated in general terms applicable to all classes of people. The Fascist system is well calculated to exclude from the advantages of a higher education all but the youth from wealthy and well-to-do classes. Rules, regulations, and exorbitant school fees make it difficult for the youth of working classes in town to get more than some training in the lower grades of a high school. As for the rural classes, still less frequently do they have a chance to go beyond the elementary school level. It is reasonable to think that Fascist education does not make a deep impression upon the boys of the lower classes, and that the environment in which they grow up both before and after they have left school, contributes most to the formation of their minds.

The problem of the youth of the lower middle classes is more difficult to analyze. In pre-Fascist times this class furnished, besides all small tradesmen and the artisans, the great bulk of "white collar workers," petty local functionaries, and skilled mechanics and technicians. Not a few of the more intelligent and able among them, by using to good advantage such educational facilities as were available, rose high in the professional ranks and became conspicuous personalities in the intellectual and political life of the country. In the Fascist regime, where there is no room for free competition, and where the system of regimented corporations does not even allow the people to elect their own officers, much less to direct their policies, the members of the lower middle classes could hardly earn a living unless they conformed. They have no incentive and no chance to better themselves except through special Fascist protection, which they can obtain only by a show of extra Fascist zeal. It is just because of this situation and because the lower middle classes have been more hit by economic conditions than the others that we expect their reaction against Fascism to be more general and more spontaneous. After all, from their ranks came many of the local leaders and a large part of the membership of the old Socialist organizations.

The problem confronting the youth of the upper classes, who get training in the universities and other institutions of higher learning, presents different features. Some of them come from reactionary families steeped in Fascist ideas, but many others come from the families of professional men who have paid only lip-service to Fascism. Their training in secondary schools has seldom failed to leave a deep impression upon their minds and characters. By the time they have reached the university, however, and have begun to widen the horizons of their knowledge and think for themselves, they almost inevitably experience an intellectual and moral crisis. The more intelligent and morally healthy among them, now that they have had the opportunity of learning history from other than exclusively Fascist sources, react strongly against their early training. Not only are they led to hate Fascism, but, if the occasion offers, they organize underground anti-Fascist activities. As early as 1932 a number of students of the University of Turin were discovered to be members of the secret society, *Giustizia e Liberta*. They were arrested and tried by the Fascist Special Tribunal and behaved heroically.

Nevertheless, the rank and file of students, though most of them have lost their naive faith in Fascist greatness and have discovered the hollow content of Fascist ideologies, are incapable of divesting themselves altogether of the prejudices against freedom and democracy which they imbibed in the Fascist schools. This combination of disillusionment and prejudice often leads them to become skeptical, cynical opportunists. They know that under Fascism, professional careers, personal success and well-being depend entirely upon Fascist party membership and Fascist profession of faith. They do not see any way to escape, nor do they actively seek any.

In 1938, one of the authors of this book, who had the opportunity to gather a considerable amount of evidence on the widespread hatred of Fascism among the Italian young people, could summarize his findings in the following words, which are even more applicable to the present:

Among the young people who have been brought up in the Fascist atmosphere for fifteen years and are now entering the Universities, there is a turmoil of restlessness, a sense of offended dignity, which bodes ill for the dictatorship. I am not addicted to wishful thinking, but I have drawn this fact from many sources of information, independent of each other and all so reliable as to dispel any doubt. In that section of Italian youth which is alive and active, Fascism has lost the match. Even among those who call themselves Fascists, young men who have sincere faith and are ready for sacrifice are scarce. Most of them are cynical. They tie up the donkey where the master tells them, but they will never do anything to defend either the donkey or its master. If this is the state of mind of the university students who, for so many years, have been kept under pressure in Fascist schools, we may be certain that something even more vast and more profound—something which we do not know about and which will probably develop in directions which we do not guess— is fermenting among the great multitudes, who, in town and country, escape the influence of the school, and whose living conditions have become tragic. One of the most striking features of present-day Italian life is that after sixteen years of victories, the Fascists are afraid. They have all the levers of command in their hands. No opposition can organize in a country where no one can talk politics with his neighbor without suspecting his neighbor. And yet the Fascists do not feel sure of what tomorrow may bring. They live always on the alert. They shout about their strength and their invincibility like a man in a forest at night who whistles to give himself courage. They have won all their battles. They have no certainty of winning the war. They feel themselves besieged by a mysterious force which, suffocated in one place, springs up in another, the force of ideas which have invisible feet with which they walk far, and invisible hands which take hold of the souls of men and suddenly uplift them. These unconquerable forces work against Mussolini.

The tragedy of Italian youth is not that they are Fascists; in fact, most of them are only negatively Fascists, in the sense that they lack the Fascist conviction and fanaticism and merely conform externally to Fascist practices, upon which their existence depends, in the same spirit in which certain Italians, who are Catholics only because they were born Catholics, conform externally to such practices of Catholicism as are required by society, remaining all the while free-thinkers and anti-clericals.

In pre-Fascist public schools no religious instruction was given, but in the elementary schools, if and when parents requested it, the opportunity was given them to provide for such instruction in the school building. It must be said that very few families ever requested this type of instruction. When, at the beginning of the Fascist regime, Mussolini made manifest his intention of becoming Pius XI's "man sent by Providence," compulsory religious education was introduced into the primary schools, but not into the secondary schools, the universities, and other institutions of higher learning. Pope Pius rejoiced in the thought that this religious instruction in the public schools was going to save the faith of Italian youth. Afterwards, when the Fascist totalitarian system of education came into being and Pius XI lost his battle with Mussolini as to what share the Church should have in that system, religious education in both elementary and secondary schools remained under regulations agreed upon by both parties in the Concordat. The Pope hoped that this religious instruction would serve as an antidote against the extreme Fascist doctrines to which the Church objected. But Pius XI could not have been ignorant of the fact that in the program compiled in 1923 for the schools by the philosopher Gentile, then Fascist Minister of Education, room had been made for religious instruction, not because it was deemed to have any intrinsic value, but only because it would "complement and crown" the whole educational structure, which was based on strict nationalistic principles. According to Gentile, Catholicism as the common and traditional religion of the Italian people, is a part of the national structure and must be maintained as an instrument of the national and Fascist element of cohesion, even if Catholic doctrine, according to Gentile's ideas, is merely a myth and, as such, has no real spiritual or moral value in human life.

When shorn of its philosophical jargon, Gentile's idea was nothing more than the old notion that religion is good for the poor in spirit and, therefore, for the masses, since it will serve to keep them more easily in subjection to their masters. From this point of view, Gentile's justification for religious instruction in the schools was the result of the same premises which led him to his famous philosophical justification of the *manganello*, the "bludgeon" which the Fascist gangsters used to refute the objections of their opponents. Gentile made his purpose very clear in introducing religious instruction in the public schools. He warned teachers of religion that they were expected to waste no time with the Catholic Catechism, but to outline the historical process of Italian Catholicism in the life of the nation.

As a matter of fact, we know from reliable reports made by both students and teachers that this religious instruction as imparted in the Fascist schools, has been, and still is, a joke played on the Catholic Church. If it has had any influence on Italian boys and girls, it has been in the direction envisaged by Gentile, who wished them to think that Catholicism is but the handmaiden of Fascism. The same textbook from which primary school children learn their elementary notions of grammar and history, and which are filled with phrases and mottoes glorifying Fascism and the Duce, also contains a few pages of religious instruction. In them, portraits of the Duce, on horseback, on foot, camouflaged as a marshal or an admiral, behind a plow, swimming—always with his chin in the air—rub elbows with the image of Christ. In the minds of the children, Christ and Mussolini are brothers who speak the same language and hold positions of equal importance in the scheme of the universe, perhaps with Mussolini a little in the lead, since he is, after all, a living being and Christ is somewhere behind the clouds. Moreover, according to Gentile's theory, this function of religion in the Fascist structure was limited to the first stages of education, because he expected that the children, the boys at any rate, when they grew up would discard all religious mythology and "ascend from a primitive, fantastic, and sentimental, to a philosophic conception of religion." What this philosophic conception consists in, Gentile has explained in his works, which are, by the way, on the Index of books forbidden by the Church.

One of the results of this linking together of religion and Fascism in children's minds is that when they reach a more mature age, if they lose their faith in Fascism, they also tend to lose their faith in religion. Since the Catholic and the Fascist doctrines are learned together as parts of the same system, they will hate them both with equal fervor. We shall not be at all surprised if many young Italians when they have become anti-Fascists will be found to have become anti-religious also.

In practice, according to reliable sources, religious instruction as imparted in Fascist secondary schools has not been taken seriously by students. Teachers of religion are often the butt of jokes on the part of their Fascist colleagues. Catholic periodicals such as the Jesuit *Civiltà Cattolica* have attacked the whole system again and again, criticizing severely teachers, textbooks, and methods. They ended, however, by consoling themselves with the remark that this kind of religious instruction was better than none. In actual fact, this distortion of religion was far worse than none at all. This seems to have been also the opinion of Pius XI, who, speaking in his encyclical *Non abbiamo bisogno* of the work done by Catholic chaplains in the *Balilla*, an organization of children in their teens, stated that even that minimum of effectiveness which the Church expected from the presence and the instruction of the chaplains was nullified by what he called "the environment." In conclusion he stated: "Recent events have proved beyond the shadow of a doubt that a few years have been sufficient to cause the loss and destruction of true religious sentiments and education."

The truth was perhaps even darker than the Pope knew. Religion in the Fascist schools, worse than destroyed, had been adulterated. The image of the crucifix had been hung once more in the schoolroom, but Christ was not there. He was being sent again from Herod to Pilate. The religion which was taught in the schools, instead of being a spiritual appeal to elevate the minds and souls of Italian youth to a higher moral and idealistic plane, assumed in their eyes the function of a mere pillar of the pagan Fascist State. How deep and widespread this moral and intellectual crisis has been, and still is, for Italian young people will be fully known only when Fascism is wiped out and these young people find themselves free to speak of their experiences. Then we shall know also what traces twenty years of Fascism have left on their souls. We are confident that Fascism has not robbed them of the qualities that an age-old civilization has impressed on the Italian people: a hatred of war and a deep sense of humanity.

The success of the Ethiopian campaign and the resistance to the would-be sanctions inflicted upon Italy by the League of Nations, both of which were adroitly magnified by Mussolini as examples of heroic Italian Fascism's ability to stand alone against fifty-two nations, inflamed the imagination of the Italian populace, and many a youth whose faith in Fascism had declined returned to the fold with his hopes and expectations revived. This was the period in which Fascism appeared to have finally conquered the Italian people. But it was only a short interlude, followed soon by the revelation of what Italy had really gained in Ethiopia, then by the Spanish expedition in which Fascist legions found for the first time, on the battlefield of Guadalajara, other Italians who fought against them and beat them. If these disillusionments were not enough, surely Hitler's rape of Austria in March, 1938, which brought about so much disappointment and bitterness among the rank and file of Italians, made it clear even to those who wished to be blind, that Fascism was leading Italy into the abyss. It marked a turning point in the history of Italy and it utterly demolished Mussolini's prestige.

The treaty of alliance with Germany, made public in May, 1939, and the military and moral disaster of the present war have done the rest. Britain and America do not need to wage a "war of nerves" as far as the Italians are concerned. Mussolini has accomplished this task himself. The Italians say: "If Hitler loses, we also are the losers; if Hitler wins, we are lost."

When this war is over, the youth of Italy will find itself immediately confronted with misery, humiliation, bitterness, not to speak of the more concrete fact of foreign armies in control of the country. What will we give them to relieve the misery, to soothe the bitterness, and to awaken new hopes? Will we wave before defeated eyes the flag of liberty and democracy? From the day on which Mussolini boasted that Fascism had trampled down the corpse of liberty, Italian youth has been taught that democracy was the refuge of scoundrels and criminals. Undoubtedly they know better now. But it will be of vital importance that the first contact of these young people with democracy should not be with a travesty of it when peace comes. They must be made to understand the spirit, the moral and civil values of the democratic system.

We are told that Americans are being trained in special schools so that they may be sent when the time comes to Italy and to other countries under military occupation, where they will hold executive offices in the provisional administrations. Theirs will be a task fraught with difficulties and heavy responsibility. They will come in close contact with all classes of Italians and will be looked upon as exemplifying our democratic ideals, manners, and education. What line of action are these representatives of America expected to follow? By what method have the teachers and pupils of these special schools been chosen? Why is this whole matter so shrouded in mystery? Is it a military secret, or is there something in this whole affair which might stir up public opinion?

From occasional indiscretions we gather that strange methods are followed in some of these schools. In one of them, for example, the pupils are supposed to learn how to "re-educate the Italians" by radio broadcasts, when the time comes for this "re-education." One of the teachers is a gentleman who has no other qualification than that of owning a beauty parlor and being an Italian. As a matter of fact, he speaks a Sicilian dialect. In one of his lectures he gave his audience a summary of contemporary Italian history which ran like this:

Under the liberal regime in Italy all cabinet ministers and members of Parliament were illiterate. There were two Socialist parties, one good and one bad. The good Socialist party was led by Mussolini, the bad one by Modigliani. There were also two Catholic parties, one good and one bad, the good one led by Don Bosco and the bad one by Don Sturzo. The good Socialist party and the good Catholic party made an alliance, put Mussolini in power, and Fascism saved Italy.

By way of interpreting these extraordinary statements, we may add that Modigliani was a Socialist much hated by the Communists and that Don Bosco, a saintly man, died in 1888 when Mussolini was five years old.

There are some strange misconceptions current about this matter of "re-educating" the Italian people. Everybody seems anxious to "re-educate" somebody else. Mussolini wanted to "re-educate" America, and he very nearly succeeded with his twenty years of "propaganda." The Vatican also wishes to "re-educate" America because, as Pius XII said, in most of our schools we have been brought up as infidels and pagans. In our turn, we wish to "re-educate" the Italians. The term itself "to re-educate" is unfortunate and will not be relished by the Italians or by any other European nation. By saying that the Italians need "to be re-educated in the ways of democracy," we are expressing a thought which is historically true and has no disparaging implication. Unfortunately, the matter of re-education is commonly regarded at present in much the same light as we think of missionary work among uncivilized peoples, and we are training teachers by the method we use to train our missionaries.

Political re-education of a people does not consist in teaching the grammar of politics or the theories of government. It consists first in giving them the opportunity of adopting a democratic system in their political life. Then they must be allowed time to conduct experiments for themselves in the principles and practices of democracy in action. It is fundamentally a process of self-re-education, which the people themselves must carry out under the guidance of leaders in whom they have confidence. Democratic propaganda spread through the medium of the press, the radio, and other sources is vital to this process of re-education. But when this work is carried on by foreign agents, it assumes the aspect of an imposition, or, more dangerously, of a calculated interference in domestic affairs which is neither disinterested nor altruistic.

We must not forget that Fascism, bad as it is, did not transform the Italians into savage brutes or automata of ruthlessness. There is no other school of liberty than liberty itself.

In our opinion, there is not much need to worry over the course the new generation will take in post-war Italy, so long as we keep our promises and fulfill expectations of the new order of political liberty, economic opportunity, and social justice which we have proclaimed to be our goal in the post-war world.

3. The Transition Period

The fundamental issue in our inquiry on what to do with Italy is whether we intend to destroy Fascism, root and branch; to help Italy start life once more on the solid foundations of liberty and democracy; and to let the Italians choose their own political system—or whether we intend to thrust upon them, willy nilly, a reactionary regime in order to protect the special interests of groups which are not working for the good of either Italy or America. It is because of the contradiction between what we promise in high-sounding official declarations and what we do through backstage intrigue that so many difficulties arise, and will continue to arise, in our international theatre.

The armed forces of the United Nations, among which those of Britain and the United States will have the last word in Mediterranean occupation, will not be able to occupy the whole Italian peninsula at one stroke. A crisis will be unavoidable in large sections of the country, between the moment of military breakdown and the time when the armed forces of the Atlantic powers have firmly established their control over the whole peninsula.

During that period of crisis, in both the occupied and still unoccupied sections, the men who have run the machine of the Fascist administration—a machine shattered and discredited by defeat but not yet demolished—will find themselves face to face with the members of the anti-Fascist underground groups, who will burst into the open. If the majority of the people joins these anti-Fascist groups, and a general upheaval takes place, unchaining the long-repressed hatred against Fascism, acts of violence, revenge, and destruction against Fascist leaders, and eventually against some ecclesiastics who have distinguished themselves for ardent Fascist zeal, are to be expected. It is natural that the Vatican should be apprehensive of this danger and should have planned in advance, and in accord with our State and War Departments, how to cope with such a possibility. Its plan is to keep intact the whole machinery of the Fascist state and of local administration. One condition necessary to the success of this plan is that the army remain faithful to the Monarchy and to its own chiefs, so that it will not hesitate to machine-gun the rebels.

It becomes obvious, then, why our diplomatic strategists in

Washington could not permit the formation, either in this country or elsewhere, of anti-Fascist legions. It becomes equally obvious why British authorities changed their policy of setting
apart the anti-Fascist Italian war prisoners, put them again under their Fascist officers, and did not allow any anti-Fascist propaganda among them. These anti-Fascist legions, were they to be
formed and taken to Italy at the time of the crisis, would certainly fraternize with the people in revolt and attract to their
side many soldiers of the regular army and even large sections
of the militia.

Such a development must be avoided at all costs, according
to the Vatican. Hence, our Washington strategists, no doubt in
compliance with Vatican insistence, have imported from British
prisoners' camps a dozen Italian generals captured in the Ethiopian and Libyan campaigns to work out with them the plans
of what the Italian army must do when Italy surrenders. It seems
that the Lend-Lease system provides for the export of goods from
America to England and at the same time for the export from
England to America of Fascist politicians, pretenders, and discredited generals. At the right moment, they might be flown to
Italy to have the privilege of machine-gunning the people in revolt, a task which would be very unpleasant for the American
army to perform.

Once the first attempt at general revolt has been quashed and
the American forces have got hold of all the key positions of communications and public services, order would be easy to maintain. While Mussolini and the highest Fascist leaders were running for safety to Spain, the old King would abdicate and his
son, the new King, would issue a proclamation promising the
restoration of the pre-Fascist constitution. Following a regular
procedure, he would invite the President of the Chamber of
Fasces and Corporations, which is supposed to have taken the
place of the old Parliament, and, therefore, to be a representative body, to act in the interim as head of the government. The
President of the Chamber of Fasces and Corporations happens

to be Dino Grandi, the man who, after Spellman's visit to the Vatican was made a "cousin to the King."

Meanwhile, all Fascist titles and emblems will have disappeared, a mass conversion will have taken place by means of which all former Fascists will appear as champions of the constitutional monarchy and will thus remain in control of all the offices in the central and local administrations. The Chamber of Fasces and Corporations will be called the Parliament. It will be convoked, together with the old Senate, and will give a unanimous vote of confidence and grant full emergency powers to Grandi and his cabinet, thus regularizing their position. Some of the extreme Fascist laws will be repealed, but, in fact, under the pretense of emergency, and under the guise of martial law, the government will continue to keep the press, the associations, the assemblies, and all labor and trade unions under strict control. What was formerly the Fascist militia will don a shirt of another color and take another name, but it will continue to act as the political police of the regime.

Thus protected by foreign armies of occupation, recognized by the United Nations as the "legitimate" government of Italy, supported in every way possible by the Vatican, and having several divisions of its own police force, the new regime could now proceed to the demobilization of the army and to a general disarmament. Having got a firm hold on the whole country, and having eliminated all opponents in the good old Fascist fashion, the government could postpone to the indefinite future a return to normalcy, and even take a further step. The so-called Parliament and the Senate, survivals of the Fascist period, would be put to work passing a series of "amendments" to the old constitution, by which the executive bodies would be given extensive powers and made independent of the whims of the legislative bodies. This would be called "the American system," thus saving the face of the Atlantic Charter, as well as the faces of all President Roosevelt's other proclamations.

In fact, following such a pattern as this, the old Fascist system, under a new name, and with only a few changes in matters of detail, will survive in its essentials with the same men, the same methods, and the same practices. Everybody will be happy except, of course, the crazy democrats and republicans who have come out of the underground or found a way into Italy from exile, making a nuisance of themselves. They will have to swallow the new by-product of Fascism, and if they do not do so with sufficient good grace, they will be dispatched to jail, or to the next world altogether, waving flags emblazoned with President Roosevelt's famous "four freedoms everywhere in the world." Peace be to their souls!

At this point, Mr. Sumner Welles, Under Secretary of State, will tell us not to worry, because "surface developments must not be taken as indication of the basic policy when they are in fact merely temporary steps in the process of achieving that policy" (Letter to Professor Ralph Barton Perry, *New York Times,* April 11, 1943). Of course, because of the "need for secrecy," Mr. Welles cannot explain fully why and how "surface developments" appear to lead in the precisely opposite direction to the "basic policy." Secrecy has always been the screen behind which the most astounding miracles of diplomatic alchemy have been concocted. As an evidence of the success of the devious and secret policies of the State Department, Mr. Welles hinted at the North African muddle, which seemed then to have taken a better turn. But was it also a diplomatic secret that Darlan was to be murdered by an aristocratic assassin?

As far as Italy is concerned, the plan of the State Department, which we have outlined, hinges primarily on the assumption that the Italian generals indoctrinated in Washington will be able to deliver the goods, that is to say, to swing the Italian army over to their side and render it willing to conclude its inglorious career—before being disbanded forever—by the supreme gesture of machine-gunning the Italian people in the streets and squares of Italian cities which will have been thoroughly shattered by British and American bombers. Will the Italian soldiers back from the battlefields and prisoners' camps be willing to commit such an act? We may well doubt that they will be in the mood for performing this ghastly task. Let us suppose that they refuse, that they shoot their generals and superior officers instead and join the people in revolt. What will the British and American military chiefs do then? Will they order British and American soldiers to turn on the civilian population—for the sake of the King, the Fascists, and the clericals? We have no answer to this inevitable, but dread question. The mere thought of such an occurrence fills our souls with anguish, and we are sure it would fill American soldiers and the American people with indignation. Would it not be wiser to make plans which do not entail even the remotest possibility of such a prospect?

Common sense suggests some considerations which might have value for those who know Italy, not through the drawing rooms of the Fascist aristocracy, nor through the libraries, archives, and museums where once they browsed, nor yet through the antechambers of the Vatican, but through its whole history and, much more, through intimate acquaintance with the present history and psychology of the Italian masses.

First of all, we must remember that the anti-Fascist forces now alive in Italy are represented by a large group of people who want liberty and free institutions. In a broad sense we may call them believers in democracy. Side by side with them there is a group of extremists whom, broadly speaking, we may call Communists. The Democrats are either isolated individuals who never joined the Fascist party, or who did so in a perfunctory fashion for practical reasons, but always remained aloof from all Fascist activities; or they are underground groups, mostly local, loosely bound together, without any central organization. They are the "Republicans," the Liberal Socialists, the Socialist, and the groups of *Giustizia e Libertà*. It seems that more recently groups of Christian-Democrats have broken away from the pro-Fascist "Catholic Action" and have started a movement of their own with underground anti-Fascist activities. The Communists are better organized and, above all, are well instructed in the tactics of revolution. When a crisis offers the opportunity, they mingle with all the other groups, irrespective of the latters' political ideas; they take advantage of their lack of cohesion and of central direction to bring about confusion and chaos, and thereupon seize key positions for themselves. Once this is accomplished, they turn upon their erstwhile associates, break them, and assume control of the government.

Will it be possible to prevent the anti-Fascist forces from coming into the open at the moment when the Allied armies set foot on Italian soil and the defense gives up the fight? And once these anti-Fascists come out into the open, will it be possible to prevent them from giving vent to their hatred of those who have oppressed them for twenty years, have murdered their brothers and fathers and sent thousands of boys to be killed in Russia fighting for the Germans? During the days or weeks which must pass before the army of occupation can get full control, many things will happen. Even if the democratic groups keep themselves in check and avoid excesses, the Communist groups will see to it that peace and order are not preserved.

In a personal dictatorial regime such as Mussolini has built up in Italy, the cohesion of the whole structure is secured only through a highly developed and highly centralized police system spreading its tentacles all over the country. The pivot around which the whole system revolves is the dictator himself. Once he disappears, the structure collapses. Policemen, secret agents, Black Shirts, and their helpers are efficient only so long as they feel sure of the power behind them, only so long as the machine works. When the moving power stops at its source, they think first of themselves and their own safety; either they disappear from circulation or go over to the enemy.

We do not share the optimism of the men in Washington who think that the transition from Mussolini to a regime such as they contemplate for Italy will take place as peacefully as if it were what Mussolini used to call "a change of the guard." We realize that a revolt of the Italian people, if it is actively opposed by the American and British armies of occupation, will have no chance, but certainly it will mean bloodshed. Since our wise men in Washington have decided that Italy must continue to be ruled by Fascists and according to Fascist methods, no matter under what guise, we would like to suggest in all humility a way to avoid useless bloodshed: Keep Mussolini in power, deal directly with him, and leave the whole machinery of the dictatorship intact. After all, it would make no difference. Mussolini has changed his political skin so many times that he would experience no difficulty in changing from a pro-Nazi Fascist to a pro-American Fascist, especially now, when he has nothing to hope for from Hitler and much to gain from allying himself with America. If what the American newspapers were saying in April, 1943, were true—that Hitler himself was eager to withdraw his troops from Italy and take refuge within the "European fortress" behind the Alps—then the Italian problem was already solved and there could be no need of our sending soldiers to run the risk of being fired on, as happened when they landed in North Africa. A little armistice with Mussolini, who was bound to be more than eager to meet us halfway, could have been concluded in a matter of hours, and Mussolini would have kept Italy in as perfect order as if it were a nunnery. No substitute for Mussolini could have performed this task without difficulty.

If, however, our leaders in Washington should change their views and decide to keep America's promise, which has kindled so much hope in the hearts of all the conquered and oppressed countries, and see to it that democratic regimes are established everywhere, then trouble, revolt, and bloodshed will be unavoidable. In Italy it will be simply impossible to make a democratic omelet without breaking a lot of Fascist eggs. Should our Washington cooks finally make up their minds to prepare the omelet, we might just as well begin breaking the Fascist eggs now and collecting the other necessary ingredients.

That the Italian people be psychologically prepared is of prime importance. We have been urging them to start a revolution, or demanding that they do something to earn the right to be helped, or advising them to stand pat and listen to current news. In the Atlantic Charter and, more explicitly, in President Roosevelt's speeches, we assured them that Fascism would be destroyed and a real democracy built upon its ruins. But at the same time we notified them that we share our ideals and purposes with the Vatican and make common cause with it, thereby linking ourselves with an institution which is known to patronize the Monarchy and a reactionary clerical-Fascist regime. When Archbishop Spellman went to Rome, the official broadcasters to Italy ceased altogether to attack Mussolini and Fascism; they confined their program to current news without comment. It is reasonable to assume that the broadcasts were following instructions.

Were such contradictory steps part of Mr. Welles' "surface developments in the process of achieving our basic policy"? Actually, their immediate result was the creation of a state of confusion and misgiving that could paralyze the Italian people, especially the anti-Fascist forces. On the other hand, this state of confusion was most helpful to the Communists, whose hopes of success depend precisely on a condition of chaos bewildering to anti-Fascist groups when the crisis comes.

An effort must be made to convince the Italian people, by actions rather than by vague, generic declarations, that our solemn promises concerning democratic liberties and institutions to be established after the war will be faithfully kept. We must revive their faith and their confidence, both of which were shaken by the Darlan muddle, and even more by our sinister backstage dealings with Fascist politicians through the intermediary of the Vatican, and by our consorting with Fascist generals.

If our intentions are pure, as we claim, and if we really mean what we say about liberty and democracy, why do we not reassure the Italian people about their future? Let us tell them frankly that we, for the sake of the world's peace, will not tolerate the establishment in Italy of any military or party dictatorship, red, black, or white; let us tell them that, apart from this, we have no interest in keeping the Savoy Monarchy in power, if they wish to get rid of it. Let us tell them, too, that we have no interest in the matter of their relations with the Church, provided freedom of conscience, religion, and association is fully guaranteed to all.

Once we have regained the confidence of the Italian people, we can expect their full cooperation when the crisis comes. Practical suggestions and instructions as to what we expect them to do at that time could be given through radio broadcasts or through the medium of leaflets dropped from the air or sent by other means. Such methods of warning the people as have been employed by the British and the Free French in France could easily be developed in Italy on an even larger scale. The danger, so much to be feared, of a bloody revolution following on the heels of the Fascist collapse would thus be reduced to a minimum. Any contemplated plot to establish a dictatorship of the Left would be discouraged by our declaration that we would not tolerate it and by the encouragement which we would thus give the forces opposing all types of governments based on the absolute and intolerant rule of any one political party.

Our wise men in Washington, and the American press which follows in their wake, have been convinced that British and American armies landing in Italy will be welcomed by the Italians with triumphal arches, waving flags, and streets strewn with flowers. The Italian people are in no mood to justify this unwarranted optimism of our press. As far as the British are concerned, we must realize that from 1935 the ungrateful Mussolini, who owed so much to the British Tories, carried on a very effective anti-British propaganda. To be sure, there was no anti-American feeling in Italy until recently, but the present complete identification of America with Britain in the war in the Mediterranean, the idiotic disparagement of Italian soldiers in our press, our contradictory statements and policies concerning the future of

Italy, and above all, American bombing of the southern cities—all have done much to create a current of hatred against the Americans. In this anti-American work, the Fascist press and Mussolini, who revels in insulting President Roosevelt, "the Jew of the White House," have been joined by some high ecclesiastical dignitaries, such as Cardinal Ascalesi, Archbishop of Naples. This rather mundane Fascist prelate has been very conspicuous in his zeal, even more so, perhaps, than his colleague, the ascetic-looking Benedictine Fascist, Cardinal Schuster of Milan. In a speech delivered in March, 1943, Ascalesi deplored the bombing of Naples and complained of the fate of innocent civilian victims. His remarks were consistent with his character and pastoral duties. But he concluded his address with an eloquent prayer in which he called upon God to insure Italian youth the victory over the "bestial" and "atheist" enemy. Cardinal Ascalesi, who blessed Italian troops sailing from Naples to the rapes of Ethiopia and Spain, never protested against the bombing and gassing of Ethiopian villages. His Eminence, like a good Fascist, saw nothing wrong when Mussolini sent his bombers to share in the glory of destroying London and other European cities in the fall, winter, and spring of 1940. It is very significant that His Eminence should have stigmatized an American bombing squad as being composed of "atheists."

It is likely that His Eminence has listened to the broadcasts of the Vatican radio station, such as the one of January 21, 1943, in which the reverend speaker said:

According to latest figures in America there are only twenty million Catholics. The remainder constitute a mass without ideas and religious color. They are moving towards the negation of any principle of Christian civilization. The country of "liberty and progress, of welfare and wealth" is suffering one of the most serious religious crises. Sympathy towards communist doctrines which, even among intellectual classes has been nurtured for years, had its roots in the spiritual disorientation of America. . . . The American soul is thirsty for God and being unable to find him is led to atheism.

Pius XII himself started this denunciation of American "atheism" in his encyclical to the American hierarchy of November 11, 1939. After having widely praised the American bishops and Catholic people and rejoiced because "the triumphal progress of divine religion has contributed in no small degree to the glory and prosperity which your country now enjoys," he raised his voice "in strong, albeit paternal complaint that in so many schools of your land Christ is often despised or ignored, the explanation of the universe and mankind is forced within the narrow limits of materialism and rationalism, and new educational systems are sought after, which cannot but produce a sorrowful harvest in the intellectual and moral life of the nation."

These remarks were general enough and merely stated once more a century-old complaint of popes, bishops, priests, and ecclesiastical writers. But the extraordinary zeal with which the campaign against American "atheists" has been pursued since the Nazi attack on Russia is very significant. Still more significant is the fact that most of the broadcasts against American "atheism" have been in Italian and therefore for an Italian audience. What has been the purpose of this attempt to make the Italians believe that the Americans were just as bad as the Russian "atheists"? Our readers may draw their own conclusions.

We are well aware of the fact that the Vatican has, on previous occasions, disclaimed direct reponsibility for what is broadcast from its station. No one can be fooled by such a declaration who knows how, in Vatican City, all services are centralized under persons directly responsible to the Pope himself. It is difficult to say whether branding the American people, Catholics excepted, with the mark of "atheism" has made any impression on the Italians or not. If it has not, as we believe, the fault does not lie with the Vatican radio.

There can be no doubt that the bombing of Italian cities, the destroying of valuable artistic and historical material, and the toll of innocent victims weighs heavily upon those of us who are

American citizens of Italian extraction, even though we recognize the tragic necessity of destroying military material and enemy supplies. The responsibility lies with the Fascist government which declared war on us. We hope and pray that such bombing be limited to military objectives, and that it may hasten the collapse of the criminal Fascist regime. But from our own reactions to this ghastly affair we can measure with some accuracy the reaction of the Italian people, who are misinformed as to which party began the ruthless bombing of cities without discrimination and who are confused as to the plans we have in store for them when the war is won.

We understand the heroic spirit which prompts French and Belgian peasants to wave to British aviators, though they know that the next bomb may fall on their home. They realize that no matter where bombs fall, each one brings them a little nearer to the day of liberation. But the Italians have no such assurance. Up to the present, our propaganda has consisted mostly in threats of destruction, boasts about our own prowess, and infantile stories about past, present, and future Italian history.

The American State Department indirectly informed all of us through the authoritative article of Mr. Kingsbury Smith in the *American Mercury* (February, 1943, p. 136) that "in Italy we stand ready to deal with any leader other than Mussolini who will help open the gates to our armies." No Darlan could open the gates while the Germans held Italy; with a German withdrawal, and the winning of the confidence of the Italian people, there could be no need of a Darlan. The gates could open by themselves.

Once the American and British armies of occupation get hold of Italy, the problem of establishing and maintaining public order will offer no serious difficulties if common sense and decency has not vanished from the earth. The nine-point plan adopted by the British in Tripolitania may be recommended as a model:

1. British military courts have been set up. War crimes such as sabotage and obtaining military information have been defined.

2. Arrangements have been made for central food supplies and for the medical treatment of civilians.

3. Guards have been posted at post offices, telegraph and telephone offices, public utility concerns and banks in various centres of the occupied territories.

4. The military government will adopt a firm but just attitude towards the Italian population of Tripolitania.

5. Fascist leaders and prominent members of the Fascist party, whether officials or not, will be interned.

6. Fascist clubs, so-called cultural centres and similar institutions will be closed. The teaching in schools and other institutions of Fascist ideas, Fascist political economy and any subjects with a Fascist bias will be forbidden. All text books to which exception is taken will be withdrawn.

7. The display of Fascist flags and emblems over houses and the wearing of Fascist uniforms and emblems will be forbidden.

8. All Fascist funds in banks will be permanently frozen. Fascist funds found in private banks will be taken over for safe custody by the military government. Control will be exercised over charitable funds to prevent their being used for Fascist or subversive purposes.

9. Existing Italian courts of justice will continue to operate to judge cases of civil crimes. They will act under the control of the military government.

It is obvious that several of these regulations and measures, which fit a colonial province, cannot be applied to a large and overpopulated country like Italy. The internment of the Fascists could not be extended to embrace all the members of the Fascist Party, but could and should be restricted to high-ranking officials down to a certain level. Moreover, while such an arrangement can be kept going for a considerable time in a colonial province, in Italy, on the contrary, this complete control of the whole political and financial system must be replaced very soon by a civilian provisional government. The task of the military occupation will be restricted to the prevention of acts of treachery, either by Fascists, Communists, or other groups.

The immediate abolishment of all Fascist laws limiting personal and political rights would enable the Italian people to reorganize their press, their associations, and their political parties. After a few months, municipal elections by universal suffrage could be called. A few months later, the election for provincial councils could be held, and finally, at the end of the year, a National Constituent Assembly could be similarly elected. When a regular government has been established by the Constituent Assembly, the peace treaty should be signed and the army of occupation withdrawn.

Our administration is preparing plans for the gigantic task of providing, after the war is over, immediate relief to lessen the suffering of war-torn and desolated Europe. Certainly Mr. Herbert Lehman will not overlook the needs of Italy. We are sure that Mr. Lehman intends to carry on this work of relief without discrimination in matters of religious and political belief. But we know only too well how the best of intentions can be sidetracked and nullified. All will depend upon the organization that is set up for the distribution of relief. Well-intentioned Americans, who have not had sufficient experience with Italian conditions, and who have been influenced by the general trend of thought which prevails in our official circles, may, for instance, rely primarily on ecclesiastical authority as the most suitable channel for humanitarian activity. But in Italy, as we have pointed out, the Church has been, and still is, closely connected with the Fascist regime. Thus, to entrust the distribution of relief to ecclesiastical persons is to give this distribution a political significance which will inevitably serve political purposes. To be sure, in forming local committees, the Catholic priest should not be overlooked. In communities where there are Jewish groups the local rabbi should not be overlooked. In every community all groups and classes must be represented. Only the Fascist leaders must be excluded, and their activities must cease altogether as a necessary precaution against the disturbance of public order. Such small committees can easily be formed everywhere. There are in every community respectable citizens whom the people trust. There are labor and trade unions everywhere, which, after they have discarded their Fascist officials and elected leaders of their own choosing, should be called upon to cooperate in the distribution of relief.

Britain and America, by demolishing the Fascist military structure, preventing any *coups de main*, and granting the Italians a cooling period, during which they can freely organize themselves, would thus empower them to choose according to their own lights the form of government they find most suitable. America and Britain would earn respect and gratitude by their fair dealings and humanitarian activities.

VI. Italy of Tomorrow

1. Italy in the New Commonwealth of Nations

THE Italians, having been defeated together with the Germans, will have to surrender along with the Germans all their military equipment. To be sure, German Nazis and Italian Fascists will feel humiliated by such an "unconditional surrender." But this is the law of war, and war is not a football game in which the loser need feel no humiliation. They have gambled, they have lost, they must pay. They have no choice. As for the German anti-Nazis and the Italian anti-Fascists, they have made their choice: rather than remain forever humiliated under the heel of Hitler or Mussolini, they consider the humiliation of military defeat a lesser evil.

After they have made their "military" surrender, the Axis powers will be forced to bow before any "political" decisions the victors may impose upon them. They will have to surrender unconditionally to a "dictated" peace as well.

Influenced by German propaganda which has for many years condemned the Versailles *Diktat*, some people shrink in horror from a dictated peace, that is, from a treaty imposed on the vanquished by the victors at the point of a sword. But anyone with the least knowledge of the history of international relations, knows that after a war there has never been a peace in history which was not "dictated," unless the war bogged down into a stalemate and the weary competitors had to negotiate some compromise. After a victorious war, even if the vanquished is permitted to discuss the peace terms with the victor, the discussion is like a contest between an English bull dog and a dachshund. The vanquished may obtain some changes in the minor technicalities of the *Diktat*, but the treaty always remains an imposition. No vanquished party ever subscribed to a peace treaty in a joyous mood or felt that the treaty was freely negotiated. The Treaty of Frankfurt in 1871 between Germany and France was not freely negotiated by Bismarck and the French plenipotentiaries, and no German historian (at least up to present) has thought so. The treaties imposed by the German government on Russia at Brest-Litovsk and on Rumania at Bucharest in 1918 were "dictated." In 1919, even if the anti-German powers had granted the German plenipotentiaries at Versaillles more time to formulate counter-proposals, and even if they had consented to greater changes in the original provisos, the Versailles Treaty would have remained a *Diktat*. German relations with the rest of Europe since 1938 and Italian-Greek-Jugoslav relations from 1941 on have been but a history of *Diktate*.

A "dictated" peace may be wise or unwise. In 1866, Bismarck "dictated" a wise peace to Austria, leaving no permanent aftermath or rancor in its wake. In 1871, he "dictated" an unwise peace to France and left the question of Alsace-Lorraine an open wound. Both these peaces, however, were "dictated." Let us, therefore, put aside the delusion that there should be no political unconditional surrender after the military one. What matters is that the peace be a wise peace, one which will not sow seeds of permanent hatred, and one that decent people in all countries will regard as just and worthy of being upheld in the face of any forces aiming at its destruction. Of course, German Nazis and Italian Fascists will never be content with even the most generous peace treaty. Since some have to feel discontented, let it be they.

Let us now assume that the leaders of the victorious powers are not maddened by blind lust for revenge and that they aim at making a wise settlement of the problems which have been raised by the present war. What peace terms would they then impose on the Italian people?

War Guilt. The United Nations cannot take any responsibility for the reprisals which German Nazis and Italian Fascists will have to face in the occupied countries and in their own countries when the Nazi-Fascist military machine breaks down. But when the immediate post-war upheaval is over, the Fascist officials (both civil and military) who are responsible for the crimes committed in occupied territories should be handed over to the governments of the countries in which the crimes were committed to be tried and sentenced according to law, provided that the Italians themselves have not already made short work of them in the meantime. On no account should the common people of Italy be held responsible for the crimes of the Fascist officials.

Reparations. Within the limits of their capacity, the Italians will have to make reparations for material damage done and looting perpetrated in the occupied territories. To be sure, the Italians cannot pay either in gold or in raw materials. They will have to pay in labor. The Italian shipyards, which are among the best in the world, might be pledged for a few years to build a specific amount of commercial shipping. The victorious powers would furnish raw materials; the Italians, skill and labor. The victorious powers would get the ships and the Italian government would pay salaries and wages to the personnel of the shipyards. The Italian government should meet this expenditure by confiscating the properties of the men responsible for the crimes committed in the occupied territories. Not only should the houses and lands of these people be confiscated but their bank deposits as well. The banks should be summoned to freeze these deposits and make them known to the government. Some international agreement should make possible the confiscation of funds which have been deposited in foreign banks. (For instance, the King of Italy has a part of his personal assets deposited with the old Bank of London. Count Volpi has very large assets in both England and America. We are afraid, however, that the international racket of kings and financiers will help Italy's King and tycoons out of their predicament.) The government would cash the assets resulting from such confiscations and use them to pay for the work done in the shipyards. Thus, not the Italian people as a whole, but only those responsible for crimes committed in the occupied territories would bear the brunt of financial reparations, as well as the more personal punishment of being handed over to the interested countries. It would be unfair to demand in reparation more than the confiscation of these properties would yield. If the victorious powers have sense enough not to demand absurd reparations from a people which is not renowned for its wealth and to refrain from making such reparations a pretext for permanent unfair extortions, this matter might be settled with no great difficulty. No sensible and decent Italian would evade this duty of justice.

Territorial provisos. The Italians will have to evacuate all the territories occupied during this war in Greece, Jugoslavia, and France, not only because they must obey the voice of force, not only because they must be taught that war does not pay, but primarily because they have no right to be there. But the government of the United Nations should repudiate every idea of severing from Italy her own national territories and opening wounds which would act as a permanent source of hatred.

How should one define Italian "national territories"?

The Dodecanese Islands are not a part of Italian national territory. Their population is Greek. They have been brutally misgoverned. They want to join Greece; they have the right to do so and must be allowed to do so.

Albania is not a part of Italian national territory. But the population of northern and southern Albania should not be handed over to the Jugoslavs and the Greeks merely because Albania is a small country and her neighbors are stronger. The present boundaries of Albania were defined in 1913 by an international conference which was anything but hostile to the Jugoslavs and the Greeks, and which made extensive readjustments at the expense of the Albanians. Rather, there should be some revision of these boundaries in favor of the Albanians. The administration of the country should be entrusted to an international committee under the control of the new League of Nations. From that international governing committee not only Italians, Greeks, and Jugoslavs, but also the citizens of all great European powers should be excluded, since all great European powers have shady records in Albanian affairs. America and the smaller countries of Europe can furnish plenty of honest men capable of governing Albania. The international committee we have suggested should direct the Albanian people in the work of economic and political reorganization which is needed to place the country substantially on its own feet. The funds required to construct roads and railroads, open schools, reclaim marshes, maintain a police force, and so on will not be large and should be raised by loans from other countries in proportion to their wealth. As soon as Albania can take care of herself, she should be allowed to do so without outside interference. This work of rehabilitation will require the span of at least one generation. The whole problem of Albania is a small one, which will present no great difficulties if handled in good faith. However, the handling of it will prove beyond a doubt whether the political leaders of Britain and America are men of wisdom.

South Tyrol. An Italian of high moral character, Leonida Bissolati, maintained in 1919 that German South Tyrol should not be annexed to Italy. But President Wilson gave in to the demands of the Italian negotiators on this point and thereby did a great wrong. The Germans of South Tyrol never accepted their fate, and the Fascist dictatorship, by maltreating them in the same way it maltreated all Italians and by endeavoring, in addition, to force them to forget their own language, did not increase their love for Italy. If the German population of South Tyrol were still there, there would be no doubt that this territory should be severed from Italy and re-annexed to Austria. But in 1939, Hitler and Mussolini agreed to settle the question by allowing all Germans in the South Tyrol who did not want to become Italians to move to Germany. A plebiscite was held for that purpose. R. G. Massock, chief of the Rome Bureau of the Associated Press from 1938 to December, 1941, in his book *Italy From Within* tells us that "the official figures of the plebiscite were made public in January, 1940. Of the 266,985 German-speaking inhabitants, 179,085 elected to go to Germany. The 89,000 who voted to remain were less than one-third of the population. . . . Italy agreed to buy the property and possessions of the emigrants and enter the cost—variously estimated at four to ten billion lire (200 to 500 million dollars)—on the trade balance as a credit to Germany. The German government then would reimburse the evacuees with bonds."

It is not known where Hitler settled those people who left South Tyrol, or whether and how he paid them for their lost possessions; however, there is no doubt that he got full value from the price paid by Italy.

Since the evacuation was not a *Diktat* forced by a victorious power upon a vanquished one, but the result of a deal through a plebiscite, and since compensation was fully paid to Germany for the possessions of those who freely emigrated, one is inclined to think that the question may be considered settled. Undoubtedly, it was a cynical deal which inflicted great suffering upon the population, but to reopen it would be to cause worse trouble and to precipitate political and economic complications. Should those who emigrated of their own will be allowed to return and buy back ther lands, their shops, their houses, for which Italy has already paid a fair price? Should the Italians who have occupied them be forced to resell them?

The problem of the *Italo-Jugoslav frontier* is much more involved. Any Italian who is not blinded by nationalistic acquisitiveness (quite different from national consciousness) is bound to admit that to the east of the cities of Gorizia and Trieste, and to the east of Istria, that is, beyond the Selva di Ternova (Trnovaski Gozo) and the Monti della Vena (Porgorse Ucke Gore), there is a compact population of about 250,000 Slavs. These want and have the right to secede from Italy and to join Jugoslavia. This is not Italian national but Slav national territory. There remains the western section of Venetia Giulia. This includes the Italian cities of Gorizia, Trieste and western Istria, and the country districts, which are Slav but which cannot be severed from the cities. Here about 400,000 Italians and about 400,000 Slavs are inextricably intermingled. This is neither an exclusively Italian nor an exclusively Slavic territory. It is a mixed Italo-Slav territory. Should this mixed Italo-Slav territory be transferred from Italy to Jugoslavia? Could any sensible man expect a city like Trieste of about 300,000 inhabitants, of whom no more than 60,000 are Slavs living mostly on the outskirts, to be ruled by the Slav minority of its suburbs and by the Slav peasantry scattered over its stony and sparsely inhabited districts? Could any sensible man expect the Slav peasantry to assimilate the Italian nuclei gathered in the cities of Gorizia and Trieste and those of Istria?

The exchange of populations has become rather appealing in these last years, not only in Nazi Germany but also among governments-in-exile. Hitler is conquering the minds of the politicians-in-exile before they return to their countries. But exchange of population, if not freely accepted by those concerned, means nothing less than the brutal and barbaric expulsion of minorities, or even majorities. Is it possible to believe that the Italians of Gorizia, Trieste, and Istria would like to leave their homes and businesses and go—where? What territory would Jugoslavia grant them while the Slavs of the countryside or the politicians of Belgrade, Zagreb, and Ljubljana established themselves in the houses and shops of the departed Italians?

The problem of intermingled nationalities exists in all territories of Europe from the Baltic in the north to the Adriatic, the Aegean, and the Black Sea in the south. It cannot be solved by exchanging populations. It can be solved only by the method which has insured its solution in Switzerland and in the United States of America: by granting equal personal and political rights to every man, irrespective of his nationality. In the case of the Italians and the Slavs of Venetia Giulia, it could be solved satisfactorily on four conditions: 1. the largest possible share of home rule should be granted to each municipality so as to leave the Slavs free to run their rural communities, and the Italians their towns and cities (the same home rule to be granted to municipalities in the whole of Italy, as we shall see later); 2. in the municipalities where Italians and Slavs are intermingled, each group should be allowed to keep its own schools, paying the school tax to a school board of its own, so that there would be two different school boards in the same municipality, and no Slav would be forced to support Italian schools with his money or vice versa; 3. the whole territory should be administered by two different provincial boards for those affairs which can be divided between two boards; for those affairs in which such division is not feasible (such as building and maintenance of main roads, sanitation services, etc.) the administration should be entrusted to a joint committee consisting of an equal number of members delegated by each of the two provincial boards; 4. a body of umpires chosen by the Hague Court of international justice, not including Italians and Jugoslavs, should be assigned to settle disputes on the spot, according to common sense.

This system would not work smoothly from the beginning. The Fascist government, by brutally mistreating the Slavs, has aggravated a problem which can only be relieved by a regime of justice for all, Italians and Slavs alike. Hatreds have been created during this past generation which only time can heal. But if an end is put to violence and reprisals, time's work of healing can at least begin.

The administrative system which would solve the problem of peaceful Italo-Slav coexistence in Venetia Giulia, would solve the same problem for *the city of Fiume, the city of Zara, and the small Italian nuclei which are scattered along the coast of Dalmatia.*

The solution of these small local problems would be hastened if Italy and Jugoslavia became partners in the same customs union, so that the Italo-Jugoslav frontier would no longer be a political and economic, but merely an administrative boundary. A man would then be able to go freely from Trieste to Ljubljana or from Fiume to Zagreb, and vice versa, in the same way as an American citizen, be he of British, Irish, Italian, or Slav extraction, now goes from New Jersey to Connecticut through New York State without noticing that he has crossed two frontiers.

The local problem of Italo-Slav coexistence in Venetia Giulia, Fiume, and Dalmatia has nothing to do with the problem of Trieste and Fiume as ports. These ports serve a Middle European hinterland. Even if there were no local national Italo-Slav problem in Trieste and Fiume, the economic problem of these two ports would exist, and a right or wrong solution of the national local problem would not necessarily bring about a right or wrong solution of the international economic problem. This latter is not only a problem of port charges and local facilities; it is, above all, the problem of railway rates and customs tariffs in Central Europe. It cannot be solved in Trieste or Fiume alone. The ports of Constantsa, Salonika, Venice, Genoa. Amsterdam, Hamburg, and Danzig must be taken into account, since Central Europe is a hinterland for all of them. There is plenty of work for all ports, if they cooperate according to intelligent plans made through an international agreement. If they refuse to cooperate, they are doomed to kill each other off by mad cutthroat competition.

Ethiopia obviously will not be restored to Italy. This can be said without arousing resentment in the great majority of Italians. They have lost all the illusions which Fascist propaganda built up in 1935 and 1936 about the opportunities for work they would find in that country. Furthermore, they will be quite content not to have to sink into it more than the four billion dollars which it has already devoured. One's heart bleeds to think what might have been done in Italy itself, had that money been spent to improve conditions in a land not ruled by criminals.

Eritrea, Somaliland, and Libya have been lost as a result of the present war. The pleasure of collecting deserts and sinking money in them has already been too costly for Italy. But from talks with many citizens and residents of Italian extraction in this country, we have reached the conclusion that if the old Italian colonies were taken away from Italy and given to someone else, Italians of all parties would consider this loss an unpardonable injustice. The same frame of mind prevails, no doubt, in Italy as well. If colonies are coveted for reasons of prestige, there is no reason why some countries must monopolize this prestige to the exclusion of others. If colonies are desired for reasons of self-interest, there is no reason why some countries may see their interests satisfied and others not.

The only way to deal with the colonial problem is to internationalize the colonies. All colonies should be considered as a trust of the entire civilized world, and they should be put under the surveillance of an international administration in which all countries participate. In this collective trust there must be neither privilege for one nation nor unfavorable discrimination against another. Each must have the right to work and trade under equal conditions. Gradually, the administrative personnel should be internationalized. Newcomers will take the places of those colonial officials who will retire because of old age. They should be chosen according to their technical ability and moral standing and not by virtue of their national origins. The British Liberals and Laborites have long accepted this solution of the colonial problem. The British Tories will have to decide to swallow this pill, if the American government remains true to its promises.

The Problem of Italian Overpopulation. A problem of overpopulation exists in Italy. The Fascist regime aggravated it by forbidding emigration and seeking to promote an increase in the birth rate, while at the same time it demanded new territories for its increasing population. More people for more land and more land for more people! Thanks to the natural good sense of the Italian people, the Italian birth rate continues to decline. One may hope that in the second half of this century the problem of overpopulation in Italy will have reached a satisfactory solution. But for the time being, the fact remains that overpopulation cannot be eliminated all of a sudden; only emigration can relieve it. The Italian people care little about Ethiopia, Gibraltar, Suez, or Dalmatia. They want to live in peace with other peoples, but they want to be sure of their own work and their own bread.

No nation has the right to exclude from lands which are sparsely inhabited and which can be tilled those people who can no longer find work in their own overcrowded lands. In this respect the Italian people have interests in common with all the peoples of southern and eastern Europe. The Anglo-Saxon world passed without transition from the policy of *laissez-faire* to a brutal policy of absolute prohibition, which increased the misery of these peoples. To be sure, the Italians cannot expect unlimited freedom of immigration to be re-established. If this should take place, Italy would be depopulated overnight, and millions of Italians would turn the labor markets topsy-turvy in all the countries of the world.

The evils of disorderly emigration and the injustice of suppressed immigration can be avoided by an international system of planned migrations. The planning authorities, representing the countries which import manpower as well as those which export it, should admit into sparsely populated territories more immigrants than present measures allow. But care should be taken that the immigrants settle in the places most fitted for productive labor and do not gather in the cities to lower the standard of living of the local working classes.

Aside from this, the Italians must be convinced that their government cannot continue to organize Italians, wherever they go, into segregated communities, under a separate clergy, with separate schools and separate papers, so that they form compact "national minorities" ready at the beck and call of Italian ambassadors, consuls, or secret agents to serve the interests of their mother country without any concern for the welfare and rights of the country which has received them. This is no longer economic emigration. It is political deceit detrimental to the receiving country. So long as such practices are continued, not only by the Italians, but by all governments of countries needing emigration, no concessions should be made.

Mussolini has turned large sections of the Italian people against the British by making them believe that Britain wanted to rob them of their work and bread. A solemn promise made by both the British and American governments to the effect that the immigration laws would be reformed in accordance with more humane principles, would gain immense favor among the Italian working classes, especially those in the south.

In November, 1942, a representative of the American Federation of Labor delivered an address in New York wherein he stated that "the sort of post-war world which we must seek, cannot be selfish"; that we must "base our efforts on the recognition that the peoples of the earth are neighbors"; that "there is a brotherhood of man"; that "justice among nations will not arise merely by defeating the gangsters or by winning the war"; that we "must win in the hearts and minds of men" by proving that "democracy not only can win, but deserves to win"; that "we must be willing to play our part and assume our responsibility in building a post-war world on a firm foundation of decency and progress"; that "labor is not fighting for the well-being of any one race or any one people"; that "we are fighting to remove the *Verboten* sign from the eyes and ears and the mouths and souls of men and women all over the world"; that "men and women of every nation have the right to work and earn a decent standard of living." While reading these high-sounding statements in the *New York Herald Tribune* (November 22, 1942), we could not help recalling that elements of the American Federation of Labor have been in the vanguard of the fight against the admission of foreign workers into this land, and has never given any sign that such a selfish attitude would be changed. Therefore, we said to ourselves that it was ridiculous to talk cant about the brotherhood of man while ruthlessly refusing to allow the labor from overcrowded countries to settle in vast and sparsely inhabited territories. The first step towards confirming the brotherhood of man should be taken by the American Federation of Labor; in other words, it should practice what it preaches.

One of the problems requiring great tact and wisdom is the handling of Tunisia. In 1881, when France placed the Regency of Tunis under its own protectorate, there were approximately 20,000 Italians settled there. In 1931, according to the French census, there were 91,178 Italians and 91,427 Frenchmen in Tunisia. The Fascists claimed that the Italians numbered 130,000, and Mussolini quoted this figure in a speech to the Chamber on November 12, 1924. They overlooked naturalizations, many of which were voluntary. On the other hand, the French authorities omitted from the census some 10,000 non-naturalized Italians. The French officials falsified their census by understatement; the Fascists falsified their statistics by overstatements. One can safely state that there were in 1940 approximately 100,000 Italians. The majority consisted of agricultural laborers and small farmers, in great part of Sicilian origin. Most farmers in vineyards and most fishermen were Italian. The manual labor in the mines of Kel and Gafsa was done by Italians. In the city of Tunis and its vicinity, they numbered approximately 60,000. Italian penetration tended to increase in Algeria as well. If ever there was a country which Mussolini should have left alone on account of the population problem, that country was France. France gave generous hospitality to Italian labor. If she had followed the same policy as the United States, Canada, and Australia, Italy would have had to reabsorb one million workers who had been imported by France. France needed labor and Italy was able to furnish it. The economic conditions of the two countries were complementary and not antagonistic. In attacking France in 1940, Mussolini created new and terrible obstacles to the solution of this problem of Italian labor in France and the French colonies. Yet the crime of "one man" and his accomplices should not be laid to innocent people. The hatred that Mussolini has fostered between France and Italy must not continue to poison the two countries after this ill-starred war. If this hatred should continue, it means that Mussolini and Hitler will have enjoyed a posthumous triumph, for it would prevent that Franco-Italian cooperation in Europe which is one of the prerequisites for convincing German nationalists that another war would not pay. To be sure, all Fascist teachers, lawyers, journalists, physicians, druggists, priests, and other vermin with whom Mussolini has honeycombed Tunisia and all the Mediterranean countries must be removed. They should not be sent back to Italy to make things there even more difficult than they will be without them. They should be sent to work on the Trans-Saharan railway, taking the place of the anti-Fascist refugees, victims of the Vichy government. But the bulk of the Italian settlers who have fertilized the land with the sweat of their brows, and of the laborers who are only concerned with the hardships of their daily life, should be left alone. If they were evicted and returned to Italy, they would not only create an insoluble economic problem, but they would also harbor in their hearts a bitterness which they would spread. Inevitably, when this war is over, many Frenchmen will be blinded by hatred and a desire for revenge against "the Italians." Confusing peoples with their governments is a common mistake and Americans should not make such a mistake. They should keep cool and forestall future dangers through the exercise of common sense and humanity. Many Italians settled in France are now performing, hand in hand with the French, a work not only heroic but wise, in opposing the Germans. Six of them, Rohegger, Foscardi, Vercellino, Buzzi, Bertone, and Guisco were shot by the Gestapo late in 1942 in Paris and Brussels though readers of most American newspapers, including the *New York Times,* were not aware of this. Let us hope that the sacrifice of these men and their fellows bears fruit for Franco-Italian reconciliation and cooperation after the war.

Peace in the Mediterranean. The only solution for the problems of peace and free transit in the Mediterranean is the establishment of a supranational police force. No nation should be authorized to keep armed forces in the Mediterranean. In this way the question of Gibralter and Suez, and even the question of the Red Sea, would be settled. To be sure, during its first years this supranational force ought to be controlled by Britain and America. But this should not become its permanent status and should be changed step by step as soon as possible. An announcement of this kind would produce an enormously beneficial effect in all the countries of the Mediterranean.

The theory, according to which British control of the seas was beneficial during the nineteenth century, is historically correct. But it is based on the moral assumption that all other peoples are in duty bound to have faith in the sentiments of justice and generosity of the British, whereas the British have the right to suspect the intentions of all other peoples. Hitler, too, asks the rest of the world to entrust its destiny to the superior intelligence and technical ability of the *Herrenvolk,* who will put each group in its proper place like horses in a well-kept stable. Other people cannot be expected to reject the doctrine of the *Herrenvolk,* when it is made bitter by German brutality, and then be summoned to swallow it, when it has been sugared over with a coating of British cant. Britishers must make up their minds either to accept the principle of equality of rights for all nations under a supranational governing body, or to admit the necessity for a world war every twenty years.

2. *Domestic Reconstruction*

We believe the great majority of the Italian people, if left free to choose, will prefer a democratic republic to any other form of government. Don Luigi Sturzo states that, though the republican tradition in Italy from 1860 to 1922 was kept alive by a small group, "yet the feeling was fairly widespread even among members of other parties that Italy would never know true democracy under the monarchy, given the coalition formed around the throne by powerful forces representing the upper bourgeoisie, the old aristocracy, the army and the bureaucracy" (*Foreign Affairs,* April, 1943).

In another, earlier article (*The Review of Politics,* Notre Dame University, January, 1943), the same author wrote that the Italian "Christian Democrats were in part republican-minded," and added that he himself "had always been" one of them. According to Don Sturzo, when the Allied armies invade Italy, the disintegration of the monarchy will be inevitable:

When the Allies reach Rome one of three things will happen; either the king will abandon the capital, to continue the war together with his government and his German ally; or he will give himself up, while his armies continue the struggle alongside the Germans; or he will give himself up, order the cessation of hostilities and ask for an armistice. In the first case, we shall have still further confirmation of the fact that we are dealing with an unyielding enemy. In the second case, the king will become an illustrious prisoner, without authority over either his armies or the people of the occupied territory. In the third case, Hitler will supplant him in the provinces still under German control until he himself is expelled or withdraws.

These various hypotheses help to demonstrate the proposition that the problem of the monarchy was not created by the anti-Fascist Italians living abroad, but was inevitably posed on the day the king signed the declaration of war and thereby assumed responsibility for what was to happen as a result of that act. When the armistice is signed, Mussolini and the Fascist leaders will be fugitives or prisoners; perhaps Victor Emmanuel will have abdicated. The generals and the admirals will be there to sign the capitulation, and after that a provisional government will become the heir to all the burdens of the past. It is necessary, however, that such a government be free of any responsibility for the past (*Foreign Affairs*).

Having so well dissected the problem, Don Sturzo concludes by saying that "in any case the question of the monarchy is not urgent," and that its solution may be left to the post-war period. Though we agree with Don Sturzo as to the general lines of possible happenings in Italy, we do not think that the transition can take place as smoothly and as simply as he foresees. Above all, we think that the question of the Monarchy *is* "urgent."

The constant and unscrupulous propaganda which is carried on here, especially by some representatives of the Catholic clergy with the encouragement and blessing of the State Department, tries to mislead the American public into believing that the Italian republicans are only a few desperadoes, revolutionary socialists, and what not. The Reverend John T. Ellis, professor of history at the Catholic University in Washington, speaking dogmatically from his cathedra and addressing, not the small group of friars and nuns who attend his classes, but the American public stated in an article published by the three hundred-odd Catholic weeklies of this country (October 30, 1942) that those who advocate a republican regime for Italy are "socialist revolutionaries under the cloak of republicans"; that they wish to bring about "an international socialist revolution and to destroy the helpful beginning which the American government has made in attempting to beat the Axis by taking Italy out of the war. . . . Fortunately the delicate issues of that problem are in the competent hands of men such as Secretary Hull and under-

Secretary Sumner Welles and their able collaborators. . . .
They are men who know something of history."

To many priests and bishops, Mr. Hull and Mr. Welles were
little more than devilish jackasses at the time of the isolationist
campaign, in fact, until Pearl Harbor. Now Rev. Ellis has pro-
moted them to the ranks of those who at least "know something
of history." Perhaps, if they behave and continue to please Professor Ellis, Mr. Hull and Mr. Welles will get a further promotion,
even a Ph.D. apiece *honoris causa* from the Catholic University.

We suppose that Father Ellis at least reads the publications
of other Catholic universities in America, and that he is acquainted with the *Review of Politics* of Notre Dame, in which
Don Sturzo said that not only he himself but many of the progressive wing of the former Populist Party were "republican-
minded" both now and before the war. We do not know how
large their group may be in Italy now, but certainly, when the
time comes, they will not be found in the ranks of the Monarchists; neither will that part of Catholic youth which will
follow their leadership, nor those who have broken away from
the Fascist policy of the Catholic Action and have engaged in
anti-Fascist underground activities. Father Ellis could not have
been ignorant of the fact that the progressive forces in Italy,
those of Catholic youth included, are primarily republican-
minded, and that only Fascists and unrepentant reactionaries
stand behind the Savoy Monarchy.

In outlining the measures which we believe will be best suited
for the solution of the most immediate problems of post-war
Italy's internal reconstruction, we have made no room for the
Savoy Monarchy, under which, as Don Sturzo says, "Italy would
never know true democracy."

1. *Post-war Unemployment and Relief.* The most urgent and
dangerous problem will be that of post-war unemployment. If
the millions of men who are now under the colors were released
haphazardly and in haste, utter social breakdown would occur.
We have been told by the *American Mercury* of November,

1942, that "one of the primary armistice terms to be imposed upon the vanquished countries is that their military forces shall be disarmed but not immediately demobilized. A defeated nation's discharged soldiers on the loose are ripe for trouble. Under the control of the United Nations' occupation forces, it is intended that the defeated armies shall be kept in orderly groups, subject to discipline and put to work on rehabilitation projects in their own countries until arrangements are provided for their gradual return to peacetime employment. . . . The demobilization of the armed forces of all the nations must be on a gradual scale, corresponding with the transfer of each country's internal economy from a war to a peacetime basis."

There is no doubt that demobilization should be gradual. But many objections must be raised against the idea of keeping the soldiers under military discipline and employing them on rehabilitation projects. Anyone who knows what an army is, knows that soldiers are good (too good) as consumers and not at all good as producers. No man is less efficient than the soldier who is commanded to do civilian work. A foremen who knows the technical job to be done and who supervises the workers on that job is one thing; an N.C.O. or a colonel who supervises soldiers doing the same job is something entirely different. If the vast destruction brought about by war in Italy (and elsewhere) is to be repaired rapidly, this task should be entrusted to experts in the various trades and not to military men who know nothing outside their own profession. We suspect that the plan to keep defeated armies under military discipline is prompted by the idea of utilizing them as media of political reaction rather than as tools of economic rehabilitation.

Plans for rehabilitating the devastated areas and for carrying on such works as marsh reclamation, which cannot be discontinued, should not be made on the assumption that carpenters under military discipline would be digging canals, longshoremen would be building houses, and colonels would be creating confusion everywhere. Let the shoemaker stick to his last. The army must be demobilized with the greatest possible speed on the assumption that each demobilized man will find work for which he is suited under the leadership of experts ready to start work. A well-planned program of public works would go far towards providing general employment, if the ingenuity of those who know their jobs is left unhampered. Thousands and thousands of private houses and public buildings will have to be repaired or replaced. It is a well-known fact that when the building trades are active, all trades are active. There will be work for all in Italy when the war is over, if recovery is not paralyzed by military men who presume to be able to do everything.

If the evil of unemployment is avoided, there will be no need for any long-drawn-out relief on the part of the forces of occupation. We feel uneasy when we read that American plans are being drawn up to feed the whole world, and perhaps even other planets, when the war is over. Such extravagant promises are dangerous. They raise expectations which cannot be fulfilled, and unfulfilled expectations leave in their wake disappointment, recrimination, and hatred rather than the kindlier emotions of gratitude and friendliness. Let us remember that America's resources are not boundless, and that the American taxpayer will revolt against excessive and protracted sacrifice when the war is over. A few months of large-scale relief for Europe's starving masses, especially for the children, will no doubt be endorsed by the generosity of the American people. But the Europeans must be told that America cannot be everybody's Santa Claus forever. We have no doubt that the Italians, aided by their habits of thrift and hard work and by common sense which some foreigners stupidly mistake for cynicism, will get themselves out of trouble through their own efforts without waiting for any ration of ham and eggs to pop into their mouths from the American market basket.

2. *The Financial Problem.* The provisional government will have instantly to cope with the financial situation.

As we have said above, the Fascist dictatorship, at the end of

1922, found a national debt amounting to 93 billion lire. By June, 1942, the national debt had jumped to 315 billion lire. According to reliable estimates, it was to reach 415 billion lire by June, 1943. The hidden debt in the form of "deferred payments" which do not appear in the figures of the national debt must be added to the avowed debt; it amounts to no less than 100 billion lire. Since the present war seems to entail a yearly outlay of 100 billion lire, Italy will be saddled, at the end of the present war, with a national debt of no less than 600 billion lire, granted that the European war comes to an end by 1944. The wealth of the Italian population was estimated at 600 billion lire in 1938. Thus, the Italian national debt will be equal to the entire wealth of the Italian people.

If in post-war Italy the present average rate of interest (five per cent) were to be paid, 30 of the 42 billion lire which was squeezed by the central government from the Italian people through taxation in 1942 would go into the service of the national debt. It is obvious that no government could devote about three-quarters of its revenue to defraying the interest of the national debt. On the other hand, further inflation of currency should be stopped at all costs, if a terrible economic disaster is to be averted.

There will be only one way to straighten out Italian finances and that is to reduce the interest on the national debt from five to one per cent so as to burden the budget with no more than 6 billion lire a year—the burden which existed in 1922. Bankruptcy? Of course. But bankruptcy has already occurred when the national debt has reached the sum of 600 billion lire, the sum total of Italy's entire wealth. The only thing the provisional government of the Italian democratic republic can do is to recognize and admit a bankruptcy which has already taken place and for which the republic is not responsible.

While the interest on the public debt should be cut down to no more than 6 billions a year, the disarmament which will be enforced by the victorious powers (if the victorious powers mean business) will bring about a yearly saving in the ordinary budget of 13 billion lire. The loss of colonies—which, from the economic and financial point of view, have always been a mad adventure—will free 6 more billion lire a year. Last but not least, the police expenses which have soared to at least 3 billion lire a year under the Fascist dictatorship should be brought down to a normal level, and that of 1922 might be regarded as normal. No less than 2 billion lire would thus become available.

On the other hand, fresh liabilities would arise. The reduction of the interest on the national debt from 30 to 6 billion lire would upset the budgets of all local charitable institutions and savings banks, which have been forced by the dictatorship to invest all their assets in state securities and would go bankrupt if they saw their incomes reduced by four-fifths. The central government should compensate them with subsidies. These could amount to no less than 5 billion lire. Then there is also the problem of the present crushing burden of taxation, which must be reduced if the country is to be enabled to breathe, work, and save. Then the vast destruction brought about by bombing will have to be repaired and the government must pay for it. Then more attention will have to be given to national education on every level. Let us remember that a considerable share of the rural population in southern Italy is still illiterate because there are no school buildings and no teachers at its disposal. No appreciable cuts would be possible in the other civil services, since they have already been cut to the bone. And finally, social security, which under the Fascist dictatorship has been but an imposing façade of words and boasts with little or nothing behind it, must become a reality, if the working classes are to be won over to the post-Fascist regime. All this means that what will be saved in military, colonial, and police expenses will have to be allotted to reducing taxation, keeping up roads, reclaiming land, developing education and social security, and improving other civil services. It is safe to estimate that when, out of the present yearly income amounting to 42 billion lire, the Italian democratic republic has devoted 6 billions to the service of the national debt, 5 billions to tax reductions, and 5 billions for subsidies to charitable institutions, savings banks, and like purposes, it will be left with no more than 26 billion lire a year to meet the bare necessities of the people and to keep them from sinking into utter destitution. The Italian republic will certainly not swim in plenty, but neither will it be impossible for it to make its way lamely along the path to a slow recovery.

This rough outline of a financial plan may seem too simple and too optimistic to those who are familiar with the endless and difficult problems of state finances, taxation, and all the complications attending any system of national economy. We realize that specialists may have objections to raise and perhaps better plans to offer. By suggesting these few general ideas about the state finances of post-war Italy, we wish only to convey to our readers our opinion that, although bankruptcy will be the bitter inheritance from the Fascist regime, there is no reason to despair. Above all, we have confidence in the Italian people.

3. *Industrial Democracy.* In the fall of 1918 the German Socialists and Democrats proclaimed a republic. But they left all the higher-ups of the former regime undisturbed and then sat back while the latter reorganized their forces to kill the republic. This mistake should be avoided in Italy in the approaching crisis.

There are some social groups which ought to be rendered harmless immediately, if the new regime is to establish itself on solid foundations. Today we are facing the crude realities of an iron age in which extraordinary measures are necessary in most European countries to secure an enduring resettlement. An upheaval of such magnitude as that which will take place in Europe after Hitler's and Mussolini's debacle cannot be met by resorting to the rules and regulations of a football game. Tender-hearted people should prepare themselves to admit the weight of extenuating circumstances in a good many harsh happenings, unless they have taken a vow to live always in the clouds.

The charitable advice given on April 16, 1939 by Pope Pius XII to Franco, the Spanish dictator, might well be taken: "Justice towards crime and benevolent kindness towards those who had been led astray." In applying this rule there should be no exceptions and no hesitations. Several high-ranking Fascists must appear before the court of justice as murderers, mandataries of murders, or as criminals guilty of other dark deeds, deeds for which they were honored instead of punished by the Fascist regime. To all these criminals immunity must not be granted; their stations in life must make no difference. No amnesty or prescription should be allowed to interfere with the rigid application of the law. The names and the crimes of these men are known to all; the evidence is at hand. Swift trials, deprived of all dramatic exhibitionism, should get rid of this cancer as soon as possible, before its poison can seep into the new republic.

Besides these assassins who murdered their victims in cold blood, there is another class of criminals which must be brought to account. To this class belong all those Fascist leaders who have used their political power and influence to amass fortunes through graft and through the misuse of all kinds of public funds and gratuities. Mussolini during the first days of his advent to power assumed a Spartan attitude, telling his followers that it was their duty *di arrivare nudi alla meta,* "to reach the goal naked." He meant, of course, that they should appear to the people as heroic examples of men who remained poor and lived modestly, though they held the highest government positions. It was merely one of those theatrical gestures by which Mussolini attempted to present himself as a hero out of Plutarch. In fact, however, from the very first day after their victory Fascist leaders engaged in a mad scramble to see who could make the most hay while the sun was shining. Within a short time a new aristocracy of wealth emerged from the Fascist ranks; they filled the highest positions in the regime: the Duce's cabinets, the Fascist Grand Council, the Senate, the High Courts of Justice, the diplomatic corps, the commanding offices of the militia, and gradually those of the army as well. It was not long before they also took control of the boards and directorates of banks and big business concerns, of public services and all the economic resources of the country. They invaded even the universities and institutions of higher learning. This new Fascist aristocracy spread its tentacles everywhere like a monstrous hydra, growing fat on the misery of the taxpayers. To make these men disgorge their ill-acquired wealth will be an act of elementary justice.

One must not overlook the fact that big industrial firms, banks, shipping and insurance companies, in Italy no less than in Germany were, together with the army, responsible in good measure for the creation of the dictatorship. For twenty years, under the protection of the regime, they have monopolized the Italian market, cornered all government contracts for public works, war supplies, and weapons, and exploited the minor concerns and the helpless Italian people. Under the Fascist regime there has been extensive capitalistic concentration of big business, and those companies are now interlocked with each other in the hands of a few dozen tycoons, who form the directorates of most of them. In our opinion, these big, monopolistic concerns should be nationalized both for political security and economic readjustment. By this we do not mean to suggest wholesale confiscation. Of course, most of the tycoons who hold and control a large share of the stock of those companies will fall under the axe of the law against profiteers and grafters who have enriched themselves by illegitimate means. But there will be no reason to punish the common stockholders of those companies. On the other hand, it is obvious that all the shareholders have, with the political connivance of the dictatorship, made large profits. They gambled on the stability of the Fascist regime. Our suggestion is that the shareholders be compensated by giving them state securities bearing interest at one per cent as do all other securities of the national debt.

The chief opposition to these measures will come from British and American capitalists who have shares in the big Italian business corporations and would, therefore, be interested in preventing their nationalization. If Washington espouses the cause of these capitalists, then we know what will happen. The American experts who are now being trained to "govern" Italy after the invasion will be instructed immediately to freeze the Italian economic system at the point it had reached under the dictatorship, and the Fascist tycoons, their helpers, and their abettors, will express their gratitude to American democracy.

But the problem of running nationalized big business concerns without making heavy bureaucratic machines of them will not be an easy one. Let us remember, however, that nationalized big business is no novelty in Italy. The railroads and the telegraph systems have been the property of the Italian state since pre-Fascist days. The manufacture and distribution of salt, tobacco, and other products have long been state monopolies. Furthermore, most public services in great cities have been municipal concerns and there has been also inter-municipal and inter-regional public ownership of common enterprises. The Italians have already had sufficient experience in these matters. Nor must it be forgotten that the most important of big business concerns, such as shipyards, automobile and airplane factories, and iron and steel works, have already been nationalized —in the wrong way. The Fascist state assumed all their liabilities and losses, at the same time guaranteeing dividends to the stockholders and high salaries to the technical experts. The state treasury, which gets its funds from the taxpayers, has already sunk large sums of money into those concerns, while the profits have been pocketed by directors and stockholders. A total nationalization of them is, therefore, fully justified for economic reasons and becomes imperative for political and social reasons.

The confiscation of ill-gotten properties and the nationalization of big business will be the first steps towards the setting up of a new social and economic order. This is the only way in which the ideal of an industrial democracy may at least partly be realized and provide that freedom from want preached in a major key by President Roosevelt and in a minor key with undertone restrictions by even the so-called social encyclicals of the last popes, especially the *Quadraginta* of Pius XI.

Democracy must be positively supported by the huge majority of the citizens, if it is not to be doomed to failure. The Italian democratic republic must be established on the confidence, devotion, and faith of the great masses of the Italian people. They will not expect immediate economic miracles of their democratic republic. Nevertheless, they should be made to feel that their social and juridical status has changed for the better as a result of the transition from the Fascist to a democratic regime. They must be made to realize that, having regained their free institutions after much suffering and loss, they must guard them jealously, because their possible disintegration would also mean a fatal deterioration of their economic and social conditions.

It is vitally necessary that the foundations for an industrial democracy in Italy be laid wisely in order to counteract all possible attempts by Communists, demagogues, and doctrinaires to bring about the nationalization of medium-sized and small industrial and commercial concerns. According to the industrial census of 1927 there were at that time: 692,313 concerns with from 1 to 10 persons employed in them; 35,951 concerns with from 11 to 100 persons employed in them; 4,150 concerns with from 101 to 500 persons employed in them. Any attempt to "socialize" all these industrial and commercial enterprises would meet not only with tremendous technical and administrative difficulties, but with the most stubborn resistance in large sections of the urban population. The problem of creating an industrial democracy in Italy must be approached without fanaticism and along practical lines of action, and certainly not according to abstract theories and ideologies conceived in a vacuum.

It has often happened in history that when a regime has collapsed under the weight of its mistakes the men who make the new regime, led by blind hatred against their predecessors, destroy without discrimination everything that was done by them. If possible the new leaders would destroy even the memory of that unpleasant past. Such indiscriminate destruction is always unwise because, just as there is no government, however good, which does not make mistakes, so there is no government, however bad, which does not build up something worthy of preservation.

In the field of relations between capital and labor the Fascist dictatorship, when it took over the government, found already in existence in Italy a wide network of associations of employers and employees. These associations had been formed by spontaneous and free action on the part of the members, and were administered by officers freely chosen by them. But these organizations were not connected among themselves so as to form an organic whole, and their membership embraced only that part of the population which had chosen to join. The Fascist regime disbanded them, confiscated their assets, and then created the so-called corporations, that is to say, associations of employers, professional men, and public officials side by side with unions of workers of all classes and categories. It would be a great mistake to destroy this framework of coordinated organizations only because it was a creation of the dictatorship. This framework ought to be preserved and so modified as to fit the new order. At present, the whole Italian population is regimented into these organizations, which have national, provincial, and local headquarters, but which are managed by officials appointed from above by the Ministry of Corporations. They are not free organizations, but the passive instrument of the dictatorship and the Fascist Party; their members have no rights, but only the duty of paying their fees, which the employers subtract from their salaries and wages and pay directly to the officials in charge of the union treasuries.

By dismissing the Fascist officials and returning to the members their former right to choose freely their local, provincial, and national secretaries and to plan their policy and program of action, these organizations would be vitalized and would function effectively in the new republican regime. Of course, in learning over again how to manage their unions the Italian workers will make mistakes; they will have to go on learning through trial and error. Such has also been the case with American and British labor unions. The Italians may profit by the experiences of the latter and avoid some of the evils which have beset our unions here, such as exorbitant initiation fees, the formation of an aristocracy of high-salaried labor czars responsible to no one, and the monopoly of labor claimed by special groups to the detriment of other bona-fide organizations.

Italian workers will demand that they be regarded as partners with the shareholders, managers, and white-collar workers in the concerns which employ them. This development cannot be avoided in democratic countries if democracy is to be a reality and not an empty word. We can even envisage for the future a society in which intellectual and manual labor, freely organized, will abolish the tithe which labor has to pay to the persons who finance production by the loan of their capital. Whether we like it or not, the radical changes which are taking place in our whole economic system, and which are now undergoing a more rapid and more complete transformation than ever under the pressure of a war economy, seem to point toward a new economic order in which private ownership of the means of production will be very much restricted without suppressing the personal rights and political liberties of the citizens.

This solution of our social and economic problems cannot be brought about by political upheavals, by outside imposition, or by dictatorships and bloody repressions. It can be achieved only by more and better education of working people and a higher sense of responsibility on the part of their leaders. What matters now is that social and political organizations grant equal educational opportunities to all newcomers in the family of democratic nations. We must realize that the time has passed when political democracy could exist apart from economic democracy.

Those who oppose economic democracy must renounce political democracy as well and choose between Fascism or Communism. There is no reason to assume that such things will be any different in Italy than they are in other countries.

Mussolini had and still has many admirers in England and America. It will be well to remind them that Fascist propaganda has always given Mussolini credit for granting the Italian workers a share in the management of Italian industry. The truth of the matter is that Fascist officials appointed from above to represent the members of the so-called unions, but not responsible to them, settled all questions regarding wages, hours of work, individual disputes, and everything else through negotiations with the agents of the employers' associations. Still other officials appointed by the dictatorship thrashed out general economic problems in the so-called National Corporations and in the Chamber of Fasces and Corporations. We shall deal with the political function of this Chamber later on. In post-Fascist Italy deceptive words and sham must be replaced by real, active, and responsible organizations. Let us hope that Mussolini's admirers will not cease to admire him on the day when someone else fulfills the promises which he so lavishly made and never kept.

3. Agrarian Reform

The government of the Italian republic, in its provisional stage, must face and begin to solve the problem of "the land to the peasants" and not leave it as a convenient springboard for Communist propaganda.

The small landowners and small tenants make up the largest agricultural class in Italy. Unfortunately, the Italian census does not distinguish clearly enough among the various classes of landowners, tenants, share-croppers, day laborers, and so on. In round numbers one can safely state, however, that there are in Italy about 1,000,000 landowners who do not cultivate their lands and live mostly in the cities. Most of these do not own large estates but relatively small family possessions which they rent while making their living in various professions. The owners who cultivate their lands number about 1,500,000; among them a minority of something like 100,000 are well-to-do people who direct the work, which is done by hired hands. Within the large tenant class, too, there is a minority of about 60,000 sufficiently provided with capital to rent considerable estates. They also direct the work which is done by hired labor. About 1,300,000 are small tenants or sharecroppers, who cultivate the soil with their own labor and that of their families.

Below these classes of landowners, tenants, and sharecroppers there is the humble category of day laborers, who number about 1,500,000. Many of them, however, also belong to the class of small landowners or tenants, who, unable to obtain a sufficient income from their little property or tenancy, work also as hired hands part of the year. It is impossible to know or even guess how many belong to this class of hybrids.

There is a notion current among foreigners that Italy is honeycombed with large estates, and that this is one of the causes of the low condition of the Italian peasantry. In fact, large estates are rather the exception than the rule in Italy. Certainly there are *latifundia*, especially in Sicily, Calabria, in the province of Rome, and in the southwestern part of Tuscany. But most of these so-called large estates would seem ridiculously small in comparison with the great estates in England or North and South America. Furthermore, the great Italian estates are not as a rule uncultivated and fallow lands; usually they are under cultivation by tenants or sharecroppers.

When one bears in mind these conditions of the Italian agricultural classes, one realizes that in Italy an agrarian and social revolution similar to that which took place in Russia in 1917 could not happen, even in military defeat and the resulting confusion. In Russia in 1917, the peasants, almost all landless, deserted the army *en masse,* went back home, and drove the property owners from the land which they had formerly cultivated as a rural proletariat. In Italy the class of rural day laborers is not so large.

Italy certainly needs agrarian reform, but the reform must be planned and carried out so as to improve the existing conditions, not in a haphazard, revolutionary fashion. The lands of the so-called large estates, which, as we have already noted, are under cultivation by tenants and sharecroppers, as well as all other estates of absentee landlords, should, by an act of government, become the property of those same tenants and sharecroppers who now cultivate them according to systems to be worked out with an eye to local conditions. Other lands equally available should be parcelled out to rural day laborers.

By these measures we do not mean to suggest an outright confiscation of private properties. The grant of lands to tenants and laborers who till the soil with their own hands, should be conditioned by their assumption of the legal obligation to pay their former landlord an annual sum of money. The amount of this sum could be calculated in each case by taking as a basis the average of the income received by the landlord during the last ten years and then subtracting from the total the average amount of direct taxes paid during the same period. Since direct taxes have gone up to a crushing degree in these last years, the annual sum due from the new owners to the former landlord would be modest. Thanks to the parasitic and destructive Fascist regime, the ownership of land for those who do not cultivate it directly has become highly unprofitable and sometimes even burdensome. Such being the case, not much opposition may be expected from the average landlord to this conversion of his income from the form of rent to that of a fixed compensation, small as it may be.

On the other hand, the lot of the former tenants and sharecroppers, now landowners, would not be much improved so long as the present high rate of taxation remained unchanged. It becomes necessary, therefore, for the government to step in soon after the transfer of property has taken place, abolish the government land tax, and lower the land tax of the provincial and municipal administrations. In order not to deprive these local administrations of their main resources, the central government should reimburse them, at least in part. These reimbursements would come from funds reserved, as we have already explained, precisely for the purpose of lightening the burden of taxation. The above measures—namely, the transfer of property titles from the absentee landlords to the peasants who work on the land and the lowering of the land tax—will immediately double the class of small landowners, give all a sense of great improvement and security, and make them most reliable supporters of the republican regime.

There are large estates which could not be divided without ruining their value. This is the case with the irrigated lands in lower Lombardy and in a few other places which are usually tenanted by men with capital who are at the same time agricultural experts and direct the work done by sharecroppers and laborers. These lands are among the best-cultivated and most highly productive in the world. It would not only be a technical impossibility to divide them among small landowners; it would also be an economic blunder. The ownership of these lands should be transferred to farmers' cooperatives under the same conditions applying to other lands. The technical direction should remain in the hands of experts.

Before the Fascist tornado destroyed the Italian labor organizations, a flourishing cooperative movement existed in Italy. There were many societies set up by agricultural laborers who cultivated estates of considerable importance rented from landlords. With such modifications as the transfer of property requires, this cooperative system can be revived and extended into various parts of Italy, and through it the problem of land which needs capital investment for its exploitation can be easily solved.

Socialists and Communists will raise against this type of land reform the objection that it maintains private ownership of land

and, in fact, increases the number of small property owners. These parties have always shown slight knowledge of agricultural problems. Anyone possessing the agricultural experience which many Socialists and Communists lack knows that land is no respecter of hard-and-fast rules. In the same district, hilly land requires treatment quite different from that needed in the plains. On the same plain, a slight difference in level demands the adoption of different methods, depending upon whether a particular level can or cannot be irrigated. Agriculture can be socialized on land suited to intensive-industrial methods (as the technicians call them), such land, for example, as the irrigated farms of lower Lombardy. But where the quality of the land does not permit these methods, the socialization of agriculture may lead to economic disaster and give rise to acute social crises. Orchards, vineyards, vegetable gardens, flower beds require individual care. To attempt to socialize agriculture in cases where each plant needs special care, where the machine cannot take the place of the hand of man, is to kill production.

It is a fact that as soon as conditions improve for the agricultural classes and enable them to buy land, the small rural owners not only do not disappear, they multiply. The reason is not far to seek. In most cases, the small owner is the one who succeeds in wresting from the land the greatest possible production. It is a known fact that the cultivator ruins the land, if he foresees that he will have it for only a short time. Without thinking of the future, he squeezes from it as much as it can give. The vine does not bear grapes within a few months, but within four or five years; the olive tree must wait ten to fifteen years. The cultivator plants the grape and the olive tree only if he is the owner of the land. If he rents the land for a few years, he sows wheat or uses up the trees that are already there without planting new ones. In Italy one can reasonably predict that if the ownership of land is transferred from the landlords who do not cultivate them to the tenants and sharecroppers who do cultivate them, production will be augmented owing to the greater interest taken by the cultivators in their *own* land.

The small owner often leads a wretched life for one or several reasons: he lacks capital, he is bled by taxes, or he is exploited in the acquisition of raw materials or in the sale of his produce. What he needs is not the socialization of land so much as freedom from excess taxes, education in the cooperative system of buying and selling, and relief from customs systems that protect industry to the detriment of agriculture.

The most difficult problem will be determining what to do with the day laborers who cannot be provided with land grants. The dream of every Italian peasant is to become a small land-owner. Unfortunately, there is not land enough in Italy for all of them; the country is overpopulated and one third of it consists of bare mountains and sterile lands. Though the day laborers are a minority, they can readily become the tools of Communists who wish to create disorder and discontent. The latter would set them against the small landowners and invoke Russia as the model to be imitated, even though they are well aware that Italy is not Russia.

The government of the new Italian republic must do something tangible for this class. It might, for instance, reserve for them the lands which become available from works of reclamation undertaken at public expense. It might set aside a fund for financing new agricultural cooperatives, or plan public works for the reforestation of mountainous regions and similar rural improvements. The new government must realize that it is duty bound to eliminate or at least mitigate unemployment by planned public works. Last but not least, it might do well to secure an outlet for a regulated emigration.

The lot of the day laborers who find work will be improved by the action of their reorganized unions and by government protection. The government can hardly be expected to do more, and it would be unwise to promise the impossible.

4. Parliament and Municipalities

The Constituent Assembly of the Italian democratic republic should endow the country with parliamentary institutions that work more satisfactorily than those of pre-Fascist Italy.

Towards the middle of the nineteenth century, when parliamentary institutions were first adopted in Italy, a single legislative organ could deal with all the problems of national life. At that time, the government did not take cognizance of all the matters which, during the past century, have gradually passed from the sphere of private initiative into that of public law. A member of parliament could examine conscientiously the bills he was called upon to sanction. Today, no man exists who has at his command the technical knowledge necessary for an intelligent opinion concerning all the bills which await the judgment of a representative. No man, even with a technical equipment far above the average, could master the enormous volume of matters calling for his consideration, though he were to specialize in a single branch of public administration. Difficulties grow as a government's activities expand. Parliament is no longer able to exercise legislative power in the full sense of the word. Actual sovereignty has passed from parliament to the high permanent officials who first prepare the bills, and then interpret and operate the laws according to their own judgment. Above the heads of the high permanent officials waves the whip wielded by the vested interests, which control the press and impose their will upon influential politicians and high officials alike.

Many of the drawbacks of parliamentary government today could be eliminated or attenuated by the adoption of reforms simplifying its constitutional duties. The national parliament ought to reserve for its own exclusive jurisdiction all problems affecting the nation as a whole, such as general principles of law, foreign policy, customs duties, budgets, and the like; but it should delegate all other matters to other national representative bodies on a smaller scale. At this point, at least a part of the framework of the so-called National Council of Fasces and Corporations could be used for building a new structure. This council, created by the dictatorship in 1938 to usurp the functions of the old parliament, has the fatal drawback of merging and confusing together the political functions of a national parliament and the technical and administrative functions of technical bodies. The members drawn directly from the Fascist party are supposed to represent the whole people, while those who come from the "Corporations" are supposed to represent the various groups of trades, professions, and occupations into which the Italian employers, professional classes, and wage-earners are divided.

In actual fact, however, they represent no one but Mussolini, who appoints them, opens and shuts their mouths, tells them what to do and how to vote, and throws them out when he gets tired of them. It goes without saying that the National Council of Fasces and Corporations must disappear and its place be taken by a national parliament elected by universal suffrage.

Besides this parliament, which will move in its assigned sphere of what we may call "political" affairs, there must be other representative bodies to whom "technical" affairs may be entrusted. The various Councils of corporations, purged of all Fascist connotations and composed of members elected by the various trades, could very well be assigned this task. They would form, so to speak, a series of small technical parliaments. Each of them would study and discuss only a specific group of problems, such as the relations between capital and labor, social security, public works, public education, local government, public health, and so on. Each would formulate the by-laws necessary to carry out the general principles of law already approved by the national parliament. Within the limits of its jurisdiction, each council or small parliament would watch the daily work of the permanent officials entrusted with executive powers to put laws and by-laws into practice.

At first sight it may appear as if the institution of a series of small parliaments side by side with the national parliament, rather than simplifying, would make the whole machinery of government more complex and more cumbersome. This objection vanishes when we reflect that these small parliaments would in reality take the place of the numerous committees of parliament which, in the old system, were each charged with a specific set of problems and reported their conclusions and their proposals to the assembly. The difference between the old system and the new would consist primarily in the fact that while the committees were formed before by members of parliament chosen by their colleagues for political reasons, regardless of whether or not they lacked that special knowledge required in technical matters, the councils or small parliaments would now be elected by the different economic groups of the population from the experts in the special line of affairs with which each council has to deal. In the second place, while in the old system the national parliament had to discuss in all their details the recommendations of the committees, in the new system the national parliament would only establish general principles of law and policy having a normative value. Thus its work would be simplified by the removal of an enormous mass of business while each group of problems would be dealt with in detail by a specialized organ.

We realize that the system which we propose is not ideal and that many difficulties, both theoretical and practical, will arise upon putting it into effect. We also realize that the men elected to the central or minor parliaments will not become supermen merely on the strength of being elected instead of appointed by a dictator. They will not forget the often selfish interests of the special constituencies. Conflicts among the delegates in each council and quarrels among the various councils will of course arise. It will be the task and duty of the international parliament to act as arbiter in all such conflicts and to have the final word, after having summoned the delegates of the councils involved for the purpose of submitting their cases and their arguments to its judgment. In these discussions, also, each side would inevitably seek to persuade the majority with good arguments, or with bad arguments when good ones were wanting, would prolong the discussion when defeat seemed imminent, and would content itself with a compromise when it despaired of victory. In short, everybody would use the methods and devices characteristic of governments based on public discussion and majority decision, and not the hidden tricks of dictatorship and the violence of civil war. In the democratic state, no less than in any state, the vested interests would try to pull the strings behind the scenes, control the press, and corrupt officials and politicians.

Democratic institutions take men as they are. They offer no solution for all woes. They are merely instruments used by civilized people to debate and decide their problems, instruments more desirable than civil war or authoritarian regimes, which are but disguised and constant civil war. To the man who has the capacity and the will to act, democratic institutions grant the right to act without danger of brutal suppression; they cannot, however, assure victory to the man who does not want or know how to act. It is not the fault of democratic institutions, if the majority of the citizens take no interest in public life, elect representatives who allow themselves to be corrupted, and prefer to read the demagogue rather than the intelligent newspapers. In any case, a democratic government, however organized, offers greater obstacles to the domination of vested interests than does a despotic-oligarchical government. So true is this that as soon as social groups appear which are capable of utilizing democratic institutions against vested interests, the latter try to do away with democratic institutions and set up a despotic-oligarchical system of government.

Be that as it may, one fact must be made clear. In a democratic state, the higher parliament and the lower parliaments should be legislative organs which the government bureaucracy must obey, and not merely consultative bodies subservient to the will of a dictator or of a government bureaucracy pulling the strings behind the scenes. Moreover, both higher and lower parliaments should be freely elected, the higher parliament by the generality of the citizens; the lower parliaments, by those social groups having a special interest in the problems with which they are to deal. Finally, all problems should be publicly and freely discussed. This is the essential procedure of democracy.

Aside from decentralizing the legislative work among one higher and many lower parliaments, there is another suitable way of bringing about a healthier political life in Italy: the re-establishment of municipal administrations, not only freely elected, but also made really independent of the central government. One of the worst stains on the pre-Fascist escutcheon was the Home Office's strict control over the local government. The town councils and mayors were elected by the citizens, but the Home Secretary kept a delegate in each province called the "prefect," who was entitled to dismiss mayors and disband town councils whenever he considered that they had misbehaved. There was no redress against his abuses. Thus, the prefect was in a position to bring pressure to bear upon the mayor and town councillors, especially in the backward sections of the country. The mayors and the town councillors who used their influence in favor of the government's candidate during electoral campaigns remained in office, even if they were the worst public rascals. Those who supported the opposition's candidates were replaced by government "commissioners," even if they were good administrators. This method, unscrupulously applied, sufficed to put at the service of the prefect most of the mayors, and at the service of the Home Secretary many, indeed too many, deputies to parliament. There was a saying in Italy to the effect that the Home Secretary sold the prefects and bought the deputies.

If the Home Secretaries of the republic return to such shameful practices, Italian democracy will be stillborn. The prefect should no longer be entitled to dismiss mayors and disband town councils. The judiciary and not the prefect should determine whether a mayor and town council have violated any law and should be deprived of their authority. As a consequence of such a reform, a deputy would no longer fear the prefect's reprisals and be forced to vote blindly for the cabinet in order to shelter the mayors and town councils of his constituency.

This simple outline of some major reforms which, in our opinion, will be necessary to secure the democratic character of the future Italian republic and to prevent some of the evils of the old parliamentary system is merely the expression of personal views resulting from actual experience in political life and from a close acquaintance with modern Italian history. It should be fully apparent that we are neither revolutionaries nor conservatives. We are firm believers in democracy, as being the least imperfect system of our times; and we conceive of politics as the science of what is possible under circumstances special to time and place, not the science of what is desirable on merely theoretical grounds. There will be other plans inspired by different principles from ours. The Italian people will have their choice. We have confidence in the practical common sense, the spirit of moderation, and the courage and will to survive of the Italian people.

VII. Church and State in Post-War Italy

1. The Background

THE problem of the relations between the Vatican and the Italian state, and the problem of the relations between church and state in Italy, must be kept distinct, since they have different natures and different implications. The first is essentially the question of how the liberty of the Holy See as center of the international Catholic Church is to be guaranteed. This problem concerns not only the Italians but all Catholics everywhere. That of the relation between church and state in Italy, on the contrary, is a local problem, parallel to similar problems in other states, and concerns Italy alone.

Pius XI and Mussolini thought that they had settled both problems by the Lateran agreements of February, 1929. They contain three distinct but connected parts. The conciliation treaty is a political document, by which the Pope officially recognized the Italian state and made a solemn perpetual renunciation of all claims of the Holy See to the former pontifical territories. In return, the Italian state recognized the independence of Vatican City. The second document is a financial agreement, by which the Italian state paid the Holy See an indemnity of 750 million lire in cash and one billion lire in state bonds yielding five per cent per annum. The third document is a concordat, by which the exercise of the Catholic religion and the relations of church and state in Italy were regulated in detail by the mutual consent of the two parties.

It is obvious that in these agreements the political and the religious questions were, to a certain extent, considered interdependent and were, in fact, solved together. But why did this confusion of things which should have been kept separate take place? Dr. D. A. Binchy, a Catholic professor of legal history at the University of Dublin, admits in his recent book *Church and State in Fascist Italy* (Oxford, 1941) that the two problems are distinct, but thinks that they became so entwined in modern Italian history that they were inseparable and called for a common solution.

The historical origin of this supposedly inseparable connection of the two problems is correctly given by Dr. Binchy as follows: The government of the Kingdom of Piedmont, or Kingdom of Sardinia, as it was officially known—the only Italian state that kept a liberal constitution after the revolutions and the war of 1848–49—during the fifties under the leadership of Cavour proposed a series of reforms for the laws concerning the Church and the clergy. These reforms, Dr. Binchy admits, were "not really drastic and some of them were long overdue, for mediaeval conditions had previously obtained in the ecclesiastical framework of Piedmont." The government tried first to bring about those reforms with the consent of the Vatican, "even choosing as its envoy the illustrious and saintly Rosmini." But Pius IX "was in an unyielding temper, perhaps because the political ambitions of Piedmont had already roused his suspicions," and he refused to negotiate. Hence, the government went ahead and introduced the reforms by unilateral legislation. In other words, Pius IX, because of his political suspicions, refused even to negotiate a religious agreement with reforms which were much needed for the improvement of religious life in Piedmont. Once the government had enacted the new laws, the Pope protested, excommunicated those who supported those laws, and from that time on considered the Piedmontese state as a persecutor of the Church.

Meanwhile, the problem of the national unification of Italy began to reach a solution. Here again, history and geography made it unavoidable that the Pope should resign himself to the loss of his temporal states and make an agreement with the new Kingdom of Italy which would fully preserve and guarantee the complete independence of the Holy See. Once more the Pope refused to negotiate, this time because he was unwilling to deal with a government which persecuted the Church. "Had it not been for the religious question," says Dr. Binchy, "Pius IX might well have made a generous, perhaps even an imprudent arrangement with the House of Savoy." Hence, the Italian government was again forced to settle the question by a unilateral action, the Law of Guarantees of 1871. And thus, as Dr. Binchy concludes, "a vicious circle of disagreement was erected," from which "escape was only possible by a comprehensive settlement of both problems."

From these facts set forth by Dr. Binchy it is evident that the vicious circle started by the Holy See when it refused to make a religious agreement for political reasons, and then refused to make a political agreement for religious reasons, was an artificial creation for which the Vatican alone was responsible. It is interesting to note that the Vatican's dealings with the Fascist and Nazi regimes are usually justified on the grounds that the Holy See is not only willing, but anxious, to make concordats and agreements with any kind of government, be it pagan or atheist, because the Holy See has in view primarily the religious and spiritual interests of the people. Evidently this was not the principle which guided Pius IX when he refused even to negotiate with the liberal government of Piedmont the much needed revision of a concordat. It is obvious that, having created the vicious circle, the Vatican should choose to remain within it; but it is no less obvious that it was not to the interest of the state to accept the situation created by the blundering policy of Pius IX.

The Italian state acted within its rights and duties in settling by unilateral legislation both the religious and the political problems, and in letting the Vatican revolve at ease in its own vicious circle. Dr. Binchy's opinion notwithstanding, the only escape from this circle is by breaking it and not by remaining within it. The Vatican was so well aware of this fact that, when it finally realized that there was no use in keeping the Roman question alive and made the first contacts for a settlement with the pre-Fascist government in 1919, it thereby showed itself willing to come out of the circle. Pope Benedict XV, as Dr. Binchy grants, was "prepared to settle with the government without a concordat," because he knew that to obtain a concordat from the pre-Fascist parliamentary regime was out of the question. His successor, however, Pius XI, hastened to get back into the vicious circle and asked for a concordat as a condition for the settlement of the Roman question; he knew that with the Fascist dictatorship he could do business to his own satisfaction. A realistic view of the situation reveals that, after the first World War, it was the Vatican which felt the urgent need to settle the Roman question.

The reason for this need was frankly stated by writers connected with the Vatican. Here in the United States Cardinal Gasparri's nephew, Monsignor Bernardini, then Professor of Canon Law at the Catholic University in Washington and now Apostolic Delegate in Australia, stated in an article published by the *Catholic World* in February, 1929:

The Italian new generation have gradually become used to the existing state of affairs. . . . This acquiescence to existing conditions has been very dangerous to the principles which the Catholic Church could not renounce, and which, nevertheless, year by year, were becoming more inexplicable to the Catholics of Italy and of the entire world. . . . Hence the necessity on the part of the Holy See of finding an early solution for the so-called Roman Question.

More bluntly, the Roman question was dying, if not already dead, and the Vatican had to hurry in order to get something out of it before it was too late. But for the same reason the pre-Fascist government of Italy had no need to hurry; delay was to its advantage. With the advent of the Fascist state the situation changed, because Mussolini was even more eager than the Vatican to make an agreement, and he was, therefore, prepared to go as far as possible in accepting the papal terms. Being a dictator, he could negotiate in complete secrecy and conclude an agreement without asking anybody's consent. He wanted the personal glory of having settled the Roman question; he wanted the support of the Church in Italy and throughout the world for his regime. It is little wonder, then, that he was willing to pay the price asked by the Vatican, that is, a concordat.

Pius XI, a good Milanese who had inherited a shrewd business sense, and his Secretary of State, Cardinal Gasparri, who came from a family of hardbitten shepherds in the Roman mountains, could not let such an occasion slip. Mussolini was the man they needed; truly, he was the man sent by Providence at the right moment. Of course, they knew Mussolini was neither gullible nor reliable, and that he was a past master in the art of mental reservation. They knew that the Fascist regime was pagan and ruthless, both in theory and in practice. Above all, they knew that they were tying up the fortunes of the agreement to the fortunes of the Fascist regime. But on the other hand, Pius XI, as Dr. Binchy remarks rather casually, had no love for democracy and parliamentary institutions; furthermore, he was convinced that Fascism was already so solidly entrenched in Italy that no change was to be feared for a long time. Finally, as a good pope, Pius XI had great confidence in the assistance of the Holy Ghost and in the Divine Providence which takes care of the Church. To be sure, the negotiations were long and laborious, because there were limits to the concessions which the negotiators could make, and there were several compromises which, after the signing of the agreements, gave rise to sharp controversies. Even after the edifying public quarrel between Mussolini and the Pope, neither party was willing, or could afford, to step back, and in spite of everything the agreements were ratified.

Thus the vicious circle of Pius IX—the interdependence of the political and religious questions—instead of being broken, was turned into an iron ring which linked them together so strongly that Pius XI could say, "The Treaty and the Concordat stand or fall together." This ring must be broken, if a lasting solution of both problems is to be achieved.

2. *The Lateran Treaty*

The new Italian democratic regime cannot be expected to accept the inheritance from the Fascist period of any laws, treaties, or obligations which are contrary to the principles of democracy, and which do not respect the rights and liberties of the citizens. Obligations assumed by Fascism in accord with its totalitarian nature and policies cannot be recognized as binding, and cannot be assumed by the new regime, if it is to be a democracy.

The Lateran Treaty contains at least two articles which cannot be reconciled with the fundamental principles and laws of a democratic state; namely, Articles 1 and 23. Article 1 states: "Italy recognizes and reaffirms the principle consecrated in article 1st of the constitution of the Kingdom of March 4, 1848, according to which the Catholic Apostolic Roman Religion is the religion of the State." This article of the century-old constitution had long before ceased to have any value in Italy. Parliament, which was the interpreter of the constitution, had again and again enacted laws which were not consistent with the principles, laws, and prescriptions of the Catholic Church. Furthermore, the Fascist dictatorship had done away with the constitution, which, for all practical purposes, had been superseded by Fascist totalitarianism and all that it implied. How the first article of a dead constitution could be revived in a political treaty with another power is something that no jurist has been able to explain.

A treaty of peace is a contract between two parties, to be sure. Religion in a democratic state, however, is not a matter to be handled by the making of political contracts between secular and ecclesiastical powers. Whether the Italians are Catholics or not, no Italian government has the right to make a contract with a third party engaging the religious faith of the nation and assuming obligations which are beyond the sphere of political and temporal matters. This article is out of place in the Lateran Treaty. It has no justification, unless we return to the principle of the German states during the wars of the Reformation: *cuius regio, eius religio.*

In principle, the state which adopts a state religion becomes a confessional state. In other words, it accepts officially the whole dogmatic teaching of the church—all the rules and regulations of canon law, all ecclesiastical decrees concerning morals and piety—to the exclusion of all other cults and denominations. As a matter of fact, Pope Pius and the Jesuits of the *Civiltà Cattolica,* together with the many Catholic polemists who came to the surface immediately after the signing of the Lateran agreement, rightly maintained that the Italian state had become a confessional Catholic state and had assumed all the obligations thereof. Mussolini refused to accept this interpretation, confiscated the Catholic newspapers and periodicals, and thus put an end to the controversy. But this does not mean that the Catholic Church has given up its claim, even though that article of the treaty has become a dead letter, just as the article of the old constitution was already a dead letter. The new Indian democratic regime cannot be expected to accept this article of the treaty. It does not belong and is meaningless. The question whether the new Italian democracy will or will not have a state religion must be decided first by the new Italian republican constitution.

Likewise, Article 23 of the treaty cannot be accepted. This article states that "the judgments and provisions of the ecclesiastical authorities when officially communicated to the civil authorities, concerning ecclesiastical and religious persons and spiritual or disciplinary matters will have automatically full juridical efficacy even in regard to the civil effects of them." The rather involved phrases mean that the judgments, decrees, and measures taken by ecclesiastical authorities against ecclesiastical persons or members of religious orders would automatically have the same value as the judgments and measures of the civil and criminal courts of the state, and that the officers of the law must see to it that they are applied.

There are two objections to this article: first, it violates the principle that all citizens are equal before the law, because it submits a class of citizens to a jurisdiction which is not that of the state; second, it makes the officials of the state executors of the judgments and orders of the ecclesiastical authorities, that is, it reestablishes in a limited way the medieval practice of the upholding of the ecclesiastical courts by the *secular arm*. In a democracy, where freedom of religion is one of the cornerstones of the whole system, ecclesiastical persons are free citizens who enjoy all the rights of free citizens, and who cannot be punished for actions which are not crimes according to the law of the state. This article is also out of place in a political treaty; it belongs in the concordat, which deals with the relations of church and state.

The presence of these two articles in the Lateran Treaty would be sufficient reason for the new Italian regime to reject the whole instrument as being incompatible with the fundamental principles and laws of a democracy. In our opinion, however, such a rejection would be a mistake, because the treaty, no matter how or when it was made, contains the final and solemn renunciation of the papal claims, and closed the Roman question forever. Though this question had already lost all its political importance, and was no longer troubling the consciences of even the Catholic clergy in Italy, the papal assent to regularize the situation *de jure* was a further contribution to the spiritual unification of Italy. It is always very helpful to bury the ghosts of the past.

But there is another, more important reason why the Lateran Treaty ought not to be cancelled and declared void by the new Italian republic. In his speech of May 14, 1929, to his puppet Chamber of Deputies, Mussolini, in the course of acid remarks upon the interpretation assigned to the newly signed Lateran agreement, made this statement:

We must convince ourselves that between the Italian State and Vatican City there is a distance which may be calculated in thousands of miles, even if by chance five minutes are enough to go there and ten minutes to make the tour of its boundaries.

Mussolini was wrong. The "imaginary distance," by which he set far apart the Italian state and Vatican City, was but one of his many empty phrases. The geographical fact is that the Papacy is in the heart of Italy, next door to the Italian state, and this fact makes it impossible for any Italian government to deal with the Papacy as can the governments of other countries. Other governments can, if they wish, ignore the existence of Vatican City with little or no trouble. Italy cannot do so for the simple reason that the Papacy is in Rome in a small area surrounded on all sides by Italian territory and depending upon it for its material existence. This condition was not created by the Lateran agreement; it has existed *de facto* since 1870. Italy's position in this matter is unique, and unique is the problem which history has given the country. It is a problem which must be faced as long as the Papacy lasts.

Liberal Italy solved it by the Law of Guarantees of 1871, which even the American Jesuit, Father Parson, who cannot at any time be suspected of having liberal sentiments, described as "a masterpiece of legislation . . . in many ways extremely wise and even generous" (*The Pope and Italy*, New York, 1929, p. 32). According to a statement commonly repeated in Catholic history books, and also reproduced by Father Parson, the great drawback of the Law of Guarantees was its being a unilateral law of the Italian state and not a treaty arranged with the Vatican. As a consequence, the Pope refused to recognize that law, but "all these years the Popes have stood ready to accept most of the terms of the Law of Guarantees if they came in treaty form, but not if they were merely a law" (p. 34).

This is not the least of the many inaccuracies in Father Parson's book. The assumption that the Popes were ready, during those sixty years, to accept the Law of Guarantees if it came in the form of a treaty must be a special revelation received by Father Parson. None of the Popes down to Benedict XV ever made any definite gesture in that direction. Did not Father Parson know that the Italian government, before and immediately after the occupation of Rome in 1870, not only stood ready, but practically begged the Pope to make a treaty? If the Law of Guarantees did not come in the form of a treaty, the responsibility was not the Italian government's, but the Vatican's for not having yet learned that its temporal power could not be restored again, and for making the mistake of thinking that the national and political unity of Italy would not last. It took sixty years for the Vatican to learn this lesson. Had it been learned sooner, much trouble would have been saved for both the Vatican and for Italy. In such circumstances, there was no alternative left for the Italian government except that of making its own law; and this law, as Father Parson says, was wise and generous.

The Law of Guarantees was wise and worked well in practice because the men who were in the government, in parliament, and the Italian people themselves realized only too well that the independence of the Pope, where governmental and spiritual administration of the Church is concerned, is a matter of prime importance, not only to Italian Catholics, but to all Catholics. True democracy abhors the use of religion as an *instrumentum regni*, but it abhors no less both sectarian anti-religious bias and petty persecutions. It applies its principles of freedom and respect for all religions both in the national and in the international sphere, whenever religious problems with international complications happen to arise. A future Italian Republic will have enough harrowing problems to face in the political, social, and economic reconstruction of the country, and it will need the good will of all its citizens to solve them. Internal conflicts of a religious character must be avoided as far as possible. Furthermore, Italy will need the good will and assistance of other nations within the system of international organization that will be set up to insure peace and a new order in the world. The Catholic Church, whether we like it or not, has recently gained, thanks to the policies followed by the American State Department and the British Foreign Office, a considerable political influence. To provoke the hostility of various governments against Italy only for the pleasure of threatening the independence of the Holy See would be sheer folly. Those Italians who have suffered persecution, imprisonment, and exile at the hands of the Fascist dictatorship, and who invoke harsh reprisals against the Vatican for its share of responsibility in the Italian tragedy, seem to forget that the Italian people will regain their freedom, not through victory, but through military defeat—a defeat which will impose stringent limitations upon the policies of the future Italian government.

There is another, more cogent reason why the Lateran Treaty ought not to be denounced by the post-war Italian regime. This treaty has for Italy one great advantage, that of having excluded the possibility of any international guarantee of the agreement. At present, the only guarantor of the independence of Vatican City is the Italian nation. To denounce the treaty means to re-open the whole question, and, in view of the political support which the Vatican now has in many quarters, the demand for international guarantees would inevitably be revived in a new settlement.

Unfortunately, there is not only the possibility, but the great probability that the question will be revived, even if the new Italian regime accepts the Lateran Treaty. There may be various plans as to the way of securing an international guarantee for the independence of the Vatican. The first may be by going back to the idea of Benedict XV, the admission of the Holy See to membership in any kind of international organization which might be established after the war. On December 24, 1939, Pope Pius XII advocated the creation of such an international body as one of the five points of the new order. Another way would be that the victorious powers bestow upon the Lateran Treaty an international guarantee, while the Holy See would not ask to be admitted to membership in any international organization. A third possible way would be to let the treaty remain as it is, a mere arrangement between two powers, but to bestow directly on Vatican City an international guarantee of its neutrality and independence.

In the first case, the new Italian government would have a good reason to object to the plan: the provision of the Lateran Treaty (Article 24) which excludes the Holy See from participation in international political assemblies. But we must realize that should the leading powers of the future League of Nations urge the Vatican to become a member of the international organization either as a special mark of distinction or because all small states shall be invited to join, the objection raised by the

Italian government would be overruled. Since, however, the participation of the Holy See in the League of Nations would imply the abolition of Article 24 of the Lateran Treaty, the Italian government would have the right to ask for a complete revision of the whole treaty and to expunge from it not only Articles 1 and 23, but several other articles containing concessions which were made having in view the fact that the Vatican was to remain outside all political assemblies and competitions.

The acceptance by the Vatican of the membership in the future international organization would imply a complete reversal of the "isolationist" policy of Pius XI. It would mean that the Holy See by taking part in the discussions and decisions of the League should also share with the other members the responsibility of its policies and of its actions. We doubt very much that the Vatican is ready for such a radical change. At any rate, the international guarantee which in this case would be bestowed upon Vatican City would not be a special international agreement aiming directly at the protection of the Vatican against Italy, but would be only the general guarantee of territorial integrity and independence which all members of the League, and among them Italy, mutually and severally promise to respect and to protect.

In the second case, the problem would be more difficult and fraught with dangers; it would mean the internationalization of the Lateran Treaty by an act of the victorious powers. The matter is not so simple as it may appear at first sight. It involves many questions of the utmost importance; here are some of them: Would the internationalization of the Lateran Treaty in its present form imply that the Italian state assumes a solemn international obligation to remain a confessional state, with the Catholic religion as the state religion? Would the internationalization of the treaty carry with it the internationalization of the concordat, which, according to the Holy See, is indissolubly united with the treaty and forms one agreement with it? Would the internationalization of the treaty impose upon Italy a perpetual obligation to carry on the heavy financial burden of the Church, irrespective of the economic situation of the country? Last but not least, would all the obligations assumed in the agreement, even those which are contrary to the principles and practices of democracy, become international obligations binding the new government?

To ponder these questions even for a moment makes one realize how absurd in its implications the internationalization of the Lateran agreement would be. These absurd implications are the inevitable consequence of the policy of the "vicious circle" which Pius XI wished to perpetuate by making the existence of the treaty depend upon that of the concordat and vice versa. Though this principle is nowhere explicitly stated in the texts of the Lateran agreements, it cannot be denied that the interdependence of treaty and concordat was a fundamental point in the mind of Pius XI. Not only did he say so during his polemics with Mussolini, but the insertion into the treaty of such articles as 1 and 23, which deal with matters belonging to the concordat, had no other purpose than to establish, so to speak, a physical connection between the two parts of the agreement, and to merge together the political and religious solutions of the old conflict.

Mussolini, on the contrary, denied ever having accepted the Pope's view, and there is no reason to doubt this statement. It is evident that, during the negotiations, this controversial point, though it was of fundamental importance, was either dodged altogether or settled by some ambiguous declaration off the record. So anxious were both parties to conclude the pact that they were content to leave that problem for the moment. As far as the question of the internationalization of the Lateran agreements is concerned, it matters little, after all, which of the two contradictory statements was true, the Pope's or Mussolini's. The essential points bearing on the problem are: first, that a concordat is by nature an internal affair of no concern to any foreign nation or government, and, as such, is incapable of assuming an international character; second, and more important, that in making the Lateran agreements both parties declared it their intention that the pact was not to be submitted to any international guarantee. On this point there cannot be the slightest doubt. Pius XI explained again and again why he did not ask for any foreign guarantee and Mussolini made it clear that, on his part, the exclusion of any outside guarantee had been a condition *sine qua non* of the agreement.

With this evidence at hand, the post-war Italian government will be more than justified in taking the point of view that any attempt to bestow an international guarantee upon the Lateran agreements would automatically render them null and void. To these few remarks we must add also that this international guarantee, far from helping to better the relations of church and state in Italy, would provoke a new and painful conflict. It would act as a boomerang against the Vatican, which would be held responsible for the violation of one of the essential conditions under which the Lateran Treaty was concluded; it would add fuel to the flame of anti-clericalism and promote general hostility to the Church on the part of the Italian people. The international guarantee, especially if extended to the concordat, would in practice reduce Italy to the condition of a nation under a regime of capitulations, precisely at the time in which capitulations are being abolished even in backward countries.

Pius XI, immediately after the conclusion of the agreement, said that in his opinion any international guarantee had no value. It had had none in the past; it could have none in the future. In addressing the diplomatic corps on March 9, 1929, he stated again that an outside guarantee was neither desirable nor acceptable as far as the Holy See was concerned. The purpose of a guarantee, he said, was to serve as a defense against enemies, but the Holy See had no enemies. If the motive of defense were excluded, then the guarantee would assume the character of a protection and tutelage, but the Holy See does not need protection and rejects any kind of tutelage. It is our hope that at the Vatican the words of Pius XI have not been forgotten, and that the men who will be in the government of post-war Italy will not assume the attitude of "enemies" threatening the independence of the Holy See.

Finally the United Nations, or some of them, might propose to guarantee only the independence and neutrality of Vatican City with its present boundaries, but without any reference either to the Lateran Treaty and the Concordat, or to any other question pertaining to them. In this case, the subject matter of the guarantee, that is, the independence and neutrality of Vatican City, would not raise any objection, since Italy herself has taken a solemn oath to respect and guarantee both the independence and the neutrality of that territory. The only point requiring discussion would be the necessity of having other guarantors besides Italy.

The answer to this question will depend upon the general policy adopted by the victorious nations towards post-war Italy. They will, of course, have the power, not only to impose absolute disarmament and other inevitable humiliations upon Italy, but also, if they so choose, to force the Italians to accept a government not of their own selection. Such a government would be entirely at the disposal of the victors, and would last only as long as foreign armies were on hand to protect it. The victors should be aware of the fact that, if they impose their will in this fashion, the government they set up will have no prestige and will not represent the will of the people. If such is the plan of Washington and London, then they will soon have reason enough to doubt that the obligations assumed by such a government can be fulfilled, or that its promises can be respected for long. In such a case, the United Nations ought to guarantee, not only the independence of Vatican City, but also the existence and perpetuation of the crypto-Fascist or authoritarian government which they would be imposing upon Italy. In addition, they must keep always at hand sufficient military force to protect such a government from the Italian people.

But if the victors keep the solemn promises they have made concerning the establishment of democratic governments everywhere possible, and if Italy is thus allowed to choose a government of the people, then Washington and London may rest assured that engagements and promises made by that government will be faithfully kept. An act of confidence, such as allowing Italy to be the natural guarantor of the independence and neutrality of Vatican City, would go a long way towards gaining the wholehearted support of the Italian people in the post-war order to be established in Europe.

Our diplomats in Washington ought to think twice before they decide this question. They must realize that a legal guarantee of the independence of Vatican City without the consent of an Italian government chosen by the Italian people would be a humilitating imposition reacting against the Vatican itself. They must realize that to ask or force the Italian government to give its consent to this international guarantee would be to discredit it with the people and to increase the difficulties of Italy's post-war reconstruction. It would be wiser to abstain from making such plans as long as there is no actual evidence that the independence of Vatican City is being threatened by the Italian people.

We speak of real and not imaginary threats, because the relations between the Vatican and post-war Italy must be readjusted according to the exigencies of the new regime. It is obvious that a treaty and a concordat which fitted in with the policies of the Fascist dictatorship cannot be expected to be consonant with the policies of a democracy. Changes must be made, and frictions will be inevitable. We shall deal with this problem, as well as with the financial problem, in the following pages. To conclude our discussion of the Lateran Treaty, let us repeat that the ratification of the Lateran Treaty by the democratic gov-

ernment of post-war Italy will be the only way of avoiding unnecessary complications and difficulties, both in the national and
in the international fields. In our opinion, the new Italian government ought to take the stand that the treaty is "intangible"
and that no revision of it is needed. Italy has fulfilled all the essential obligations assumed in that treaty; it has turned over to
the Holy See all the territory, palaces, buildings, and possessions
that were agreed upon. It has paid a heavy indemnity to the
Vatican. It has guaranteed the independence and the freedom of
the Holy See in its government of the Catholic Church the world
over. In return, the Holy See has renounced all past claims, has
recognized the legitimacy of the Italian national government,
and has most explicitly engaged itself not to seek or accept any
foreign guarantee of its independence.

The presence in the treaty of those objectionable articles
which we have mentioned above is not an obstacle against its
ratification. Those articles do not affect at all the essential content and form of the treaty; they are extraneous bodies artificially
inserted into it and have no direct connection with the political
problem settled by the treaty. Those articles will become automatically a dead letter, when the new Italian constitution declares that there shall be no state religion and guarantees the
equality of all citizens before the law. It is obvious that the ratification of the treaty which takes place after the promulgation of
the new constitution will not cover such articles of the agreement
as cannot be applied.

It is rather difficult to imagine that the Holy See would start
a hopeless controversy over the treaty. The real and very serious difficulties will arise in connection with the Concordat.

3. The Concordat

We have already disposed of the presumed juridical bond
which does not allow the concordat to be separated from the
treaty. Legal historians such as those extensively quoted by Dr.
Binchy may go on quibbling to their hearts' content about

whether or not this bond does exist, and whether or not treaty and concordat stand and fall together. Separation of church and state will break the vicious circle once and for all. The question of the concordat must be considered by itself and not in relation to the treaty.

According to an O.W.I. report, the Vatican radio, in a German-language broadcast on May 15, 1943, quoted Pope Pius XII as saying that he longed for peace, "but not peace at any price." The Pope invoked "a peace guaranteeing true veneration of God," and then added:

Render unto Caesar the things which are Caesar's and unto God the things which are God's; one would like to add: Give unto man the things which are man's; give man his freedom and personality, his rights and religion (*New York Times,* May 16, 1943).

The words which the Pope quoted from the Gospel have often been twisted and tortured to fit any political-religious scheme, whatever the point of view. Incidentally, we would much prefer to leave Caesar's name out of it. Whatever we may think of the historical Caesar, the false cult by which his name became the object of Fascist verbosity, and much more the Fascist dictator's ridiculous aping of Caesar, make us dislike to use his name as the personification of the state. After all, the democratic state represents the people and acts by the authority of the people, and is not dedicated to the service of any Caesar, legitimate or spurious.

In general, however, these words are supposed to contain the ideal formula for solving the problem of the relations between church and state: Give to each of them its due. Nothing could be more simple or more final. Actually, this phrase is so vague that it offers no solution to the problem at all. The conflict between church and state arises from a very definite question: Precisely what belongs to the church, and what belongs to the state? Each church, according to its own theories and beliefs, maintains that it possesses certain spiritual and material prerogatives; likewise, each state, according to its structure and historical background, makes definite claims. The question of what belongs to which has never been settled. In the Catholic Church, the long and sometimes tragic history of the concordats made by the Holy See with emperors, kings, and nations in the Middle Ages, with absolute monarchies in a more modern period, and with both liberal and totalitarian states in contemporary times, shows an ever-changing picture of the claims advanced by both sides. Like shifting sands on a stormy shore the boundary lines between the domains of church and state have changed with every incoming and outgoing tide. Popes, sovereigns and diplomats have been kept busy repairing the damages and tracing new lines which were as quickly cancelled as those they superseded. The canonists and lawyers of the Vatican know this sad history so well that they have coined a significant motto to summarize it: *Historia concordatorum est historia dolorum.* "The history of concordats is a history of sorrows."

Pope Pius XI was a great, perhaps the greatest, maker of concordats in modern times. He considered the Italian Concordat with the Fascist regime to be his masterpiece. He said it was the best, that is to say, the one most advantageous to the Church, ever concluded by the Holy See; at least, he said, it was the best ever made under such circumstances. But according to Mussolini it was less favorable to the Church and more favorable to the state than any concordat previously made by the same Pope with other European states (Address to the Fascist Chamber of Deputies, May 13, 1929).

In reality, the Italian Concordat was neither better nor worse than the others. It was the result of long secret negotiations, and of hard bargaining across the counter, in which both parties yielded ground inch by inch, now struggling over a word or a phrase, now compromising on some ambiguous term which allowed them to reach the conclusion so eagerly sought by both. The result was that, after the concordat was signed, the Pope and Mussolini began to quarrel as to the meaning of several of its articles. It is very instructive to read the documents of this controversy. The Duce, in truculent language, accused the Pope of trying "to change the cards in his hands," an Italian phrase meaning "to cheat"; the Pope complained of having been cheated already by the Duce. There is no need, however, for us to rehearse these quarrels, nor to discuss such results of the Concordat as the fascistization of the Italian Church and other connected events with which we dealt in the chapter on Pius XI and Fascism.

The problem which confronts us now is what can a post-war Italian democratic government, elected by the people, do with this Fascist concordat? First of all, it is our contention that this Italian democratic government, having ratified the Lateran Treaty, and having engaged itself to respect and guarantee the independence and the neutrality of Vatican City, must be left completely free to settle the question of the relations between church and state in Italy, according to the best interests of the nation and the will of the majority. The victorious powers and the international organization which will be set up to put into effect the new political and social order based on democratic principles will have no right to interfere in this matter, except to see to it that not only in Italy but in all nations the fundamental principle of religious freedom is faithfully put into practice.

In the second place, it is our opinion that the question of making a decision about the concordat is not to be undertaken hastily by any provisional government set up to carry on the administration of the country while it is still under occupation; such a decision must be postponed and reserved to the assembly elected by the people to draw the new constitution. In the interim, the concordat ought to be respected, with the exception of those prescriptions which infringe upon the rights of the citizens. This respect for the *status quo* would, among other things, enable the provisional government to request that for obvious reasons of public order, the Vatican "purge" the high ecclesiastical hierarchy of all ultra-Fascist bishops in the Italian Church. The government's right of veto for political reasons might be used against the appointment of notoriously Fascist clergymen to ecclesiastical benefices. This experiment would at the same time give the Vatican an opportunity to declare its attitude towards the new democratic regime, and this knowledge would aid the government in making its plans for the future.

The decision as to the system of relations between church and state to be adopted by democratic Italy should then be made by the Constituent Assembly. In making such a decision, there are several very important facts to be kept in mind.

First, Italy cannot go back to the pre-Fascist hybrid system, in which the state, for the historical motives which we mentioned in dealing with the Lateran Treaty, exercised a certain control over ecclesiastical appointments and over the administration of ecclesiastical temporalities. The pre-Fascist Italian state needed that power as a weapon of defense as long as the Roman question was a menace to national unity, or at least was a factor in fostering the hostility of various sections of the clergy (especially the high clergy) against the state. This reason will not exist any longer in post-Fascist Italy, because, no matter what the Vatican does, the Roman question is dead and buried. We are confident that the guiding minds of the Vatican have common sense enough to see that, after having made the great and irrevocable renunciation, and after having pocketed one billion and three quarters lire as the price of the deal, they cannot expose the Holy See to ridicule by claiming again the old provinces of the pontifical state.

At any rate, the principles of a democratic state, if logically interpreted and applied, leave no room for the old state jurisdiction over the church. In a true democracy, freedom of religion implies in practice that religious beliefs and membership in religious organizations are matters of individual choice; therefore, there should be no state jurisdiction compelling the acceptance of one faith against another, or favoring one more than another.

This point suggests that a rejection of the old system will make it impossible for Italian democracy to accept and ratify the Fascist concordat. The primary reason why this concordat cannot be accepted by a democratic regime is that it was negotiated by a dictatorship for the benefit of its totalitarian regime and as an instrument of Fascist policies. In its spirit and in its letter the concordat is as thoroughly Fascist as are many other Fascist laws and practices of the Fascist regime. The oath of allegiance to the regime, which bishops and priests in charge of Catholic souls had to take—a survival of medieval and modern absolute monarchies of divine right— (Article 20); the right of the government to a political veto in ecclesiastical appointments (Articles 19, 21); the obligation of the secular arm to put into effect decrees of ecclesiastical authorities (Articles 5, 29, i); the loss or limitation of civil rights by a class of citizens for religious motives (Article 5); all the privileges and exemptions granted to special classes, again for religious motives (Articles 6, 8, 20, 41, 42); and lastly, the articles which impose upon the state heavy financial obligations in support of the church —all are measures which may have been justified in a Fascist dictatorship. They are measures devised to secure to the state a certain control over the church and to secure to the church a larger share of political and financial help. Above all, they were measures taken at the expense of the people's rights to freedom of religion, freedom of association, and equality before the law—the cornerstone of democracy.

The governments of Poland, Lithuania, Latvia, Austria, Rumania, Hitler's Reich, Salazar's Portugal—all states with which the Vatican concluded concordats along the same lines as the Fascist Concordat—were not democracies, but open or disguised dictatorships. The only concordat made to date by Pius XII is that concluded with Franco in Spain, and it is particularly objectionable because of the abject formula of the oath to be taken by the Spanish bishops and priests to the regime of the Caudillo. The truly democratic states of pre-war Europe, Czechoslovakia and France, both having a population largely Catholic, could not make concordats but only such a *modus vivendi* as did not engage the government to resort to undemocratic practices. In view of this historical fact, and in view of the fact that the modern democratic state and the authoritarian government of the church have no common ground upon which to meet, there remains only the alternative of separating the church and state once and for all.

It is well known that the Catholic Church condemns the separation of church and state on theological grounds, which have their beginning in the assumption that Catholicism is the only true religion, revealed by God and possessing alone the divine mission of leading men to eternal salvation. All other religions and all other non-Catholic Christian groups are either pagan or heretical, and as such have no right to exist. Whether or not these claims have any validity on theological grounds is a question which theologians may discuss as much as they like. But the modern democratic state recognizes freedom of worship as a fundamental right of all its citizens, and, therefore, it is confronted with the actual existence within its boundaries of various religions and denominations, all of which claim unique and exclusive possession of a divine revelation. Surely, the state can neither attempt to pass judgment upon these various claims, nor allow any one religion to gain a monopoly detrimental to the others. Since it seems that God's plan is to have a variety of religions, the best and only way the state can honor God and fulfill its religious duties is to let all individuals and groups worship Him as they wish, and to protect the rights and freedom of them all.

In reality, the opposition of the Catholic Church to the system of separation is dictated primarily by the fact that in this system the religious monopoly and the privileges and control of society, which the church has enjoyed for many centuries, are lost. Under the system of separation the church is offered freedom from the fetters of state control, but the church prefers a gilded cage, so long as it is the only bird in the house, to flying in liberty with other birds. The legalistic tradition, with its consequent institutional rigidity, has so compenetrated the whole ecclesiastical mentality and outlook, that even today the learned Roman canonists who rule the church are unable to look upon the present world from any other angle than that of the *iura ecclesiae*. Even today they warn us that to force a priest to pay a tax to the state from his ecclesiastical income is to violate the rights of God; that to thrash a cleric caught committing a crime and to drag him before the criminal court of the state is to incur the excommunication of God; that to send a policeman to arrest a murderer who has sought refuge in a church or a convent is to offend the majesty of God; that to allow freedom of speech, freedom of the press, freedom of association to everybody besides the Catholics is to grant equal rights to God and Satan. On the other hand, the church has, without a qualm, allowed dissolute kings to appoint (under the guise of nomination) all the bishops of a country; it has given Mussolini, a charlatan having neither faith nor honor, the right to veto ecclesiastical appointments; it has viewed with approval the humiliating sight of Spanish bishops kneeling before a man like Franco and swearing fidelity in the most abject terms. These and like activities are acceptable to the church, so long as the state recognizes the other *iura ecclesiae* and opens its purse to ecclesiastical beggars.

Democracy has no use for the oaths of bishops and priests. Democracy looks with disgust upon such things as the church's blessing on criminal exploits like the rape of Ethiopia, for which in Italy cardinals, bishops, and priests offered public services of thanksgiving. Monsignor Duchesne, the great Catholic historian, while describing a shameful episode of papal history in ninth-century Rome and the service of thanksgiving in St. Peter's which followed it, has remarked: "In listening to that hymn of thanksgiving the angels in heaven must have smiled a bitter smile, if the angels do ever smile."

We have few or no illusions that the Vatican will willingly yield. It will fight to the last ditch in an effort to prevent the separation of church and state. Even so, the Italian democratic regime ought to do its utmost to achieve a friendly and not a hostile separation. If this fails, however, the world will know where to place the responsibility of the conflict. To be sure, a separation, friendly though it may be, is a major operation, and the Italian clergy must be prepared to make sacrifices. They will be sacrifices much less heavy than those which must be inflicted upon the whole Italian nation as a consequence of the disasters caused by the "man sent by Providence" who was knighted by Pius XI, and by the "wise and farsighted ruler" who was honored by Pius XII.

Abolition of the Concordat. When the French Republic denounced the old Napoleonic Concordat in 1907, the Holy See protested on the grounds that a bilateral contract could not be dissolved by the action of only one of the parties. But up to recent times, the canonists of the Roman Church had consistently denied that a concordat was a contract. They maintained that it was nothing more than a gracious concession on the part of the Pope and, therefore, revocable at will by His Holiness. The civil jurists declared, on the other hand, that a concordat was a gracious grant made by the state to the church, revocable at will by the state. More recently, the canonists modified their views and accepted the principle that a concordat is, at least in part, a bilateral contract "in the likeness of an international agreement." Church and state have never concurred as to the nature of the agreement, although its purpose is to put an end to their disagreements. This divergence of views has contributed to the lack of vitality which distinguishes most concordats, and has likewise given rise to recriminations and protests on the part of the Holy See, whenever a concordat has been denounced by the state.

In the ancient concordats it was customary to insert a clause stating the perpetual character of the agreement, but modern concordats contain only the provision that, in case differences should arise over the interpretation or application of a concordatarian measure, a mixed committee will be appointed to settle the question. It would seem, therefore, that there is no legal principle preventing the state's use of its right to cancel such an agreement considering it as a matter of internal state legislation even if it may follow the procedure used in denouncing international agreements. And thus, by an act of courtesy, the state may notify the Holy See beforehand of its intention, thereby giving the ecclesiastical authorities enough time to issue the necessary regulations and instructions to the clergy.

With the fall of Fascism there will be in Italy a change of regime, from dictatorship to democracy, from a monarchical to a republican form of government. In ancient times, when changes of regime meant only the superseding of one dynasty by another, the principle usually followed was that the privileges, rights, and jurisdictions over ecclesiastical matters and institutions secured by the state through concordats or otherwise, as well as the obligations thus incurred, were inherited by the new dynasty as rights and duties pertaining to the crown. The Holy See occasionally offered some objections, especially concerning privileges, but usually acquiesced to this practice.

In recent times, particularly after the first World War, when, for instance, the new states formed out of the dismemberment of the Austrian monarchy claimed to have inherited the privileges sanctioned by the old Austrian concordat (such as that of the right of nomination to bishoprics), the Holy See took the stand that the Church did not recognize this right of inheritance in the passage from one regime to another. This was tantamount to a declaration that concordats made with a dead regime cease to exist when a new regime comes into being, for not even a Roman canonist would hold the theory that a new regime does not inherit the advantages, but only the obligations, of a previous concordat. Even in Spain, after the passage from the monarchy to Franco's dictatorship took place, the Holy See refused to recognize the dictator's claim to exercise all the concordatarian rights of the Spanish monarchs. In all such cases, the policy of the Holy See has been that of considering the old concordats as dead and of asking that a new concordat be made.

The Roman canonists explain that this change in the Roman tradition is primarily due to the fact that there have been considerable changes in ecclesiastical legislation, and that, for instance, the new Code of Canon Law promulgated in 1917 forbids the grant to anyone, be he king or chief of state, the right of nomination to bishoprics and ecclesiastical benefices, and has abolished lay patronage over churches, benefices, and other ecclesiastical institutions.

These principles, invoked by the Church to justify its change of policy, may well be appropriated by the post-war Italian state to justify its rejection of the concordat. Why should a concordat made with the Fascist regime under the Monarchy of Savoy be considered still valid under the republic, if there is no inheritance of concordats from one regime to another? Also, if it is legitimate for the Vatican to justify this policy by the changes in its legislation, why should it not be legitimate for the post-war Italian republic to justify its rejection of concordats by the exigencies of its new constitution, which provides for the separation of Church and State?

The separation of church and state must be complete, and accomplished in a liberal spirit. No remnants of jurisdictionalism, and no vindictive limitations designed to shackle the freedom of any denomination, should be allowed to thwart the purpose of this separation. When the principle of separation becomes an article of the constitution of a new Italian democratic state, there will be no need of any special legislation concerning religion, except, of course, those measures necessary to effect the transition from the concordatarian regime to the regime of separation. Declaratory and normative rules must be available to guide the executive branches of the government and the courts, so that there will be no difficulty in ascertaining the proper legal position of churches and religious institutions before the law.

Churches as Voluntary Associations. Since in a regime of separation there are no privileges and no exemptions benefiting one group to the exclusion of another, the churches will fall under the general classification of voluntary associations, and as such, will have their own legal status, their rights, and their duties.

When the French Republic denounced the concordat, it also prescribed the formation of *associations cultuelles* with officers to be elected by the members. The Catholic Church refused to accept this provision, which was subversive of the hierarchical constitution of the Catholic system. As a result, the government had to seize ecclesiastical buildings and evict the occupants by force. Such methods can only have the effect of arousing universal sympathy for the persecuted victims, and of placing the government in an unfavorable light. After World War I the French government found it necessary to modify the objectionable clauses of this law. In post-war Italy such mistakes ought to be avoided. It would be advisable to adopt the American system, in which churches are considered as corporations, ruled as far as their internal organization is concerned by their own statutes, but subject to the requirements of the law regulating the legal existence of corporations. The churches could not object to this system on the ground that it infringes upon the hierarchical constitution.

Churches and Religious Buildings. To recognize the churches as either diocesan or parochial corporations would be to give them the right to own the buildings used for the cult and for other religious purposes. In Italy, however, there are special reasons why this general principle cannot be adopted without some limitations. Most of the Italian cathedrals, many churches, monasteries, and other ecclesiastical buildings have, for artistic and historical reasons, long been classified as national monuments. They constitute a large, and perhaps the largest, part of Italy's artistic wealth. As such, these buildings have been considered, for all practical purposes, as being national property, and the heavy expense attendant upon their upkeep has been paid by the state. They, or more precisely, those of them which will be left still standing when the wholesale bombing of this war is over, should remain national monuments under state care, for the nation has a vital interest in their preservation, and the churches themselves could not assume the financial burden of their maintenance. They should continue to be used for the cult as in the past, under such rules as have been hitherto applied to the satisfaction of all concerned.

Schools and Educational Institutions. In a modern democratic state the existence of a public-school system and of higher institutions of learning supported by the state does not prevent the organization of privately owned schools. There is no reason why ecclesiastical and religious private schools should be discriminated against. In a country like Italy, where now by long tradition the whole educational system has been centralized and placed under government control, the danger of lowering educational standards, which often follows indiscriminate use of the right to organize private schools, may be easily avoided by the adoption of strict legal requirements administered by a competent representative body.

Religious Orders and Congregations. There seems to be no reason why, under the principle of freedom of association, the right of groups to form religious organizations with a rule of common life should be denied. Like the churches, these organizations would be free to organize themselves as corporations having a legal existence under general laws.

Matrimony. It would be deplorable to revive again all the old controversies over matrimonial legislation. The system adopted in the Fascist Concordat has much to recommend it. In this system, priests and duly authorized ministers of all denominations, in performing the ceremony of marriage, act not only in their religious capacity, but also as delegates of the civil law. Furthermore, the marriage is recognized by the civil law and has civil effects only if it is registered with the proper government bureau. There is no obligation to celebrate the marriage ceremony in a church; those who wish to do so are free to have the ceremony performed before a civil magistrate. No innovation is necessary, since the rights of the state are fully protected in the present system.

It is a different matter in the case of the prescriptions of the concordat which recognize the jurisdiction of the church where the nullification of a marriage is concerned. The civil effects of the marriage contract are dependent upon, and are regulated by, the civil law, and they cannot be altered or destroyed by any other agency than the civil law. There can be no compromise on this point. This fact, however, does not prevent anyone who cares to do so from seeking ecclesiastical sanction as well.

Divorce. The various attempts made in pre-Fascist times to pass a law legalizing divorce failed to obtain the support of the majority. Many Italians would like to have such a law enacted in post-war Italy as soon as possible. In our opinion, this is not an urgent matter, as long as the large majority of the Italian people do not seem ready for this innovation. When the time is ripe for a modification of the law concerning divorce, the new measure should first be submitted to a referendum of the people and enacted as a law only after it has received the approval of the majority. To provoke a storm of discussions and protests over the question of divorce at the very beginning of a new democratic regime would be unpractical and unwise.

Ecclesiastical Privileges. There is no room for ecclesiastical privileges in a democratic system based on the equality of all citizens before the law. Nevertheless, the law must, even in a democratic system, take into account special conditions which necessitate exceptions to the rule. Such common duties as jury service and military service are incompatible with the ecclesiastical profession, and exemption from these obligations should be granted to all clergymen in major orders. With the complete disarmament of post-war Italy, the problem of military service for clergymen will cease to exist, and the large organization of military chaplains under a bishop will not be needed any longer.

Economic and Financial Settlement. The new Italian state will find that this problem will be the most troublesome of all those with which it must deal in passing from the concordatarian regime to a regime of separation of church and state. Any plan conceived for the purpose of untangling this problem must not lose sight of two considerations: first, the economic condition of the nation and of the state finances in post-war Italy; second, the principle that, in a democratic state under the regime of separation, no contributions by the state to any religion or cult are allowed.

As we have already seen, the new democratic government will inherit from the Fascist regime a disastrous condition of financial bankruptcy. If a state of bankruptcy should be declared, either indirectly or directly (by removing all barriers to inflation and by cancelling the 600-billion lire debt at one stroke), the largest part of church investments and endowments, as well as those of other ecclesiastical institutions, would be wiped out, together with the savings and investments of all the Italian people. The effort which must be made to avoid bankruptcy will benefit the churches, but it will impose enormous sacrifices upon the whole nation. Is there any reason why ecclesiastical institutions and persons should not bear their share of these sacrifices? If the churches are heavily interested in saving Italy from bankruptcy, why should they be exempted from contributing to the common effort? The churches will be poor during the post-war period; so will the Italian people. The Italian clergy will feel the pinch of economic distress; so will the Italian population. If the very class which is supposed to live according to rules of renunciation and self-mortification, and to look after spiritual rather than worldly values, were to claim privileges and exemptions from the common misery, the whole purpose of religion would be defeated. Above all, such a claim would cause the people, not only to lose all respect for the clergy, but it would likewise cause them to hate both the clergy and the principles which they represent.

The post-war Italian government cannot go back to the pre-Fascist system, in which ecclesiastical endowments and income were subjected to general and special taxation, while ecclesiastical incomes were supplemented by government grants from the public treasury. Much less can it preserve the Fascist system whereby all taxes and contributions hitherto levied upon ecclesiastical holdings and incomes were abolished, and government contributions to ecclesiastical institutions and persons were doubled. The new Italian government must solve this problem of ecclesiastical properties, state contributions, and taxation in the only way possible—according to the principles of democratic justice and equality of rights and obligations.

The right to possess cannot be denied to ecclesiastical institutions and associations, for they will be registered as corporations. Thus, their investments in state bonds, as a consequence of the general reduction of the rate of interest paid on public debt, would yield one-per-cent interest. Their lands will be subject to the same agrarian laws as all other lands, and any limitations of capital imposed by law on corporations will apply to them. By these measures, the gradual formation of a new *main-morte,* the cornering of large estates and holdings by permanent institutions, by which lands and industrial stocks are taken forever away from the market, will be made impossible, as will be the amassing of great wealth in individual hands. It goes without saying that religious corporations will be subject to the same ordinary and extraordinary taxation as far as their holdings are concerned. It is equally obvious that churches open to public worship should not be considered taxable property.

This, however, is a question of little importance, since, as we have already noted, many of the Italian churches are national monuments under state care.

The large contributions made by the state to the support of the church in the past were at least partially justified by the fact that, after the unification of Italy, the Italian state confiscated by a special law the possessions of religious orders and ecclesiastical benefices which did not carry pastoral obligations and care of souls. The capital derived from the sale of these possessions, after making some deductions, was invested in state bonds, and the income therefrom was used to supplement the income of poor bishoprics and parishes. The state bonds representing the capital of this fund, and yielding one per cent interest like all other bonds, should be handed over to the Church.

The possessions of bishoprics and parishes were not confiscated by the law of 1867, but were also liquidated and the capital invested in state bonds. These should likewise be turned over to the Church under the same conditions as those of the fund above.

Over and above the income from the fund and from the endowment of bishoprics and parishes, the Church in Italy has received comparatively large contributions from the state treasury. These contributions were counterbalanced in the past by the right which the state exercised of control over the temporalities of the Church, and, further, by the right which it exercised to have a voice in the appointments made to ecclesiastical benefices, whether by nomination to benefices under royal patronage or by grant of the royal exequatur to the appointments made freely by the ecclesiastical authorities. Both patronage and exequatur were abolished in the Fascist Concordat, but the Fascist government, with the consent of the Holy See, reserved to itself the right to object to, or veto, all appointments to ecclesiastical offices judged unacceptable for "political reasons."

The new Italian democratic government should give up all claims to interference in ecclesiastical matters and, at the same time, free itself from any obligation to contribute directly or indirectly to the financial support of the churches.

By leaving the Church free to rule itself according to its own statutes, by returning to it what belongs to it, and by freeing the state from all financial obligations towards religious organizations, the separation of church and state in Italy can be brought about in the most friendly spirit a democracy could offer.

It is not difficult to foresee that the spokesmen for the American Catholics—men like Professor Ellis of the Catholic University at Washington, Father Parson and other Jesuits of the *America,* editors of periodicals such as the two hundred-odd Catholic diocesan bulletins, as well as Catholic apologists in other countries—men like Dr. Binchy of Dublin—will loudly protest against this plan of separation of church and state. Believing as they do that the system of separation is an evil here in America, they will argue that it would be no less than a crime to adopt it in Italy, because Italy is a Catholic country, while the United States is not yet, though, as they hope, it will be soon.

For our purposes, it is enough to mention that there are non-Catholic minorities in Italy, small though they may be. But apart from this, the separation of church and state is not going to be imposed upon the Italian nation at the point of a sword; it is a matter to be decided by the Italian people. If they decide in favor of it, the fact that they are or are not Catholics will make no difference.

Financial Settlement with the Vatican. The financial agreement between the Vatican and the Fascist regime was an integral part of the Lateran Treaty of 1929. The Vatican received a handsome indemnity, as we have already pointed out; and if, as we have suggested, the post-war Italian democratic government accepts and ratifies the treaty of conciliation, it must also accept the debt incurred with the Vatican in the financial agreement.

By a special arrangement the Vatican, which had become by this agreement one of the largest holders of Italian government stock, consented to abstain from alienating these holding over a number of years. Professor Binchy deplores the Vatican's decision to accept these bonds as part payment of the indemnity, thereby giving "the impression that the Vatican has acquired a permanent interest in the prosperity of Italian public finances" (*Church and State in Fascist Italy*, p. 314). Why only "the impression"? Whoever holds stock in the Italian public debt to the amount of one billion lire is certainly very much interested in the welfare of the Italian treasury. We have more than an impression to deal with; we have a fact. We have also another fact to deal with, a sad fact; the Italian treasury is now bankrupt.

If the Holy See has not already disposed of those bonds by some subsequent unknown agreement with Mussolini, it will share with all other creditors of the Italian government either total loss of its credit, if bankruptcy is declared, or the reduction of its interest from five per cent to one per cent, if bankruptcy is avoided.

Had Professor Binchy been Pope instead of Pius XI, he would have preferred "a single and final payment in cash, even if it had entailed a drastic reduction of the original claim." Since, however, Pius XI chose to run the risk and place his faith in Fascist finances, there is nothing to be done about it. Will the Vatican accept this loss with resignation, or will it insist upon obtaining its pound of flesh by invoking "the sanctity of treaties"?

Let us remember that the Vatican's policy on this minor question, as well as on many other questions, will be determined by its general attitude towards the whole problem of Italy's post-war reconstruction. At present, the Vatican's policy would seem to be that of attempting to prevent by all possible means the emergence of an anti-Fascist democratic regime from the ruins of Fascism. In this, the Holy See has had the support of British and American foreign policy, especially the latter. What will happen, if the Vatican is confronted with an Italian democratic republic and with the people's decision to adopt the system of separation of church and state?

Pope Gregory the Great said long ago that the events of the past are a sure promise of those of the future. If this be true, then it is not difficult to surmise what the Vatican will do. Unless a miraculous change of heart takes place and unless Vatican policy comes to be dictated by men alive to present needs instead of by canonists living in the remote past, we may be sure that the new Italian regime will have to face the hostility of the official Church. The Vatican will do again what it did in 1870; it will take the attitude that it is the innocent victim of Italian anti-religious groups bent on destroying the Church. The popes will start over again to protest against the Italian regime, denouncing its domination by Freemasonry, or by Communism, and calling the whole world to witness how the Church in Italy, deprived of all its rights, faces persecution and martyrdom. But will the Vatican again resort to the method of engaging in national and international intrigue, hoping thereby to undermine the democratic republic, as it formerly tried to undermine Italian national unity? In such an event, the Italian state must perform the duty of taking all necessary measures to safeguard the republic. After the lesson learned from the Fascist experience and from the readiness shown by the Vatican to lend the weight of its authority and influence to such reactionary antidemocratic forces as may appear on the scene, who could blame the Italian government for clamping down all threatening agitations and intrigues of a political clericalism? But we may be sure that there will be no religious persecution. Such forms of fanaticism are alien to the Italian people; the history of the sixty years which lapsed from the seizure of Rome to the Lateran agreements are witness to that.

If the governments of victorious nations will keep out of internal Italian affairs, and if the President and the State Department of the United States do not set themselves up as a kind of new Swiss guard for the protection of the Vatican and its claims, the separation of church and state in Italy would be a lasting solution of this problem. There will be recriminations and perhaps years of estrangement, but in the end the Vatican will find out, too, that freedom is the best concordat for the Church that can ever be made.

The tragic Fascist experiment and the unfortunate part played by the Vatican in it have strengthened in many Catholic circles, but especially among British and American Catholics, the old complaint about the great preponderance of Italians in the central government of the whole Church. Since the first World War, when the Vatican's finances became so dependent upon American contributions, the American clergy has often raised its voice, though in a subdued tone, to claim the right to be more widely represented in Roman ecclesiastical offices and bureaus. These requests do not seem to have met with great favor at the Vatican. The substantial indemnity received from the Italian treasury according to the terms of the Lateran agreement, by securing a degree of financial independence of the Holy See from foreign sources, undoubtedly contributed to increasing the Vatican's resistance to outside pressure.

To be sure, the Catholic hierarchy, the clergy, and the Catholic press in America are now more than ever Roman-minded. Hardly a sermon is preached in Catholic churches, or an article or a book published by Catholic authors, which does not quote on any subject some passages from papal encyclicals or speeches and which does not pay homage to the wisdom and glory of the Holy Father. But beneath the surface there is much grumbling and discontent. Many clerics and laymen think that able as the Italians have been in governing the Catholic Church, especially by virtue of their subtle "combinazioni," the time has come to wrest the Roman Curia and the Papacy from their control. Too many blunders were made in dealing with Fascism, and the Italian clergy went too far in its subservience to the Fascist regime.

Dr. Binchy, being a layman and a scholar, in his book so much praised by the American Catholic press, broached the subject more frankly, though with a great deal of tact. After having showered his contempt upon the Fascist Italian clergy, high and low, which seconded so well Mussolini's attempt to "integrate" with all other national forces the Church into the Fascist totalitarian system, Dr. Binchy remarks, not without a subtle sense of irony:

How are they [the leaders of the Church] to oppose this tendency, without destroying the obvious advantages which the Church has drawn from its good relations with the Fascist government? . . . They must be content to watch and wait . . . remaining silent about its unorthodox [Fascist] theories, covering the regime with bouquets while working in secret to counteract its more dangerous tendencies. It is an unheroic policy and the foreign observer may even feel that it is unnecessarily so, for Fascism cannot afford to break with the Church, and in any event prudence is an unsafe counsellor in dealing with a totalitarian state. But bishops are generally chosen for their prudence, rather than their heroism. . . ."

But these are the bishops who will fill the college of Cardinals and from among them the pope of tomorrow will be chosen. Even the French Jesuit Yves de la Brière, well known as a commentator on political and religious events, on the occasion of the tenth anniversary of the Lateran agreements remarked sarcastically: "If we must commemorate this anniversary, we could not do it better than by a discreet celebration *in nigris,*" that is to say, by a funeral Mass in black vestments. In conclusion, Dr. Binchy advocates, not only a political internationalization of Vatican City under a guarantee of foreign nations, but also the internationalization of the Roman Curia, by choosing the officers of the Church government and administration in Rome from all nations, may be in proportion to their Catholic population. This change, of course, would in a short time make inevitable a break in the long line of Italian popes and the election of popes of other nationalities.

Whatever we may think of this proposed radical change in the traditions of the Roman Curia, it is certain that it would also affect considerably the relations between the Italian government and the Vatican. The contingency of a non-Italian pope and of a non-Italian Curia in the heart of Italy, rubbing elbows with the Italian State, and enjoying all the rights, privileges, and exemptions granted by the Lateran Treaty might turn into a serious cause of frictions and conflicts. Who can guarantee that those non-Italian prelates will not prove more sensitive to national feeling than the Italians have been? The experiment made with the French popes of the fourteenth century is certainly not reassuring. The separation of church and state under such circumstances would not be an unmixed blessing. For instance, something would have to be done to prevent the Italian churches from being invaded by foreign prelates. This change would be a step in the dark and it might lead to a second Avignon.

At any rate, among the other disastrous results of the Fascist experience, we must note also the discredit thrown upon the Italian rulers of the Catholic Church. Mussolini, whom Dr. Binchy describes as a great man who "played for high stakes and played with superb skill and daring," dreamed the crazy dream of a new Roman Empire of which the Catholic Church, ruled by Italian prelates and integrated into the Fascist system, was to be one of the great pillars. After twenty years all that we can see is a heap of ruins among which the great pillar itself, half-cracked, is in danger of tumbling down.

Afterword

THE events of the weeks which have lapsed from the day this book was sent to the publishers to the present date have not altered substantially our picture of the Italian situation, nor have they changed our outlook as to the future. The smashing defeat and surrender in Tunisia, first of the German and then of the Italian armies, opened the door for the invasion of Italy which began with the invasion of Sicily. Up to the present, however, the dream indulged in by the State Department of a breakdown in Italy through the action of the King, the Pope, and certain Fascist leaders and army chiefs is as yet not fully realized. As far as we know, Mr. Hull has not claimed any credit for the surrender of Pantelleria.

That the North African debacle and the pitiless bombing of Italian cities and towns have undermined the foundations of Mussolini's dictatorship becomes evident when we look at the desperate effort made to revamp the Fascist Party through a radical shake-up of its National Directorate. As he did in the crisis of 1924, Mussolini has mobilized the most criminal elements among his followers to stem the rising tide of anti-Fascist opposition. The new Secretary General of the Party, Scorza, is an eminent representative of Fascist criminality. In July, 1925, he personally led the gangsters in an attack upon the liberal leader, Amendola, who died several months later of the injuries suffered in that attack. In 1928, he published an article in which he likened the Fascist Party to the Catholic Church, as having the same type of organization, the same discipline, and the same intolerant spirit. Of course, as he remarked, he did not mean the Catholic Church of such weaklings as St. Francis of Assisi, but the

Catholic Church of the "heroic" Pope Borgia, ready at all times to wage war and to dispose of his enemies by poison. Like most Fascist leaders, Scorza, the "boss" of the province of Lucca, has amassed a fortune through scandalous graft and bribery. Another Fascist of the first hour, no less a criminal than Scorza, Renato Chierici, has now been called to the key position of Chief of the Italian Police. At the end of June, eleven hundred persons were arrested; among them, seven thousand were labelled "Reds." We do not know whether those Fascists (among whom were several former prefects of provinces) who were put behind the bars were counted also as "Reds" (*New York Times* and *New York Herald Tribune,* June 25). Perhaps those in Washington and London who are so desperately seeking Italian leaders with whom to deal may find their man among these newly consecrated "martyrs" of the Fascist purge.

Nowhere else outside the high Fascist ranks has the impending doom of Mussolini created more consternation and fear than in the high Vatican circles. They foresee that the Italian people, when free from Fascism, will neither forget nor forgive the Church for its part in the Fascist tragedy. On May 12, a well-informed and keen French columnist, Pertinax, stated in the *New York Times* that Archbishop Spellman had reported from Italy that the Vatican was "deeply concerned with the social upheavals in the peninsula that are likely to be the outcome of military defeat." Then, on May 18, the *New York Times* printed another "unconfirmed report," according to which "the Vatican had informed the British and American governments that an Italian collapse now would have disastrous results unless Italy was . . . immediately occupied by Allied armies." This information was given under headlines such as the following: "Mussolini appeal to Pope reported. Italian leaders said to have asked Pontiff to use good offices with the Allies. Vatican said to have warned London and Washington of dangers in collapse." In other times, this would have been branded by Mussolini as an act of treachery against him on the part of the Vatican. Now, not even the notorious Fascist anti-clerical firebrand, Farinacci, had anything to say. It is clear that not only the Pope, but Mussolini himself admits the fact. On June 13, the Pope delivered, in person, an address to twenty-five thousand Italian workers gathered in Rome from various parts of the country, especially from Northern Italy. The most important part of the papal address was a passionate exhortation to the workers not to make a revolution. Said His Holiness: "Salvation does not lie in revolution . . . a revolution which proceeds from injustice and civil insubordination." What we need, the Pope added, is "a spirit of true concord and brotherhood animating all: Superiors and subjects, employers and workers, great and small—in a word, in all classes of the people." The Pope took care to explain that what he opposed was a Communist revolution such as would abolish "private property, the foundation of family stability," but his statements were general enough to include and condemn all kinds of revolutions and to make it clear that salvation must be sought through "evolution," or gradual and legal methods.

It is clear that this pilgrimage of workers to Rome, in such large numbers and at a time when transportation is so difficult and so much needed for military operations, could not have taken place without Mussolini's consent. It is obvious also that the approval of Mussolini could not have been secured without informing him beforehand of the content of the papal address. We may be sure, then, that Mussolini, no less than the Vatican, has reason to fear the increasing danger of a revolutionary movement. Though both Mussolini, in ordering the arrest of so many Italians, and the Pope, in addressing the workers, referred to the "Reds" as the would-be revolutionaries, there can be no doubt that the revolution which they fear is an anti-Fascist revolution. The humble workers who joined the pilgrimage—we do not know how they were mobilized—and heard the papal address could not fail to understand that the whole papal sermon was delivered for the purpose of telling them that they should not revolt against the Fascist regime and should refrain from "civil disobedience."

During this part of his address, the Pope refrained from even mentioning the war and spoke as though the workers were living under normal conditions, their only troubles being in regard to their relations with their employers. The Pope even took pains to describe in a poetical vein the happiness of a society molded according to the social teaching of the Church. Then abruptly he indulged in a long controversial tirade to refute the calumny that the Catholic Church was responsible for the unleashing of the present war. Newspapermen and radio commentators explained that the Pope intended to answer the German propaganda agent, Dr. Friedrich, who some weeks before had levelled this charge against the Catholic Church on the Paris radio.

It is rather difficult to accept this explanation. The Vatican radio had immediately protested against that fantastic charge when it was made, and the German propaganda agent himself had disclaimed the utterance of such a calumny. There was no need for the Pope to take up the cudgels to refute the incredible attack of a radio announcer who had recanted. And why should the Pope have reserved this matter for an address to Italian workers, who very likely had not heard the Paris radio and knew nothing of the whole story? It is obvious that His Holiness was countering something which was in the minds of the Italian people and not the fabulous invention of a German propaganda agent.

The Pope knows well that the Italian people do not accuse the Vatican and the Italian ecclesiastical hierarchy of having caused the present war, but only of having made common cause with the Fascist dictatorship for twenty years, and thus of having a share of responsibility for their suffering and for the final disaster of the country. Pius XII's address of June 13, together with Cardinal Schuster's address of March 20, quoted above, are eloquent indications that a wave of violent anti-clericalism is sweeping Italy today. Cardinal Schuster branded this movement as utterly irreligious and communistic. To be sure, there are in Italy, as there have always been in the Latin countries, irreligious tendencies and communistic groups; but the movement with which the Vatican is confronted now is primarily anti-clerical and political, not religious. The Vatican and the hierarchy are now reaping the fruits of the seeds which they have sown in Italy for the last twenty years. Of course, the Pope did not meet this charge directly; being a good casuist and versed in legal lore, he preferred the convenient method of attacking the weakest argument of the opposition, that is, the wholesale charge that the Church was responsible for the war, thus convincing his audience that the Vatican had had no part at all in the events which brought on Italy's present misery.

We must recognize that Pius XII's speech was the ablest piece of oratory that has ever come from his pen. Like President Roosevelt, the Pope can kill several birds with one stone. By urging the Italian workers not to revolt, he rendered a signal service to the Fascist regime. By specifying that what he meant was a "Red" revolution, he pleased Washington and London, who took the papal words as referring not only to the present situation in Italy, but much more to the situation which will develop when the Allied armies get hold of the country. Last but not least, he hopes to have appeased the wrath of the Italian people (which is not Communist-minded) against the pro-Fascist policies of the Italian Church.

The uneasiness of the Vatican as it awaits the downfall of Mussolini is strongly reflected in the Catholic circles of America. Though Mussolini has forfeited their former admiration and respect, they too seem to fear his downfall. The editor of the *Catholic World* frankly expressed his fears in June, 1943: "Catholics will be anxious to know what effect the downfall of the Duce will have upon the Church. . . . Will the Italian people, reacting violently against their former leader, visit their wrath also upon the Church? . . . But," he continued, "has the Church invited and deserved reprisals?" His answer was, of course, an emphatic negative, because there is "an essential incompatibility between Fascism and Catholicism." Therefore, no Catholic could also be a Fascist. The whole article was a severe lecture to those misguided Catholics, especially Italian Catholics, who have been ardent admirers of Mussolini and Fascism, whereas the Vatican has been the greatest and most irreconcilable enemy of Fascism:

The essential incompatibility of Catholicism and Fascism was demonstrated before the world in the David-Goliath duel [between Pius XI and Mussolini]. On the one side was the swaggering, blustering, fire-eating Duce; on the other the Pope with no weapon but a pen and an occasional speech. . . . There can be no question as to who was the victor and who the vanquished. Catholicism incarnate in the Pope defeated Fascism embodied in Il Duce. So it is only fair to conclude that no one can be a good Catholic and a Fascist at the same time. It will be neither logical nor just, therefore, to punish Catholicism for the crimes of Fascism.

One wonders where the writer of these words has been for the past twenty years, and how he has read his Bible. As far as we know, David never made a treaty and a concordat with Goliath, never bestowed upon him knightly decorations, never called him the "man sent by Providence," never sat side by side with him on the shores of a river where "olive branches were blossoming." As if it were not enough to have clothed old Pope Pius in the garments of the youthful David, the editor must also clothe him in the lion's skin: "To anyone who loves to see an old lion seated on the papal throne, and to hear him roar, the Encyclical *Non abbiamo bisogno* is a delight."

Undoubtedly, it is a delight to read in that papal document of 1931 that the pestilential doctrine of Fascism resolved itself "into a pagan worship of the state, a statolatry." But it was only two years after the Lateran agreement by which "God was given back to Italy and Italy to God," that Pope Pius saw the light and found out that Italy had been given instead to the devil. And need we remind the editor of the *Catholic World* that Pope

Pius XI, after roaring his condemnation of the Fascist doctrines, continued meekly: "We have not wished to condemn the Fascist Party and the regime as such," and that he allowed Catholics to take the Fascist oath with "some mental reservations"? The roaring of the old lion ended in a pitiful squeak.

Parallel to this campaign to whitewash the Vatican is the campaign to salvage at least part of the Fascist regime. According to the *New York Times,* May 11, 1943, a plan for the reconstruction of Italy was "elaborated in a special message from Pope Pius XII to Archbishop Spellman of New York." This plan provides that the Fascist Party should be "immediately disbanded," but that "present" Italian prefects of provinces "should not be considered to have been active Party supporters," and that, therefore, they should be left in their places as heads of the civil administration under the orders of an Allied Commission sitting in Rome. It is important to note that the prefects of the ninety-four Italian provinces were not elected by the people, as the American state governors are. They were appointed by Mussolini, who naturally enough selected them from among the most active and trustworthy members of the Fascist Party. Since 1926, the prefects in their turn have appointed the mayors or "podestà" of cities and towns, selecting them, too, from the Fascist ranks. Furthermore, the prefects were also given control over the officials of the party and over the Fascist organizations of their district. In other words, the prefects are the key men in the Fascist system of government and administration. These are the men who, according to the papal plan, are to be entrusted with the government and administration of the Italian provinces when the war is over and an Allied Commission sits in Rome.

The scheme of the Vatican provides also for a "ten year plan of political metamorphosis. . . . During this period, civil administration would be handed back to the people at certain definite stages." We are left guessing who "the people" will be. What we do know is that the ex-Fascist prefects will be there to carry on those plans. Six years of civil war were needed, from the end of 1920 to the end of 1926, before Mussolini and his men could stamp out the anti-Fascists in Italy. Ten years, according to the Vatican plan, will be needed before the revolt created by twenty years of Fascist tyranny and the material and moral disasters of the present war are under firm control. During these ten years, the governments of the United Nations, especially those of Britain and the United States, will be materially and morally responsible for what will be done in Italy to establish a new type of democracy, represented by an authoritarian regime.

In one of its leading articles of June 20, the *New York Herald Tribune,* starting from the obvious assumption that the Fascist government had been discredited in Italy, warned us that "the depth of such feeling, the manner in which it may be channeled, are not matters upon which it is wise to be dogmatic." We must realize, however, that "it would be painfully easy for an occupying force, in the interest of 'order,' to freeze Italy's Fascist organization in authority. It is less likely that the Allies would permit the opposite to occur—namely, the riotous competition of anti-Fascist groups for power—during the critical period of occupation. To avoid both of these extremes—to permit Italy to learn to function politically after her long self-imprisonment while maintaining the tranquillity necessary to Allied war plans—will require the most earnest efforts of men of vision, sympathy with legitimate Italian aspirations, and, above all, knowledge of Italian conditions."

These are, indeed, sensible statements. The most sensible of all concerns the knowledge of Italian conditions as an indispensable preliminary to any wise decision. But knowledge of conditions, to be of any use, must precede the decisions to be made. Furthermore, the decisions must, of course, be guided by certain definite principles of action. When decisions are made, not only in ignorance of actual conditions, but also with the express intention of acting according to wrong principles, plans are bound to go wrong.

In his press conference at Washington on May 25, Prime Minister Churchill, speaking of Italy, said: "Of this we may be sure, we shall continue to operate on that donkey at both ends with a stick as well as with a carrot" (*New York Times*, May 26). Had Mr. Churchill been endowed with a little more imagination and sense of humanity, he would have realized that, while he was speaking, bombs were raining on the Italian donkey, that is to say, on the Italian cities and towns inhabited by innocent men and women, old people and children—like those who fell victim to the German "stick" in London, in Coventry, and in other English cities. He would have shown a wisdom and generosity more becoming to the leader of the great English people, had he said: "We know that bombing means suffering and death for innocent people; we hate to have to do that. But there is no other way to destroy the Fascist dictatorship which has forced this war upon us." As things stand now, the Italian people get the stick and the Fascist leaders who are expected to betray Mussolini get the carrot! In 1940, when Mr. Churchill still had unbounded admiration for Mussolini, it was the Duce who for twenty years had operated with the stick upon the Italian donkey. Now the stick has passed into the hands of Mr. Churchill, but the donkey is the same—the Italian people.

The unfavorable reaction of a large section of the American people to the plans and policies of the United States government concerning several European countries seems to have made some impression in Washington. The crazy plan of organizing an Austrian Legion here under Otto of Hapsburg has been given up. But the North African political muddle still goes on. The satisfaction at the results achieved there, so complacently voiced by Mr. Hull and Mr. Welles, seems to have been a little premature. One of the tangible results of the policy of the State Department appears to be a growing anti-American feeling among the French leaders, who apparently have a very large following among the French people.

As far as Italy is concerned, President Roosevelt, on the occasion of the fall of the little island of Pantelleria, felt the need of making a new appeal to the Italian people. Far from imitating Mr. Churchill's perhaps involuntary phraseological cynicism, President Roosevelt stated that "The irresponsible acts of which the United Nations complained were not committed by the Italian people. . . . They were the acts of Premier Mussolini's personal Fascist regime, which did not actually represent the Italian people." The President expressed his regret that the United States has no other choice than to continue the war against Italy, and finally assured the Italian people that "the United Nations were agreed that, when German domination had ended and the Fascist regime was thrown out, we could promise them their complete freedom to choose a non-Fascist, non-Nazi kind of government. . . . It is the intention of the United Nations that Italy would be restored to real nationhood and take her place as a respected member of the European family of nations" (*New York Times,* June 12, 1943). To be sure, President Roosevelt's promises are couched in vague, general terms. The choice of a "non-Fascist, non-Nazi kind of government" does not include necessarily a "democratic" government, nor does it exclude an "authoritarian" government of the type desired by the Vatican. The restoration of "Italian nationhood" is a rather puzzling phrase, because Italy has not lost it. Nationhood remains intact in spite of any regime or of political dismemberment. If President Roosevelt meant the integrity of the Italian national territory, it would have been better to be a little more explicit. At any rate, the sympathetic words of the President towards the Italian people seem to suggest that a little change of heart may be taking place in the State Department. Unfortunately, on June 17, the International News Service announced from London that "*according to an Algiers radio broadcast, reported by Reuter's* . . . President Roosevelt's bid to the Italian people to overthrow Mussolini has made a deep impression on Italy. His remarks of *sincere friendship with the House of Savoy* met a very favorable echo among the Italian masses."

If this remark about the House of Savoy was included in the

text of the President's message broadcast to Italy, then the Italians who heard it could not fail to understand that they will be left free to choose any non-Fascist, non-Nazi government, provided they preserve the Savoy Monarchy. But in the President's statement as published by the American press, there is no word about the House of Savoy.

The Algiers radio is an unreliable source of information. But Reuter's is an official British agency. Why did it relay the information given by the Algiers radio? In time of war, more than in time of peace, words are weapons. And there are words which should not be allowed to go uncontradicted. If the expression of "sincere friendship" with the House of Savoy did actually exist in the text President Roosevelt read at the press conference, why was this phrase left "off the record," as newspapermen are wont to say? If the phrase was not in the text, why and by whom was it added to the text broadcast to Italy? Was it interpolated by someone at the State Department, or by somebody else in London with or without President Roosevelt's consent?

It seems incredible that any one could have tampered with the official text of the President's words. Thus, either the news given by the Algiers radio is wholly false, or the State Department is so afraid of the unfavorable reaction of the American public to any attempt to salvage the Savoy Monarchy that it must resort to methods of public deception characteristic of the Fascist and Nazi regimes.

We do not believe that the President or the State Department resorted to such methods, or that they would express such confidence in the Italian King who only twenty days before the President's speech, had sent to Hitler the following message: "On the fourth anniversary of the Treaty that unites our Nations, I send you, Fuehrer, my most sincere wishes for the greatness and prosperity of the German nation in the knowledge that the valor and worth of our armies cannot but lead to victory" (*New York Times,* May 22, 1943).

This most recent gesture of solidarity of the old *roi fainéant*

with his Fascist and Nazi overlords, followed by the significant
address of Pius XII urging the Italian working classes to be
good and not to imperil the Fascist regime with an internal revolution while fighting against the Allied Nations, might be
enough finally to open the eyes of even the most stubborn believers in the appeasement of Italian reactionary forces and institutions. Somebody in Washington seems to have begun to see
the light. In the *New York Times* for June 17 Mr. Harold Cal-
lender, who is said to be close to the Office of War Information,
wrote as follows:

Neither military nor political observers here count upon an early
breakdown of Italian morale, in spite of the bombings. Military men
point out that the Italians in Tunisia fought well and that those in
Italy will be defending their homeland. Some think the impending
danger may stiffen Italian resistance. There have been reports of
additional German troops moving into Italy and of Italian garrisons
in the Balkans being called home to ward off invasion.

One thing seems sure, as we have stated again and again in
this book: as long as the Germans are in Italy, and they are not
defeated there, no surrender is to be expected. For a while, our
newspapers and armchair strategists filled their columns with
hopeful and seemingly logical prophecies, according to which
the Germans had already decided to abandon Italy to her fate.
Italy, the strategists remarked, had become a burden, difficult to
defend against an invasion; hence the German generals were
ready to withdraw behind the Brenner Pass and entrench themselves in the heart of the impregnable European fortress. In their
wishful thinking, these strategists forgot that it must be in the
German interest, from the military and from the economic point
of view, to keep waging war on non-German territory as long as
possible, and that a stubborn defense of Italy is by no means
impossible. At least, it can be made a long and difficult affair for
the Allies.

Our hearts are filled with sadness and with a sense almost of
despair when we read of the terrific bombing which is heaping

so much devastation and death on the Italian cities. We lived in them; we loved them: Naples, Palermo, Messina, Catania, Bari —all names which revive in our minds remembrance of years of peaceful study and are associated so closely with the glorious traditions of Italian culture. We cannot bear to think that that land of beauty, those cities with their artistic treasures, are being reduced to ruins. But a still greater sadness comes into our hearts when we, old teachers in an American university, which has become a large training camp for soldiers and officers, see our boys, most of them fine young men, depart and when we bid them a melancholy goodbye. We wish them good luck with all our hearts. We wished to train them for life and for constructive work, not for death and destruction. The mistakes of politicians and statesmen have borne bitter fruits; these boys are now fighting and dying for an ideal: to maintain in America and to revive in Europe the democratic way of life. Will the men of the older generation who have in their hands the conduct of the war and the settlement of the peace continue in their blunders? We fervently hope not. We cannot bear to think that these boys shall have died in vain.

July 8, 1943

Index